HIGH CONQUEST
The Story of Mountaineering

by

JAMES RAMSEY ULLMAN

> Have we vanquished an enemy?
> None but ourselves.
> *George Leigh-Mallory*

FOREWORD

This book has been written during the second year of the Second World War. Men, scanning their horizons, are not searching for the snowcaps of distant ranges but for the smoke of burning cities; their eyes are not raised to the challenge of great peaks but to the drone of bombing-planes above the clouds. A mountain today means an international boundary line, a gun emplacement, a hideout for guerilla bands. The Alps, towering above shattered Europe, are the Mountains of the Axis. Olympus, where the gods dwelt, flies the swastika.

In such a world a book concerned with mountains and mountaineering, for their own sake, cannot but be labelled "a book of escape." And in a sense that is exactly what this volume is. The "conquest" of its title is far removed from the bloody, mindless conquest that stalks the earth today; and the human adventures which it records have precious little to do with dictators and generals, panzer-divisions and the fall of nations. They have also precious little to do with disillusionment, despair and fear.

Very well then—this is a book of escape. And the Mountain Way itself is a Way of Escape. But that does not mean that it is an escape from realities to unrealities, or from that which is true to that which is false. On the contrary, it is as real and true a way as men have ever followed. And its essence is not negation, but affirmation—of the splendour of the earth we inhabit, of the meaningfulness of living, of all that is close and precious to the human spirit.

The mountains and the men who climb mountains have more to tell us than a mere story of physical obstacles and physical adventure. They tell us that the world is old and tired and sick only to those who are themselves old and tired and sick; that there are still such things as high devotion and high enterprise under the sun; and that men have fought and died—and will fight and die again—under other banners than those of power, greed and hatred. At a time like the present—here and now—it is well to remember these things.

This book makes no pretence of being an exhaustive record of mountaineering activity. Neither is it an encyclopædia of the sport nor a manual of technique. What this book does attempt is to present in broad outline the history of the relationship between mountains and men, to re-tell some of the great climbing stories of the past two centuries in terms of interest to the general American reader, and to indicate not only what men have done in the mountains, but what they have sought and found there as well. Also, it attempts to offer a word of suggestion and encouragement to the reader who would follow the Mountain Way himself.

The stories related in the following pages have, for the most part, been taken from the original accounts of those who lived them, and my debt to these men and their writings is as great as it is obvious. In return, I can only express the hope that this book —and the appended Reading List—will lead the reader on to a closer acquaintance with these other greater books and with the almost limitless realm of adventure to which they hold the key.

I also wish to make grateful acknowledgment to the many officials and members of the American Alpine Club who have generously helped me in my work—in particular to Miss Helen Buck, Mr. Norman Dyhrenfurth, Miss Georgia Engelhard, Mr. Joel E. Fisher, Dr. Charles Houston, Mr. Nicholas Spadavecchia, Mr. Bradford Washburn and Mr. Fritz Wiessner. My thanks are due too to Mr. Edward Cushing and Mr. Erling Strom for their valuable assistance, and to William M. Sloane for his unflagging interest and encouragement.

Finally, my list of acknowledgments would be woefully incomplete if I did not express my gratitude to my own climbing companions on many mountains and over many years. For better or worse, it is they who are responsible for this book's being written and for its being a labour not of duty but of love. To them—and to all others like them who have known the adventure and freedom and companionship of the hills—*High Conquest* is affectionately dedicated.

J. R. U.

CONTENTS

PART ONE

Chapter I. Where the Demons Dwelt   page 13

II. A Sport is Born—The Winning of the Alps   22

III. A Mountain and a Man—The Ascent of the Matterhorn   44

IV. Mountaineering Comes of Age—1865–1941   68

PART TWO

V. "The Great One"—The Story of Mount McKinley   93

VI. Snowpeaks and Firepeaks—The Andes of South America   111

VII. Ice on the Equator—The Mountains of Africa   133

VIII. Highest Yet—Mountaineering in the Himalayas   147

IX. "Eight-Thousanders"—The Unclimbed Himalayas   172

X. Summit of the World—The Fight for Everest   204

CONTENTS

PART THREE

XI. Our Own High Places—Mountains and Mountaineering in North America 237

XII. Axe, Rope and Trouser-seat—The Craft of Mountaineering 262

XIII. Behind the Ranges 286

APPENDIX

I. A Note on Volcanoes 293

II. One Hundred Famous Mountains 297

III. Glossary of Mountaineering Terms 301

IV. Reading List 303

Index 315

ILLUSTRATIONS

The Last Citadel	*Facing page* 16
The White Dome of Europe	17
"That Awful Mountain"	50
White Death	51
Top of the Continent	94
Giant's Causeway	95
Hard Rock—Thin Air—A Rope	122
Capstone of the Western World	123
Highest Yet	168
The Naked Mountain	169
King of the Karakoram	198
Summit of the World	199
Ultima Thule	228
A World of Rock and Ice	229
The Void Below	276
"Have We Vanquished an Enemy?"	277

MAPS AND SKETCHES

The Mountains of the World	End papers
The Alps	24 & 25
The Matterhorn from the Theodule Pass	48
The Route to Everest	212
Ultima Thule	228

PART I

I

WHERE THE DEMONS DWELT

THE SUN IS down. Purple shadows race swiftly across the desolate Tibetan uplands, and the buildings of the ancient monastery in the valley are soon almost indistinguishable from the mountain rock. Presently, across the valley, there sounds the blare of trumpets—an eerie, monotonous note, long sustained, reverberating from the valley walls and the icefields far above. It is answered by a measured clash of cymbals and the tiny tinkling of many prayer wheels. Men sit crosslegged and motionless on the terraces of the monastery, beside rough piles of stone in the surrounding waste, and at the mouths of caves cut in the living rock. They are yellow, weatherbeaten men in homespun robes and pointed hats, holy lamas of the Buddhist faith. They sit quietly while the dusk deepens, their eyes raised to the mountain that looms white and gigantic above them to the south.

It is a magic mountain at which they are gazing—a sacred and supernatural mountain, ringed with mystery and a fear as old as night. It is the abode of spirits and demons. Great shadowy shapes with flaming eyes prowl the glaciers, and on the gaunt heights beyond the ghosts of the departed hold black communion with the howling wind. The Evil Ones are there —Sukpas and Zhidags and Nitikanji—lurking in blue crevasses and behind the walls of precipices; and the bloodthirsty Snow Men, with long hair and tails, roam the high ridges under the stars. Woe to the mere mortal who would venture into this ice-shrouded world above the world. Woe to him who would violate the demon-guarded sanctuary of the mountain goddess.

The lamas of the Rongbuk Valley gaze up at the monstrous white pinnacle above them and slowly turn their prayer wheels. "Chomolungma," they murmur, "Goddess Mother of the World——"

The long shadows race swiftly up the mountainside. They fall on glacier and snowfield, precipice and ice-wall, and now at last on a skyline ridge, ten thousand feet above the valley, where the tiny figures of two men are moving upward toward the darkening sky. These men move with infinite slowness, their feet dragging heavily on the ice-encrusted rocks, their bodies bent almost double against the howling fury of snow and wind. Their faces are not yellow, but white, beneath their frosted beards; and on their heads, instead of pointed lamas' hats, are helmets of leather and fleece. Dark goggles cover their eyes, and they carry packs on their backs and ice-axes in their mittened hands. For a dozen steps they struggle on, then for another dozen, while their hearts pound to bursting, their lungs gasp for air, and the last light of day drains slowly from the sky. Then, suddenly, they stop. For a long while they stand motionless, leaning on their axes, staring upward.

Above them the desolate ridge twists on into space. Their eyes, straining through the dusk, perceive neither beast nor demon nor goddess, nor do their ears hear the cries of the departed and damned. All that they see is the brown, snow-flecked rock slanting endlessly away; the only sound is the deep, wild moaning of the wind. Yet the two men go no farther, for they know that to go farther would be to die. The night is at hand; they have given to the last measure of their strength and will; and it has not been enough. The great white pinnacle of the mountain still looms above them in the darkness, inviolate as it has been since the beginning of time. One of the men starts slowly down. The other lingers for still another moment, gazing upward. Pain and exhaustion and bitter disappointment lie on him like a leaden weight, but his eyes, behind their snow-fogged goggles, fix the magic summit with the deep, quiet challenge of the undefeated.

"Just wait, old thing," he mutters between cracked and frozen lips, "we'll get you yet!"

Almost twenty years have passed since a young Englishman named Geoffrey Bruce stared up at the unconquered crest of

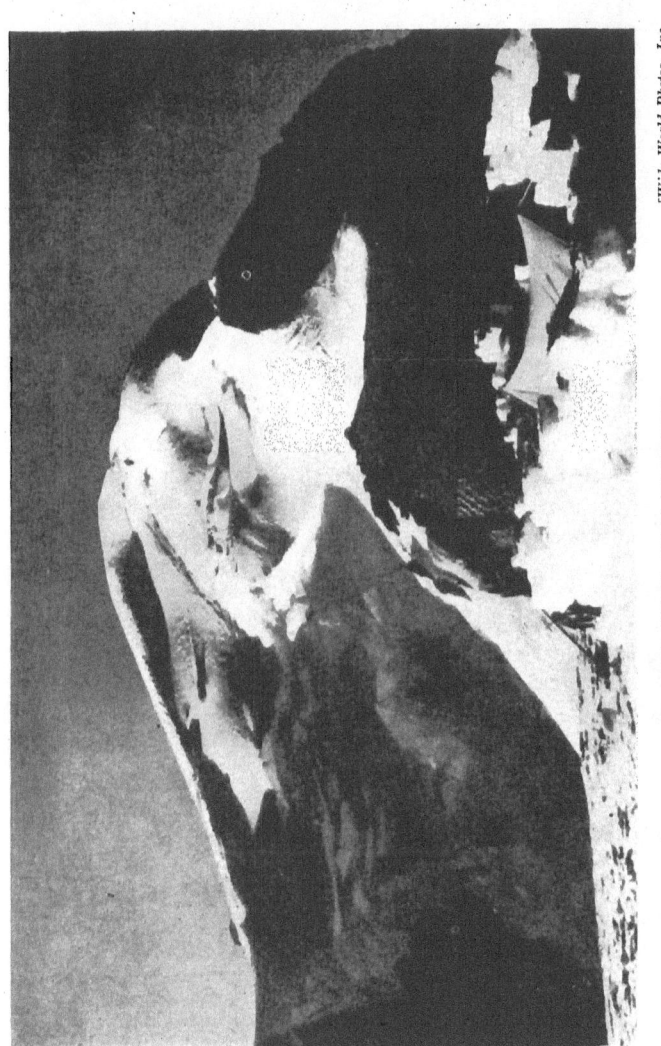

THE WHITE DOME OF EUROPE   [*Wide World Photos, Inc.*

The summit of Mont Blanc at sunrise, seen from a bivouac at about 12,500 feet. The Vallot Hut, highest on the mountain, stands on the still-darkened ridge about one-third of the way between the bivouac and the summit. The routes of the famous early ascents lie just beyond the skyline ridge on the left.

THE LAST CITADEL [*Photo by V. Sella*

The great obelisk of the Mustagh Tower in the Karakoram Himalayas.
No man has dreamed of climbing it—yet.

which have come down to us from olden times abound in references to great peaks and ranges. In some instances these are factual and historical; more often they are grounded in religion and mythology. But in virtually every case it is the spiritual rather than the physical nature of mountains with which the accounts are concerned.

Many of the most famous biblical stories have a mountain background: Noah on Ararat; Moses on Sinai and Pisgah; Jesus Himself going up into the mountain to pray and facing the supreme moments of His life on the Mount of Olives and Golgotha. The old Greek gods—though not the Greeks themselves—were mountaineers of the first order, and their fabled dwelling places, Olympus, Parnassus and Helicon, were among the most celebrated localities of early western civilization. Farther afield were the Atlas range of Africa, where the Titan whose name they bore was reputed to carry the sky upon his shoulders, and the mysterious Caucasus, where Prometheus first stole fire from heaven. Indeed, there was scarcely a mountain in the known world of ancient times' which the imaginations of men did not invest with an aura of legend and story.

Actual authenticated ascents, however, were few and far between. We know that the philosopher Empedocles ascended the volcano Etna, in Sicily (though he did not, as legend has it, kill himself by leaping into its crater), and during the period of the Roman Empire the same summit was surmounted by many climbers, among them the Emperor Hadrian. Philip V of Macedon climbed one of the peaks of the rugged Haemus range and met the not uncommon mountaineer's fate of finding only mist where he had hoped for a view. But aside from these and a few other sporadic ascents, the ancients were content to gaze up at their mountains from the plains below. They marvelled at them; they worshipped them; they created great imaginative legends about them that will live as long as civilization. But they did not climb them.

The long years of the Middle Ages, the Renaissance and the two centuries following it saw little change in the relationship between mountains and men. The horizons of mankind, to be sure, were slowly being pushed back, and factual knowledge was gradually impinging on the legends and superstitions of the ancient world; but the earth's high places still held their grip on the human imagination as realms of awe and dread. As late as the middle 1700's adventurous travellers would solemnly commend their souls to their maker before risking the crossing of what today are considered the most prosaic Alpine passes, and to the occasional unhappy wanderer on the higher slopes it was merely a question of whether a bandit, a three-headed dragon or the ghost of Pontius Pilate would waylay him first.

It was no accident that men first began climbing mountains in the late eighteenth and early nineteenth centuries. On the contrary, it was a direct result of the profound changes that were occurring in the world and in men's ways of looking at it. This was the era of Napolean and Goethe and Beethoven, of the American and French Revolutions, of the birth of science and democracy and the beginnings of industrial civilization. In every sphere of human thought and activity the bonds of ancient tradition were being broken; frontiers were pushed back with dazzling rapidity; and in the province of physical adventure, no less than in politics, science and the arts, men found themselves looking about them with fresh and eager eyes. The Alps, towering above the very nub of Europe, had for unnumbered centuries moved mankind only to awe and terror. Now, suddenly, they were a challenge, beckoning it to try its new-found knowledge and skill and courage.

And the story of mountaineering began.

The climbers of the world's great mountains have been drawn from many nations and many walks of life. The great majority, however, have been men—or women—of standing and achievement in fields far removed from mountaineering, and there is scarcely one among them who could fit the conventional mould of the professional athlete. Edward Whymper, A. F. Mummery and George Leigh-Mallory, perhaps the three greatest figures in climbing history to date, were respectively an artist, a business man and a member of the faculty at Cambridge University. De Saussure, who, if anyone, merits the designation of "the father of mountaineering," was one of the foremost scientists of his time. So too was John Tyndall, conqueror of the mighty Weisshorn and many another famous Alpine summit. Charles Hudson, one of the outstanding early climbers, W. A. B. Coolidge, the Baedeker of the Alps, and Hudson Stuck, who first climbed Mount McKinley, were clergymen. A. M. Kellas, pioneer explorer of the farthest Himalayas, was in his *alter ego* an eminent London physician. Paul Bauer is a lawyer, N. E. Odell a geologist, Geoffrey Winthrop Young a classical scholar and writer.

One of the most eager climbers in the Alps of a half century ago was a young Italian priest named Abate Achille Ratti, who was later to become Pope Pius XI. Kings and princes have also been proud to count themselves among the mountaineers, notably the Duke of the Abruzzi, of the royal house of Italy, who stalked great peaks across the world from Alaska to Central Africa, and, in more recent years, the late Albert, beloved soldier-king of Belgium. It was as a mountaineer, indeed, that Albert perished, falling to his death while on a solitary climb among the cliffs of his native countryside. Other famous men who were also accomplished and devoted climbers include the scientist Julian Huxley, the historian and United States Senator Hiram Bingham and the late author and Governor General of Canada, John Buchan, Lord Tweedsmuir. Among present-day mountaineers, as well, are many persons prominent in public life, the arts and the learned professions.

These are the sort of men who have followed the mountain way. Their personalities, backgrounds and methods of climbing have differed widely, one from another. So too have their actual accomplishments, the degree of their success or failure. With scarcely an exception, however, it has been the same underlying adventure-spirit that has motivated them all; and, taken together, they form as gallant a company as could well be assembled in any field of human endeavour.

But why? the valley-goer still asks. Why should men deliberately turn their backs on the hard-won security of their usual lives to face storm and cold, hardship, danger and often death itself on lonely and savage heights? It is not material gain that lures them, for no fortune was ever made on the mountain-tops. Nor is it fame, for the great peaks are still a closed world, God be praised, to the high-powered press-agent. It is not power or prestige or—except on Hollywood mountains—the hand of a fair lady. Why then do men climb?

Even the climbers themselves have had a hard time answering the question. In a world full of golf courses and gymnasiums it is impossible to say that one climbs simply for exercise. "The view" is scarcely a satisfactory explanation either, when one considers that one may do quite as well at the nearest airport for a charge of five dollars. And no one who has ever toiled up a mile-long scree slope under a blistering sun or contorted himself into a pretzel in a black, wet, evil-smelling chimney can say simply "recreation" and let it go at that. Competition, scientific and artistic ends, the thirst for knowledge, even that old stand-by, character-building—all these, too, have at one time or another been advanced as the motive and justification for climbing. At about this stage of the discussion, however, the true mountaineer—if he is also an honest one—resolutely closes his psychology manual and gets to work on the more essential business of oiling his boots.

Climbing needs no justification, no more than does watching a sunrise, or listening to a great symphony, or falling in love. A man climbs because he needs to climb; because that is the way he is made. Rock and ice and wind and the great blue canopy of the sky are not all that he finds upon the mountain-tops. He discovers things about his own body and mind that he had almost forgotten in the day-to-day, year-to-year routine of living. He learns what his legs are for, what his lungs are for, what the wise men of old meant by "refreshment of the spirit." He finds action and rest, solitude and companionship, promise and fulfilment. He finds the divine harmony and simplicity of the natural world, and himself alive in it, a part of it.

The key to the mountaineering spirit is not far to find. It can be found equally in the words of Geoffrey Bruce, gasping and defiant on the heights of Everest, and in the jaunty whistling of a Manhattan shoe clerk, setting out from the Fort Lee ferry for a Sunday tramp among the Hudson Highlands. It lies not in what men *do*, but in what they *are*—in the raising of their eyes and the lifting of their hearts.

II

A SPORT IS BORN

THE WINNING OF THE ALPS

    ALPS—1. *A range of mountains in Europe.*
           2. *Any large range of mountains.*
    ALP—1. *Any mountain in the Alps.*
          2. *An upland meadow or pasture.*
          3. *Any mountain.*
    ALPINE—1. *Pertaining to the Alps.*
            2. *Pertaining to any mountain.*
    ALPINIST—1. *A climber of the Alps.*
             2. *A climber.*
             (derivation uncertain)

THUS THE DICTIONARY. And if the definitions add up to something less than conciseness, they still make one fact abundantly clear: the Alps—as a place, as a descriptive term, as an idea—are inseparable from the whole subject of mountains and mountaineering.

Furthermore, in a very real sense, they are inseparable from the history of western civilization. For uncounted centuries they formed the great natural rampart of the ancient world, separating the thriving nations of the Mediterranean basin from the barbarian hordes of the north. In later times they served as the rugged highroad of conquest, the stepping-stone of Hannibal and Alaric the Goth and Napoleon in their wide-ranging forays which changed the map of the world. Today, towering between the plains of Germany and Italy, they stand at the very heart and nub of war-racked Europe—the Mountains of the Axis.

This is the political history of the Alps. Happily, however, they have also another history—one that unfolds without benefit of kings and generals, clanking armies and rumbling caissons, and dictators plotting in the Brenner Pass. It is a story of men and the spirit of men and the interplay of that spirit with the physical world in which they live. It is a story of the slow, painful conquest of fear, of the gradual spread of knowledge, of the awakening of the world to the challenge of new frontiers. The Alps were the birthplace of mountaineering and the first great range of the earth to be climbed. This in itself is not important. What is important is that they were the first place where it ever even *occurred* to men to climb mountains—where not merely a sport was born, but an idea.

Two centuries ago scarcely a peak in Europe had been ascended; today scarcely one remains that has not, and the high white world above the valleys that was once a shunned and unknown wilderness has become rich in human associations. The winning of the Alps has been a struggle, to be sure—what meaningful human activity has not? It has been marred by pettiness and bitterness, ugly rivalries and jealousies, defeat and tragedy; for mountaineers, no less than kings and generals, are only human. But, in its essence, it has been a struggle not of man against man, nor even of man against the obstacles of the physical world, but of man against his own ignorance and fear.

This is the second history of the Alps. It is less familiar than the first, less important, no doubt, by the usual standards of men. The impression persists, however, that it is a history which does considerably more credit to the human race.

In point of sheer size the Alps are not one of the pre-eminent mountain ranges of the earth. They do not compare to the Himalayas of Asia in height nor to the Rockies or Andes of the New World in extent. From the French Riviera to the environs of Vienna their overall length is somewhat less than six hundred miles, and the elevation of their loftiest summits ranges between 13,000 and 16,000 feet, or roughly half the height of Everest.[1]

[1] For the altitudes of the principal Alpine peaks see Appendix II

THE ALPS

High above the heart of Europe the most famous mountains in the world sweep in a great bow six hundred miles long—from the French Riviera to the environs of Vienna. The Alps are by no means synonymous with Switzerland. Their ramparts rise from the soil of five different nations: France, Italy, Switzerland, Austria and Germany. Their loftiest peaks, however, are concentrated in a comparatively small area between Innsbruck, on the east, and Chamonix, on the west. Here rise the three greatest sub-ranges of the Alps—the Mont Blanc uplift, the Pennines and the Bernese Oberland—containing hundreds of the most celebrated and most frequently climbed mountains on earth.

What the Alps lack in sheer mass, however, is more than offset in beauty, variety and sharp dramatic impact. Their valleys and forests, twisting trails and plunging streams present an ever-changing panorama of soft loveliness and rugged majesty such as can stir the blood of even the most jaded traveller; their great peaks, passes and glaciers remain today, as they have been since men first climbed, the unrivalled paradise of mountaineers. "The Playground of Europe," the noted English climber, Leslie Stephen, called them long ago. He might as rightly have called them the playground of the world.

It is a common supposition among many Americans that the Alps lie wholly, or almost wholly, in Switzerland. This, however, is far from the case. Only about one-third of the range is Swiss, another third is Italian, and the rest is divided equally between France and Austria, with a small segment of the latter section extending into south-eastern Germany. Also, the Alps are by no means a continuous and unbroken chain, but are repeatedly split into sub-chains and lesser ranges by deep passes and valleys and even, in some instances, by open plains. The various districts thus formed are apt to differ greatly, one from another—in terrain and geological structure, in the nationality and language of their inhabitants, in the height of their peaks and their attractions for mountaineers. No true climber would make the mistake of returning home from a vacation and announcing to his colleagues merely that he had been climbing in the Alps. The answer would inevitably be: "What Alps?"

The south-westernmost spurs of the great range rise from the Mediterranean Sea along the French and Italian Rivieras. Roughly paralleling the frontier of the two countries, they are known successively as the Maritime and Cottian Alps and, together, extend due northward for some hundred miles to the pass of Mont Cenis. The average elevation of this region is not high, and there is little to attract the mountaineer, with the shining exception of Monte Viso, in the Italian Cottians, one of the most beautiful of all Alpine peaks and literally the only one to be mentioned in the surviving literature of ancient times.

North-west of the Cottians rise the Dauphiné Alps, centring about Grenoble and wholly French. This is a district of steep

uplands and bold rock towers which in recent years has become
a favourite climbing-ground for expert cragsmen and has been
the scene of some of the most difficult and sensational ascents
ever made. The most famous summits are Mont Pelvoux, Les
Ecrins and La Meije, the last-named having been among the
latest of the major Alpine peaks to be conquered.

   The Graian and Tarentaise Alps lie north-east of the
Dauphiné, between Mont Cenis and the Little St. Bernard Pass,
the former on the French-Italian border, the latter altogether
in France. There are many fine mountains in this region—
notably the Grand Paradis, the Grande Casse and the Grivola
—but they are rather difficult of access and have been infrequently climbed.

   Beyond the Little St. Bernard, near the point where France,
Italy and Switzerland come together, the mountains suddenly
expand on to the grand scale. Here towers the Mont Blanc
range, topped by the great peak itself—the highest of the Alps.
This vast massif presents so many claims to fame in the history
of mountaineering that it is virtually impossible even to list
them. It was the scene of the first extensive mountain explorations, of the first great ascents, of the development of modern
rock-climbing, and of fully half the most famous climbing
exploits of the last seventy-five years. It was here that the profession of guiding had its beginnings. It was here that almost
every noted climber from de Saussure to the present day served
his apprenticeship and, in many cases, performed his finest
feats. Indeed, it might almost be said that no man can truly
call himself a mountaineer unless he has at some time in his
career trod the rock and snow of the great uplift between
Chamonix and Courmayeur.

   The Mont Blanc range is without rival in Europe for the
grandeur of its scenery and in the whole world for the quality
and variety of the climbing which it affords. The main peak
itself is predominantly a snow-mountain, presenting today more
than twenty recognized routes of ascent of all degrees of difficulty. Crowded around it is a veritable army of lesser summits—
domes, knobs, towers, spires—some of them also snow-covered,
more rising in bare bristling granite from their skirts of glaciers.

Most notable of all, perhaps, are the famous and aptly named *aiguilles* (or needles) of Chamonix: du Plan, du Midi, de Triolet, d'Argentière and the rest, topped by the fabulous Aiguille Verte. Others are the Grandes Jorasses, the Charmoz, the Grépon, Mont Dolent, the Dru, the Géant, the Requin—the list is all but endless; and every one is of such structure and form that it might almost have been built to specification for mountaineers. All these lie close within the shadow of Mont Blanc, ranging like great spiky sentinels around the famous glacier of the Mer de Glace. Further afield, across the valley of Chamonix, a smaller but equally fine chain of peaks known as the Aiguilles Rouges runs northward along the French-Swiss border toward the splendid uplifts of the Buet and the Dents du Midi.

Beyond Mont Blanc, however, the main backbone of the Alps makes a right-angle turn and sweeps eastward in the towering chain of the Pennines. Bounded by the famous passes of the Great St. Bernard and the Simplon, this range boasts the highest average elevation of any in the Alps and presents a galaxy of world-famous peaks. Here rise the Breithorn, the Lyskamm, the Grand Combin, the Dent d'Herens, the twins Castor and Pollux, the gigantic snow-dome of Monte Rosa and the incomparable Matterhorn[1]—a towering international rampart with its northern slopes in Switzerland and its southern in Italy. Slightly to the north and wholly in Swiss territory are a host of others no less impressive: the Obergabelhorn, the Zinal-Rothorn, the Dent Blanche, the Strahlhorn, the Weisshorn—the picture-book mountain—and, loftiest of all, the great mass of the Mischabel, which in itself comprises a whole sub-range of peaks, topped by the Täschhorn and the Dom. The principal climbing centres in this region are Zermatt, on the Swiss side, and Breuil, on the Italian, and over a period of three-quarters of a century they have witnessed many of the most celebrated exploits in mountaineering history.

North of the Pennines and separated from them by the upper Rhone valley lies the vast jumble of peaks, valleys, passes and

[1] The French call the Matterhorn Mont Cervin; the Italian Monte Cervino. The English, however, and climbers generally, know it by its German name.

glaciers known as the Bernese Oberland. This is the heart of Switzerland, and though its summits are not quite so high as those of Mont Blanc and the Pennines, it yields to neither in majesty of scenery or attraction for the mountaineer. The most famous summits, many of them rising like the walls of an amphitheatre about the little town of Grindelwald, include the Schreckhorn, the Wetterhorn, the Finsteraarhorn, the Blümlisalp, the Aletschhorn, the Bietschhorn and, pre-eminently, the great triumvirate of Jungfrau, Mönch and Eiger. The imagination can spin drama out of the very names of these three—the Virgin, the Monk and the Ogre. The Oberland, lying within easy travelling distance of Interlaken and Lucerne, is more accessible from northern Europe than most sections of the Alps and over the years has probably been the scene of greater climbing activity than any other high mountain region in the world.

Mont Blanc, the Pennines and the Oberland are the culminating points of the Alps. Further east the great range still sweeps on for hundreds of miles—to the Adriatic, to the outskirts of Munich and Vienna—but it never again quite matches the height and grandeur of these three huge uplifts.

Even more than in the west, it now spreads out into separately designated sub-ranges and mountain groups. In the south the Lepontine Alps continue the rampart begun by the Pennines along the Swiss-Italian frontier, extending for some seventy-five miles from the Simplon to the Splügen Pass and cut in two by the celebrated St. Gotthard. The outstanding summits here are Monte Leone, Pizzo Rotondo and the Rheinwaldhorn. Still further on are the Albula, Bergamasque and Rhaetian ranges, the last-named distinguished by the magnificent isolated peak of Monte della Disgrazia, and beyond them the Dolomites, the Carnic Alps and the Julian Alps, curving down in a great horseshoe toward the Adriatic. Of these, the Dolomites, centred about the Italian town of Cortina, are of special interest. Formed of a peculiar type of limestone, known likewise as dolomite, they are bold in outline, strikingly reddish in hue, and present a rough, almost sponge-like outer surface unmatched anywhere else in the Alps. Mountaineering on this range is limited in its scope, as there is virtually no ice or snow, but some of the most sensational rock-climbing of recent years has been accomplished upon its precipices, chimneys and giddy pinnacles.

The Bernina and Silvretta Alps—in reality a northward continuation of the Rhaetians—lie east of the Lepontines between the Splügen Pass and the Austrian border. This is the region known as the Engadine, and its centre is the famous international resort of St. Moritz. The Berninas are for the most part massive snowpeaks, better suited to ski mountaineering, perhaps, than to the more usual forms of climbing. Among the outstanding summits are the Piz Bernina itself, Piz Roseg, Piz Scersen and Piz Palu, the last-named ranking among the most photographed mountains of the world. The Silvretta group, farther to the north, culminate in the impressive summit of Piz Linard, and beyond it the range fans out into the numerous, but less important, chains of north-eastern Switzerland.

The Austrian Alps sweep eastward from the Swiss border, past Innsbruck, toward Salzburg and Vienna. They completely fill the narrow corridor between Italy and Bavaria, and are cut laterally into two roughly equal sections by the broad gash of the Brenner Pass. West of the Brenner the principal peaks are, from north to south, the Zugspitze, the Wildspitze, the Weisskugel and the great massif of the Ortler, perhaps the finest uplift of the eastern Alps. Actually, neither the first nor last of these lies in Austrian territory—the Zugspitze is just over the line in Bavaria, and the Ortler since the First World War has been wholly Italian—but both are nevertheless part and parcel of the Tyrolese chain. East of the Brenner are the Zillerthal mountains and the outstanding massifs of the Gross Venediger and the Gross Glockner; then, finally, comes the outpost peak of the Hohe Dachstein, and great ranges slope gradually away into the rolling forest-land of central Austria.

These are the Alps. For some thirty thousand centuries their white crests loomed above the heart of Europe, as remote from the tides of life as if they stood upon the surface of another planet.

Indeed, it is hard to say just when what we may call the human history of the Alps began. The ancient Romans were familiar with them, of course, and many records have come down to us of their legions marching through the passes of the Brenner and the St. Bernard; but there is no indication of their having ascended, or even having attempted to ascend, any of the actual peaks. In fact, Monte Viso, the great white watchtower at the source of the Po, is the only Alpine summit to be mentioned by name in all the surviving writings of the old historians. The Romans were conquerors and explorers, but they were no mountaineers.

Then came the Middle Ages and silence.

A few accounts exist of sporadic ventures in the foothills of the Alps during the thirteenth and fourteenth centuries, but the first complete and authenticated ascent of a peak did not take place until late in the fifteenth—in fact in the significant year 1492. This was the climbing of Mont Aiguille in the Dauphiné by one Antoine de Ville of Grenoble. Undertaken at the command of King Charles VIII of France, it was a truly remarkable exploit, for the Aiguille, though not high, is a steep and formidable rock tower. Even today its ascent is considered a fairly difficult one; 450 years ago it was all but miraculous.

The sixteenth century was the age of the High Renaissance and, as might be expected, marked the beginnings of the first fairly systematic exploration of the Alps. In the forefront of the pioneers was no less a figure than Leonardo da Vinci, that universal genius who made the whole realm of human knowledge his own; and we find him, as early as 1500, venturing high on the southern slopes of the Pennines in the interest of meteorological investigation. More truly mountaineers, however, were a group of men who a few years later began climbing and exploring among the ranges of northern Switzerland. Their leading spirits were Conrad Gesner and Josias Simler, professors at the University of

Zurich, and their writings are the first of which we have any record that exhibit an interest in mountains and mountain climbing for their own sake. The actual ascents made by Gesner, Simler and their followers are unimportant—the highest was probably the 7,000 foot Pilatus on the shores of Lake Lucerne—but they did more than anyone before them to dispel the age-old fear with which men regarded the high places of the Alps.

The next two hundred years, however, saw little progress, and as late as 1725 "authoritative" guides to Switzerland were being published which included detailed descriptions and classifications of Alpine dragons. Then gradually, in the middle of the eighteenth century, a profound change began to occur. It was a change, to be sure, that extended far beyond the province of mountains and mountaineering, into the whole fabric of men's lives and ways of thought. The American and French revolutions were in the making; democracy, capitalism, science, the industrial revolution—a thousand new concepts and institutions were evolving slowly out of the doldrums of an outworn and stagnant civilization. And, in key with the times, men presently found themselves eyeing the Alps with a new perspective and a clearer vision. Travellers on the celebrated "Grand Tour" no longer gazed up from their valley inns with horror, but with admiring awe. Naturalists and other curious wanderers pushed up toward the treeless slopes and the high glacial passes. Books and pamphlets were circulated in ever increasing numbers, dealing not with dragons, but with climate, flora, fauna, rock structure, glaciers. Strongest and clearest of all was the voice of Rousseau, the impassioned prophet of the new order. His *La Nouvelle Héloïse*, in fact, published in 1769 and devoted largely to the glorification of untamed nature, had perhaps the widest circulation and greatest influence of any book of its time.

The horizons of the world were expanding again, as they had during the Renaissance and in the golden age of Greece. All Europe was astir with ideas and events, and great exploits were at hand—in the Alps as elsewhere.

A SPORT IS BORN

England has its 1066, the New World its 1492, the United States its 1776. The first great date in the story of mountaineering is 1786, the year of the climbing of Mont Blanc.

Mont Blanc is not only the highest of the Alps; it is the highest mountain in Europe west of the Caucasus. Situated some fifty miles south-east of Geneva, on the high frontier where France, Italy and Switzerland meet, its 15,782-foot summit is wholly French, but its slopes build up from the territory of all three nations, making it one of the most truly international of mountains. It is as impressive as it is huge. A snowpeak rather than a rock-peak, it rises from an enormously broad base in a great sweep of glaciers, soars for thousands of feet in a complex maze of plateaux and ice-walls, ridges and sub-peaks, and culminates in a massive buttressed summit like the dome of a cathedral. Seen from whatever side, it completely dominates its surroundings, appearing from the distance less a mountain among mountains than a single blindingly white mass suspended in the sky.

Unlike most of the world's great peaks, Mont Blanc has long been familiar to men. Many of the ancient trade routes of Europe passed within view of its shining summit, and as early as the eleventh century a priory had been established in the French valley of Chamonix at its very base. Like all other mountains, however, it remained for hundreds of years an object of fear and superstitious legend, and it is not until after 1700 that we have any record of men approaching even so far as its lower slopes and the snouts of its great glaciers. These earliest pioneers were crystal-seekers and chamois-hunters, and, while they contributed little to the actual exploration of the mountain, they at least brought back the cheering tidings that the expected demons and dragons had failed to materialize. Soon others were following where they had blazed the way—scientists, travellers, adventuresome spirits from all parts of Europe. By the middle years of the eighteenth century the terrain surrounding Mont Blanc had been fairly well explored, its great snow-dome was established as one of the celebrated "sights" of the continent, and

Cc

Chamonix was already on its way to becoming the famous international resort it has remained ever since.

Scientist, tourist and peasant alike, however, were content to go about their business in the valleys and gaze up at the mountain from afar, and it remained for one man to look upon it and feel its challenge and say to himself the magic words: "I must get to the top." The man was Henri Benedict de Saussure, and he was to become the first, and one of the greatest, of mountaineers.

Looked at from the perspective of almost two centuries, de Saussure is a remarkable figure. A native of Geneva, he was both a man of great wealth and social position and a scholar whose researches in the natural sciences had made his name known throughout Europe. Visiting Chamonix in 1760 in pursuance of his study of glaciers, he conceived the idea, undreamed of by any others, that Mont Blanc could—and should—be climbed, and a great part of his labours and energies for more than a quarter of a century thereafter were devoted to that end. To be sure, there was no such thing as a mountaineer at the time—neither the word nor the idea existed. De Saussure himself, in almost all his writings, refers to his great project as a purely scientific venture, devoted to geological study and observation. But only one kind of man could have known feelings such as he recorded after one of his many visits to Chamonix. "It became for me a kind of illness," he wrote. "I could not even look upon the mountain, which is visible from so many points round about, without being seized with an aching of desire."

Whether or not the word then existed, de Saussure was a mountaineer.

Chiefly as a result of his enthusiasm and planning, several attempts were made on Mont Blanc between 1775 and 1785. All of them, including one by de Saussure himself, fell far short of the goal; but each successive venture added something to men's knowledge of the mountain and, more important still, resulted in the development in Chamonix of a sizable group of skilled and experienced climbers—the forerunners of the professional Alpine guides. By the summer of 1786 de Saussure was no longer alone in his belief that the mighty summit could be attained. The mountain had at last fired the imagination of others, and the struggle for its conquest began in earnest.

As it turned out, it was to be a struggle that is unique in mountaineering annals. The records of most great climbs are concerned primarily with physical obstacles met and overcome—with glaciers, precipices and ridges, cold, altitude and storms. The conquerors of Mont Blanc, to be sure, encountered their full share of these, and their exploits bear full witness to their skill and courage. But the basic drama of the story is concerned with the characters and personalities of the men involved. For in its whole subsequent history it is doubtful if mountaineering supplies a more pointed example of both the good and the bad that it can generate in its followers.

De Saussure was the motivating force behind every attempt to climb the mountain and the dominant figure in its conquest. But the men who were the first to stand upon its summit were Michel Gabriel Paccard and Jacques Balmat. Paccard was a physician of Chamonix, Balmat a peasant guide and crystal-hunter. Despite great difficulties in background and education, however, the two men were as one in their love of mountains, and both had been fired by de Saussure's enthusiasm to vanquish the great peak that overlooked their native valley. Over a period of several years each on his own had made extensive reconnaissances of the approaches to the summit. Then at last, on the morning of August 7, 1786, they set out together to reach it.

The external facts of their epoch-making ascent are simple and well-known. Ascending steadily all through the first day, Paccard and Balmat worked their way up the great glaciers that buttress the Chamonix face of the mountain. After several hours they traversed to the more stable footing of the so-called Montagne de la Côte, a long tongue of solid ground running far up into the higher slopes, and, following it to its top, came out on the jagged prominence where the oft-visited Grands Mulets hut stands today. Near here they spent the night, improvising a tiny shelter. The next morning, frost-bitten but undaunted, they pushed on, passing in turn over two great tilted snowfields known as the Petit Plateau and the Grand Plateau and then inching up a precarious snow-ridge between two bristling bands of outcropping rock.[1] This passage, as it turned out, was the crux of the ascent. There remained only the gentle white slopes of the summit dome, and at 6.30 in the evening the two adventurers were standing, exhausted but triumphant, on the highest pinnacle of the highest mountain in the Alps. Forty-eight hours later, after an arduous descent, they stumbled into Chamonix, to be greeted as heroes by their rejoicing fellow-townsmen.

Thus was Mont Blanc won; but the real struggle over its winning was yet to come. The peasant Balmat was unfortunately a man whose head was easily turned by success and fame, and he promptly began boasting to all who would listen that it was he and he alone who deserved credit for the great ascent. Paccard, he claimed, had been merely excess baggage. It had been he, Balmat, who had discovered the route to the summit, hacked out the laborious way and, indeed, all but carried the poor doctor on his shoulders during most of the climb. It was not long before rumours were circulating to the effect that Paccard had not reached the summit at all.

It is doubtful if much credence would have been given Balmat's fantastic tale had it not been for the entrance into the controversy of still another figure—one Marc Théodore Bourrit. Bourrit was a Swiss writer and journalist of some note at the time and a recognized authority on Alpine exploration. For several years past he had been among the forefront of those who believed that Mont Blanc could be climbed and had, indeed, made several attempts of his own to gain the summit; but all of them had been complete, and even ludicrous, failures. An inordinately vain and egotistical man, he nevertheless clung

---

[1] These rock-bands, immediately beneath the summit dome, are called the Rochers Rouges and are a distinguishing feature of the upper mountain as seen from Chamonix. Paccard's and Balmat's route passed between them, but de Saussure, on his ascent, followed the snow above the upper band. This latter route was soon to become one of the most famous in the Alps and is known today as the *Ancien Passage*.

to the hope that he would be the first to reach the famous summit, and he watched his various rivals with a sharp and jealous eye. The result was that when Paccard, whom he particularly resented, won the coveted prize, he threw himself into the work of discrediting him with all the energy and resources at his command. Soon after the ascent he published a pamphlet which supported, and even elaborated, Balmat's boastful story, and for years thereafter lost no opportunity to minimize the doctor's role in the exploit.

Indeed, Bourrit may be said to have established what is probably an all-time endurance record for spite, for, as late as 1832, when he was an old man of seventy, we find him repeating his fabricated story to no less a personage than Alexandre Dumas the elder. Dumas, unfortunately, took his account at its face value, and his subsequent "history" of the conquest of Mont Blanc, based on Bourrit's lies, enjoyed world-wide circulation and went unchallenged for many years. It is only comparatively recently that historians of mountaineering have uncovered the authentic records of the venture, which prove conclusively that Paccard was not only its moving spirit but the pathfinder and leader through most of the ascent.

In pleasant contrast to the machinations of Bourrit and Balmat was the exemplary conduct of de Saussure. Disappointed though he must have been at not being the first to the summit, he was generous in his praise of the victors and in the following summer of 1787 returned again to Chamonix for yet another try on his own. He was not even to be second up, however, for in early June of that year, while he was still busy with preparations, Balmat again reached the top of Mont Blanc, this time in company with two fellow-guides. Nevertheless, de Saussure proceeded unruffled with his plans and at last, on the first of August, set out on his long-dreamed-of venture.

From the strictly mountaineering point of view de Saussure's ascent of Mont Blanc is of interest today chiefly as a curiosity. The huge climbing party consisted of no less than twenty persons: the scientist himself, eighteen guides headed by the ubiquitous Balmat, and—of all things—de Saussure's valet,

who had never been on a mountain in his life. They were
loaded down with an enormous quantity of provisions and
heavy scientific instruments, as well as much primitive climbing
equipment and large crêpe masks to shield their eyes from the
sun's glare, and through much of the ascent were strung out
haphazardly along the steep slopes in a fashion that would
cause a present-day alpinist to shudder. The glimpses we are
given of de Saussure himself show him plodding upward
between two guides, one hand resting on an alpenstock which
they hold between him and the precipice as a railing. There
were constant minor mishaps, long arguments as to routes and
camp-sites, threatened mutinies and desertions. But in the end
de Saussure's resolute spirit prevailed over all obstacles, and
late afternoon of the second day found virtually the entire party
crowded exultantly together on the summit. A full four and a
half hours were spent there, devoted to scientific observations
and recordings; then through the two succeeding days the
caravan staggered triumphantly down to the valley.

Almost without exception it is the first ascent of a mountain
that becomes the famous ascent. This was not, however, to be
the case with Mont Blanc: de Saussure's climb was destined not
only to eclipse that of his predecessors but to become, in a
historical sense, perhaps the most important single event in the
history of mountaineering. Paccard and Balmat were obscure
French villagers, and their exploit was of small interest to a
world that had not yet awakened to the challenge of mountains. De Saussure, on the other hand, was both an aristocrat
and an internationally known scientist. All Europe, figuratively,
watched and held its breath as he struggled to the summit of
the highest Alp, and his success and subsequent writings about
it had the effect of wiping away, almost in one stroke, the age-
old terror and superstition with which men regarded the high
places of the earth.—"Lift up thine eyes unto the hills," adjure
the Scriptures. Now at last, with de Saussure's conquest of
Mont Blanc, the world lifted them for the first time without fear.

The true birth of mountaineering as a sport was, however,
still far in the future. For more than half a century ninety per

cent of the climbing in the Alps consisted of endless ascents and re-ascents of Mont Blanc, and although a few new trails were blazed and various improvements made in technique and equipment, the great majority of climbers were content to follow the routes and methods of the pioneers. The fourth ascent of the peak was made by an Englishman, Colonel Beaufoy, less than a week after de Saussure's successful climb, the fifth by another Englishman, Woodley, the following year. Woodley was accompanied on his ascent by the journalist Bourrit, but the latter gave out when only a few hundred feet from the top. Indeed, it is a pleasant instance of poetic justice that he never succeeded in reaching it.

The French Revolution and the Napoleonic Wars put a pause to climbing for a considerable period around the turn of the century, but after 1818 activity was resumed and increased steadily thereafter. Among the more noteworthy ascents were that by the first American party, in 1819, and that by the first great woman-mountaineer, Henriette d'Angeville, in 1838. Although no one knows how often Mont Blanc has been climbed in the past five score years, it is safe to say that the figure runs into many thousands.

It is elsewhere, however, that we must look for the next important developments in the struggle between mountains and men. While the great snowpeak of Chamonix basked in the spotlight and drew the tourists, a small group of adventurous men were gradually filtering into other and less-known regions of the Alps, exploring the passes and glaciers, working their way ever higher and higher toward the peaks. Outstanding among these were the members of a wealthy Swiss merchant family named Meyer, who ranged widely through the Bernese Oberland during the early years of the nineteenth century and among other exploits accomplished, in 1811, the first ascent of the famous Jungfrau. Another important pioneer was J. D. Forbes, who, though actually a Scot, may yet properly be called the first true British mountaineer. Between 1827 and 1844 Forbes visited virtually every district of the Alps, from the Dauphiné to the Dolomites, crossing the high passes and glaciers, circling the peaks, breaking new ground wherever he went. His record of first ascents, like that of the Meyers, was impressive, but even more important in the historical sense was the interest which his expeditions aroused among his fellow-countrymen. It was he, in fact, more than any other man, who was responsible for the development of that whole school of British climbers who were soon to make the realm of the Alps so completely and brilliantly their own.

As the century grew older other influences were also at work, turning the eyes and ambitions of men toward high places. The industrial revolution had created in Europe an upper-middle class with the means and leisure for extended journeys. Furthermore it had provided railroads which put the Alps within easy travelling distance of the great cities of the north, and each year such resorts as Chamonix, Zermatt and Grindelwald were thronged with larger and larger crowds of tourists. The work of the distinguished Swiss-American naturalist, Louis Agassiz, focused the attention of science on the geology of mountains and the movements of glaciers; in the field of literature, John Ruskin, picking up the torch where Rousseau had dropped it, preached eloquently not only of the physical, but the spiritual grandeur of the great peaks and ranges; and on every hand pamphlets, guide-books and travel-brochures on the Alps were making an appearance and gaining wide circulation.

To all this was presently added the phenomenal influence of one Dr. Albert Smith. Smith, by profession, was an English physician, but in inclination and talent he was a showman and high-pressure publicity-agent. Having made the ascent of Mont Blanc in 1851, he conceived the idea of making a good thing of it commercially, and accordingly, the following year, produced at a London theatre a show purporting to be based on his experiences. The show, which took the form of an illustrated lecture and featured the wildest kind of melodrama, was an instant and huge success, running for six consecutive years and bringing mountains and mountaineering to the attention of a wide public which would never have heard of them through a hundred years of scientific treatises and literary essays. Indeed, not a few of the earliest English climbers themselves, who were for the most part highly educated men, were by their own admission first exposed to the lure of the Alps through the medium of Dr. Smith's penny-dreadful thriller.

At all events, the tide was rising, and the time was at hand when it was to be in flood.

By the middle of the century a total of perhaps a hundred Alpine peaks had been ascended. These included, besides Mont Blanc and the Jungfrau, such famous summits as the Ortler, the Finsteraarhorn, the Gross Venediger, Mont Pelvoux, and all but the very highest pinnacle of Monte Rosa, as well as many others only slightly less celebrated. But the climbing had been done by only a few scattered enthusiasts over a long period of years, and it remained for the 1850's to witness the first large-scale invasion of the mountains and the emergence of climbing as a recognized and widely practised sport.

1854 is generally accepted as the date on which the so-called "Golden Age" of mountaineering began. Almost as if by a pre-arranged signal, a throng of ambitious and accomplished climbers made their appearance in the Alps during the summer of that year, reconnoitring, exploring, wandering far and high afield into the still realms of rock and snow where no men had ever been before. In 1855 their number was larger, in 1856 still larger, and throughout the next decade the invasion swelled by leaps and bounds. One by one, ten by ten, finally hundred by hundred, the great summits began to fall before the onslaught—among them vast, awe-inspiring mountain-masses which until a few years before had seemed destined to remain unclimbed until the end of time. The outstanding conquest of 1854 was the Wetterhorn. The following summer came the highest point of Monte Rosa; in 1857 the Mönch; in '58 the Dom; between '59 and '64 the Bietschhorn, the Aletschhorn, the Grand Combin, the Dent Blanche, Monte Viso, the Schreckhorn, Lyskamm, Disgrazia, the Grandes Jorasses, the Täschhorn, the Weisshorn. The list, indeed, is almost endless, and in 1865, when the tide culminated in the conquest of the fabled Matterhorn, only a negligible handful of virgin summits remained throughout the length and breadth of the Alps.

The climbers of this halcyon period were almost exclusively English. Forbes, who may well be called the godfather of them all, had retired from active mountaineering some time before, but there were now hundreds of his countrymen ready to take up where he had left off, and during the years that followed one might almost have thought the Alps were actually British, rather than Swiss and French, Italian and Austrian. The great names among these early climbers were legion, and scant justice can be done most of them in a record that must perforce skip over decades in seven-league boots. Outstanding among them were the Reverend Charles Hudson, Alfred Wills, Leslie Stephen, John Tyndall, A. W. Moore, F. F. Tuckett, E. S. Kennedy, and, pre-eminently, Edward Whymper, who was to become perhaps the most dramatic figure in the history of mountaineering. Many of these men are best remembered by posterity for the conquest of one or more specific peaks—Wills for the Wetterhorn, for example, Tyndall for the Weisshorn, Whymper and Hudson for the Matterhorn. But few of them, it should be noted, were mere one-peak adventurers like the majority of their predecessors on Mont Blanc. They were mountaineers in the truest, deepest sense—wide-ranging, catholic in their interests, loving the mountains for their own sake as well as for such triumphs as they could win from them—and their legacy to the infant sport of climbing was far more than a statistical record of "famous firsts."

Indeed, the whole term "Golden Age," signifies much more than a lot of men climbing a lot of peaks at random. Mountaineering was still primarily an adventure—in any age and under any circumstances it is primarily that—but the conquerors of the Alps were not long in discovering that it could also be a craft, a science and an art. Each year, during the 'fifties and 'sixties, climbers came to know more about the structure and behaviour of mountains, about glaciers and crevasses, sound rock and rotten rock, stonefalls and avalanches, and the other phenomena of the high, untrodden world above the trees. Route-finding, bivouacking and the use of alpenstock and rope were brought to a new degree of efficiency. The ice-axe, second in importance only to the rope among the climber's tools, was devised and perfected. The profession of guiding developed rapidly, not only in the number of practitioners but in standards of performance. Guide-books and maps were published, routes marked out, huts and shelters built. And with the formation in 1857 of the Alpine Club of London, a means was provided for the promotion and collation of mountaineering knowledge and the future of the newborn sport was assured.

So many noteworthy climbs were made during this prodigal period that it is well-nigh impossible to single out any of them as being of greater interest or importance than the others. Wills' conquest of the Wetterhorn stands out not so much because of its actual difficulties, but because it headed the parade. In 1855 came one of the historic exploits of Hudson and Kennedy—the climbing of Mont Blanc by a new route and without guides. The ascent of Disgrazia in 1862, by Stephen and Kennedy, was a remarkable feat; so too was that of the Lyskamm, a year earlier, by a party of no less than fourteen members. Perhaps the greatest of all—also accomplished in 1861—was the magnificent struggle of Tyndall and his guide Bennen up the huge snow-spire of the Weisshorn—a peak whose reputation for invincibility was second only to that of the terrible Matterhorn.

Yet the true significance of the period is to be found less in such individual exploits, extraordinary though many of them were, than in the cumulative results of them all. At its inception ninety per cent of the great Alpine summits were still untouched, unknown, as they had been for three million years. At its close ninety per cent had been ascended. Before 1854 a man climbing a mountain was simply—a man climbing a mountain. A decade later he was a mountaineer. The Alps had been won, a sport born.

III

A MOUNTAIN AND A MAN

THE ASCENT OF THE MATTERHORN

LATE IN THE morning of July 15, 1865, three dazed, exhausted men stumbled down from the glaciers into the Swiss village of Zermatt. They were returning from the conquest of the most famous mountain of Europe, but there was no spring to their step, no light of victory in their eyes. Swiftly and silently the villagers gathered around them, and in the eyes of all there was but one sombre question:
"Where are the other four?"

It was then that Edward Whymper told the story of the climbing of the Matterhorn. Today, after more than three-quarters of a century, it is still one of the great, tragic adventure stories of the world.

There are hundreds of mountains higher than the Matterhorn; there are hundreds that are harder to climb. But there is none, anywhere in the world, which has so consistently and deeply stirred the imagination of men. Rising in an immense isolated pyramid on the high frontier between Switzerland and Italy, it possesses not only the dimensions, but the stark simplicity, of greatness, and its sprawling neighbour-peaks, several of which actually exceed its 14,782 foot altitude, seem to shrink into insignificance beside it. Through all the centuries that men have known and travelled the Alps their eyes have been drawn irresistibly upward to its savage, soaring pinnacle. Other mountains were—well—mountains. This mountain was beauty and magic and terror.

In the early sixties of the last century the Matterhorn was as famous as it is today—but for a different reason. The previous decade, as we have seen, had been the great age of Alpine mountaineering, and with the first ascent of the Weisshorn by Tyndall in 1861, virtually all the great peaks of Central Europe had fallen. All, that is, save one—for the Matterhorn still towered into the sky, untouched and unchallenged as it had been since the beginning of time. But men scarcely counted it in their reckonings. The Swiss and Italian peasants of the surrounding valleys looked up at its cloud-hung battlements with superstitious awe and spoke fearfully of a ruined city on the summit where ghosts and demons dwelt. Even the unsuperstitious—travellers, scientists and mountaineers from all over Europe—stared at it in fascination, shook their heads, and turned away. True, there had been a half-dozen or so attempts to gain the upper reaches of the peak, but all had been utterly defeated, and none who returned held out any hope for future success. The Matterhorn, men were agreed, was not only an unconquered mountain. It was unconquerable.

They did not know that in the summer of 1860 Edward Whymper had made his first visit to the Alps.

In that year Whymper was only twenty and had as yet made none of the famous ascents which were to make him the foremost mountaineer of his day. Indeed, he did not know that he was a mountaineer at all. An artist and illustrator by profession, he came to Switzerland from England for a few weeks of sketching and intended to do no more climbing than was necessary to find vantage points for his easel and brush. But the great peaks cast their spell upon him, and the fever to climb and conquer came into his blood. Alone and with local guides, he made many notable ascents, but, once his eyes had feasted on the fabulous Matterhorn, all else became of secondary interest to him. Here, he told himself, was a mountain fashioned for an artist's dream: the unclimbed mountain, the unclimable mountain. Staring up at it with pounding heart, he vowed that it would be his.

Thus began what remains to this day the most relentless battle ever waged between a mountain and a man. Seven times in five years Whymper attacked the Matterhorn, and seven times he was beaten back. The obstacles that confronted him were enough to have broken the spirit—not to mention the neck—of a lesser man. In addition to the natural perils of precipice and glacier, storm and avalanche, he had also to contend with the stupidity, cowardice and treachery of men. But he kept on, undismayed—dreaming, planning, attacking, counter-attacking; on each of his seven unsuccessful attempts he made progress and learned a little more about his mighty antagonist than he had known before; and at last, on the eighth attempt, he went to the top. No mountaineer has ever had a greater triumph. Nor, as fate in the end decreed, a more bitter one.

On his first visit, in 1860, Whymper did not actually come to grips with the mountain, but contented himself with studying it, carefully and patiently. He saw that it was built in the shape of a colossal pyramid, with four principal faces and four well-defined corners, the whole mass thrusting skyward in precipice upon precipice to a height of some 5,000 feet above its skirt of glaciers. Across this vertical mile the wind howled with unchecked fury, and down its chimneys and gullies roared endless avalanches of rock and ice. For the men who ventured into that savage, slanting world death would lurk not only in the abysses below; at every moment it would be clutching at their clothing or hanging invisible above them, poised, ready to fall.

The northern and western sides of the peak seemed to Whymper to be utterly inaccessible. He therefore did most of his reconnoitring from the south and east, chiefly in the region of the Theodule Pass, a great glacial bridge that connects the Swiss valley of Zermatt with the Italian Val Tournanche. The line drawing on page 48, adapted from Whymper's own, shows the outlines of the Matterhorn from the summit of this pass, itself 10,900 feet above the sea. As can be seen, two possible routes suggest themselves: the north-east and south-west ridges, the former leading up from the direction of Zermatt, the latter from the village of Breuil in the Val Tournanche. Of the two, the north-eastern seemed to Whymper the more direct, but he judged the south-western to be less steep, and when he returned to England in the late summer of 1860 he had already determined that this would be his route of attack.

And so it was, through six fruitless attempts during the summers of 1861, 1862 and 1863. It was not until five years later that Whymper at last turned to the north-east ridge—and to triumph and tragedy.

On the morning of August 29, 1861, Whymper set out from Breuil on the first of his great adventures. He was accompanied by a solitary guide—the only man in all the surrounding villages he could induce to go with him. They spent the first night in a shed in the highest pasture of the Val Tournanche, where their herdsmen-hosts spoke fearfully of the demons of the Matterhorn and pleaded with them to turn back. The next day, however, they pushed upward, ascending the Glacier du Lion and skirting the cliffs of the Tête du Lion at its head, until they reached a high narrow saddle leading to the base of the Matterhorn's south-west ridge. On the snowy summit of this saddle, shown in the drawing as the Col du Lion, they pitched their tent.

They were now well within the domain of the great peak, almost a mile above Breuil. On one side of them steep slopes of glassy snow descended to the glacier they had crossed. On the other a sheer wall fell away to the Tiefenmatten Glacier, so far below that when they threw down a bottle no sound returned for more than a dozen seconds. At nightfall it grew bitterly cold; the wind howled and tugged against the canvas of their tent, and the water froze in a flask under Whymper's head. They succeeded, however, in dozing for a while, until "—about midnight there came from high aloft a tremendous explosion, followed by a second of dead quiet. A great mass of rock had split off and was descending toward us. My guide started up, wrung his hands and exclaimed, 'O my God, we are lost!' We heard it coming, mass after mass pouring over the precipices, bounding and rebounding from cliff to cliff, and the great rocks in advance smiting one another." Luckily only a few fragments fell near the tent, but there

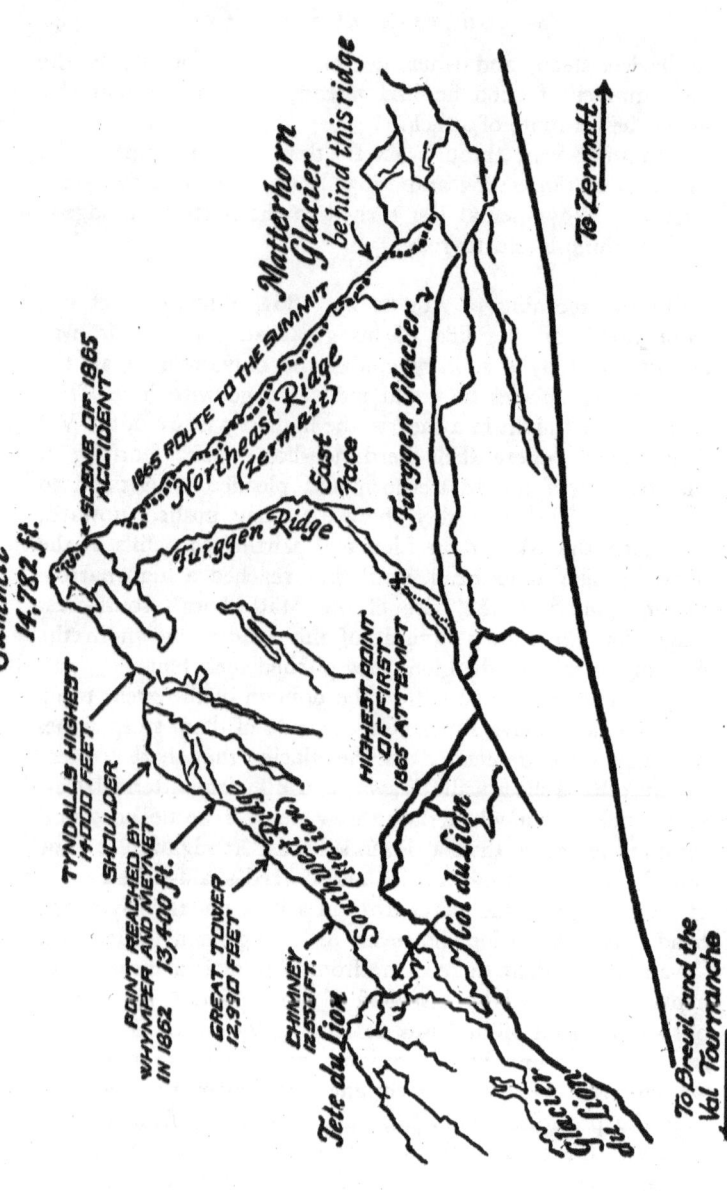

was little sleep for the two men the rest of that night. Whymper had had his first taste of the cannonading of the Matterhorn.

At dawn they began the ascent of the south-west ridge. The day was fine, the climbing was hard but in no way hazardous, and the heights above seemed very near. Pausing for a moment's rest, Whymper's heart pounded with the excitement of the artist and mountaineer.

"We overlook the Tête du Lion," he writes, "and nothing except the Dent d'Herens stands in the way. The ranges of the Graian Alps, an ocean of mountains, are seen at a glance —how soft and yet how sharp they look in the early morning! The mid-day mists have not begun to rise; nothing is obscured; even the pointed Viso, all but a hundred miles away, is perfectly defined.

"Turn to the east and watch the sun's slanting rays coming across the Monte Rosa snowfields. Look at the shadowed parts and see how even they, radiant with reflected light, are more brilliant than man knows how to depict. . . . Then note the sunlight as it steals noiselessly along and reveals countless unsuspected forms—the delicate ripple-lines which mark the concealed crevasse, and the waves of drifted snow, producing each minute more lights and fresh shadows, sparkling on the edges and glittering on the ends of the icicles, shining on the heights and illuminating the depths, until all is aglow and the dazzled eye returns for relief to the sombre crags."

His joy and exhilaration, alas, were to be short-lived. Less than an hour after leaving the Col du Lion they came to a point known as the Chimney—a smooth, almost vertical slab of rock fixed between two other rocks, equally smooth. Bracing himself against the sides and using several tiny cracks for holds, Whymper succeeded in scrambling up, but his guide, after several unsuccessful attempts, suddenly untied himself from the rope and announced that he would go no farther. "I told him he was a coward," said Whymper, "and *he* mentioned his opinion of me." Argument, however, was fruitless; the guide insisted on going down, and the artist, frustrated and angry, had to follow.

"The day was perfect; the wind had fallen; the way seemed clear, no insuperable obstacle was in sight; but what could one do alone?"

Thus the first assault on the Matterhorn ended at a height of 12,550 feet.

Whymper did not attempt the mountain again in 1861, but the following summer he was back in full cry and launched no less than four separate attacks. Warned by his earlier experience, he had determined that in future he would not depend on the whims of a single guide. His first venture of 1862 was therefore undertaken with four companions: his friend and fellow-mountaineer, Reginald Macdonald, two Zermatt guides, Taugwald and Kronig, and, as porter, a little hunchback from the village of Breuil, Luk Meynet. Of these, strangely enough, it was Meynet who was destined to play the most heroic role in the arduous days to come.

In spite of the strong party and elaborate plans Whymper's second try was doomed to quick and complete defeat. A nasty fall by one of the guides delayed them while crossing the Glacier du Lion and dampened the spirits of the others. Then, no sooner had they reached the Col du Lion and made camp than a strong wind blew up, freezing their hands and feet and causing them to spend a sleepless night holding their wildly flapping tent.

By morning a hurricane was howling at them from the great snowfields of Monte Rosa, to the east. Taking advantage of a brief lull they made a start up the south-west ridge, only to have the gales whip back at them with renewed frenzy. "Advance or return," wrote Whymper, "were alike impossible; the ridge was denuded of its debris, and we saw stones as big as a man's fist blown away horizontally into space. We dared not attempt to stand upright and remained stationary on all fours, glued, as it were, to the rocks."

It was all they could do, in the next lull, to make the return to the tent, and even their diehard leader had to admit defeat. Battered and chagrined, they descended to Breuil.

"THAT AWFUL MOUNTAIN" [*Ewing Galloway*

The Matterhorn from the north-east. The ridge in the centre foreground is that climbed by Whymper and his six companions and is to-day the "usual" route from Zermatt. The ridge on the left is the Furggen, that on the right the Zmutt.

WHITE DEATH [Ewing Galloway.
An avalanche thundering down a mountainside in the Bernese Oberland of Switzerland.

Whymper's next attempt—his third—is noteworthy in that it marked the beginning of his association with the great guide, Jean-Antoine Carrel. Carrel was famous throughout the Alps as a climber of unsurpassed skill and daring, and, in addition, he was perhaps the only mountaineer in the world, outside of Whymper, who believed the Matterhorn *could* be climbed. It had been his lifelong dream that he should be the first to stand upon the summit of the great peak—for the honour of Italy and his native Val Tournanche —and for years past he had explored the mountain and sought vainly to conquer it. Whymper had met him in 1860 and 1861, but until now all the artist's efforts to secure him as guide had failed. Proud and strong-willed, Carrel resented the intrusion of an outsider on what he considered his own personal preserve, and indeed, in 1861, had not only refused to accompany Whymper on his first attempt but had made a separate attack of his own on the very same day. Now at last, however, he came to the decision that it was wiser to fight with this determined Englishman than against him. The greatest climber and the greatest guide in Europe joined forces, and a strange relationship of friendship and enmity began.

Whymper wasted no time between his second and third attempts on the mountain. He met Carrel at Breuil the night of his return, won him over, and the very next day set out again for the south-west ridge. In addition to Carrel he was accompanied by his friend Macdonald and a second guide called Pession. They followed the now familiar route up the glacier, around the cliffs of the Tête du Lion and on to the narrow snow-saddle of the col; but this time they did not camp there. Instead, following Carrel's advice, they went on up the ridge to the foot of the Chimney, where they found a tiny level space among the cliffs and set up their tent.

The day being fine, they then pushed on farther and within an hour came to the foot of a crag. This huge rock battlement, one of the most distinctive features of the south-west ridge as seen from below, was known as the Great Tower and, at 12,990 feet, marked the highest point on the mountain which anyone had ever reached before. Whymper and his companions studied the vast rock wilderness above, discovered what seemed a feasible upward route, and descended to their tent to rest for the great effort of the following day.

It was an effort, however, that never came off. No sooner had they left their camp at daybreak and begun the passage of the Chimney than the guide Pession complained of feeling ill and declared that he could not go on. There was a long wait, and long arguments, but the man refused to budge another step upward, and Carrel declined to go further as the only guide. Whymper and Macdonald were helpless. Instead of pushing on into the unknown world above they began the long, joyless descent to Breuil.

"Three times," wrote Whymper of this stage of his campaign, "I had essayed the ascent of this mountain, and on each occasion I failed ignominiously. I had not advanced a yard beyond my predecessors. Only 1,800 feet remained, but they were as yet untrodden and might present the most formidable obstacles; no man could expect to climb them by himself. It was evident that a party should consist of three men at least, but where could the other two be obtained? Want of men made the difficulty, not the mountain."

There was reason for his pessimism. Macdonald had been called back to England, Carrel and the hunchback Meynet were busy with work in their village, and not a single other guide in either Breuil or Zermatt was willing to risk his neck and immortal soul on what had come to be known throughout the Alps as "that awful mountain."

After a week of galling inactivity Whymper returned to the south-west ridge alone. He himself declares that it was for the practical reason of looking after the tent, which had been left at the Chimney, but one suspects that by this stage of the game he simply could not stay away from the mountain of his dreams. At all events, he lingered on the heights, drinking in an artist's fill of beauty.

"The sun was setting," he relates, "and its rosy rays, blending with the snowy blue, had thrown a pale, pure violet as far as the eye could see, the valleys were drowned in purple gloom, while the summits shone with unnatural brightness; and as I sat in the door of the tent and watched the twilight change to darkness the earth seemed to become less earthly and almost sublime: the world seemed dead, and I its sole inhabitant——"

He spent the night there, wrapped in a spell of height and loneliness, and in the morning began inching his way upwards alone. Soon he had reached the foot of the Great Tower, the highest point of his previous ascent. The monstrous rock mass above him "stood out like a turret at the angle of a castle, and behind it a battlemented wall led upward to the citadel." Whymper had ventured this far only to search for a possible spot for a new tent platform, but now, suddenly, temptation was too much for him.

Slowly and cautiously he worked his way up the Tower. The first step necessitated his jumping up, grasping a ledge eight feet above and pulling himself on to it by the sheer strength of his arms. Directly in front of him now was an overhanging rock wall and immediately to his left a tremendous precipice plunging to the glacier below. He bore to the right and in a moment found himself clinging to a sheer cliff, "fixed as if crucified, pressing against the rock, and feeling each rise and fall of my chest as I breathed." Making use of the tiniest cracks and ledges, he succeeded, however, in surmounting the Tower and came out on the ridge above.

Up to this point he had been climbing on firm, living rock. Now the upper reaches of the mountain soared above him in a fearful sweep of decay and ruin. For another half hour he crept upward, threading a path between huge, rotted blocks that appeared to him like the gravestones of giants. Then, at last, prudence returned and he started back. His heart, nevertheless, was beating high with excitement and hope, for he had reached a height of 13,400 feet and was confident he had at last found the key to the summit.

Before that day's climbing was done Whymper was to have a painful—and almost fatal—object lesson in the perils of solitary climbing. Safely down the south-west ridge, he passed the col and began the now familiar passage of the snow slope under the cliffs of the Tête du Lion. All the hazards of the mountain were apparently behind him, and he was descending rapidly, his thoughts on Breuil, a warm bath and bed—when suddenly he slipped and fell.

The slope beneath dropped steeply away, narrowing as it went, and came to an abrupt end in an opening between two walls of rock. Beyond this opening was a thousand-foot precipice, falling to the Glacier du Lion. Toward it—and almost certain death—Whymper now plunged as if down a funnel. He pitched first into a mass of rocks, then on to ice, flying head over heels as he gained momentum and spinning through the air in great bounds of thirty and forty feet. But the demons of the mountains were on his side that day. At the very neck of the gully he brought up against the rocks to one side of it, and his fall was stopped. Dazed and bleeding he clung there, two hundred feet below the point from which he had fallen, not ten feet from the lip of the precipice.

After several minutes he was able to creep to a place of safety, where he fainted. Night had fallen when he regained consciousness and, summoning his last reserve of strength, he continued the descent. Many of the villages had already given him up for lost when, long past midnight, dazed and blood-soaked, he staggered into Breuil.

Another and yet another try at the Matterhorn Whymper was to have before the eventful summer of 1862 was done. No sooner had his wounds healed than he was back on the southwest ridge for his fourth campaign, accompanied this time by Carrel, little Meynet and a cousin of Carrel's called Caesar.

The four camped for a night at the base of the Chimney and the next day scaled the Great Tower and emerged on the savage upper ridge where Whymper had pioneered on his solitary climb. No sooner were they there, however, than a heavy mist descended upon them, and through it driving snow. Retracing their steps, they improvised a tiny platform among the crags at the base of the Tower and crept into their tent. Then occurred another of the bitter arguments which were constantly arising between Whymper and Carrel. The former, as usual, was hopeful and wanted to wait out the storm, which he thought would be of short duration. The latter insisted that the whole mountain would soon be coated with ice and that immediate retreat was their only salvation. In the end the guide won out. They turned back, only to discover, to Whymper's intense irritation, that he had been right after all: mist and snow soon blew away and the day shone clear and warm. But it was then too late to retrace their steps.

This was nothing, however, to the vexation that was in store for him next day. The four had agreed to set out from Breuil at dawn for yet another try, but when the time came Carrel and his cousin were off marmot-hunting. Only faithful Luk Meynet was on hand and ready, and, with him as his only companion, Whymper set forth on his fifth attempt on the Matterhorn.

The little hunchback of the Val Tournanche was as strange and lovable a man as has ever trod the high mountains. In spite of his cruel affliction he was the sole support of his dead brother's widow and children, and to earn bread for them he gladly followed Whymper into dangers before which stronger men quailed. His loyalty and devotion were absolute, and he looked upon the great peak that towered above his native valley with an almost religious adoration. Whymper has given us a touching picture of him as he stood upon the Col du Lion and for the first time stared up and out at the unclouded view:

"The poor little deformed peasant," he relates, "gazed upon it silently and reverently for a time and then unconsciously fell on one knee and clasped his hands, exclaiming in ecstasy, 'Oh, beautiful mountains!'"

Now, as the artist's sole companion, Meynet was to go higher on the Matterhorn than men had ever gone before. Together the two laboured up the endless crags and precipices of the south-west ridge—past the Chimney, up and over the Great Tower and onto the desolate, shattered heights beyond. They passed Whymper's previous highest point and pushed on until they were a bare half-dozen rope lengths beneath the great shoulder of the upper mountain. Here, however, the razor-edged ridge became so steep that it was unclimbable, and when they turned to the cliffs on the right they found themselves "both spread-eagled on the all but perpendicular face, unable to advance and barely able to descend." Further progress was impossible for the two men, but Whymper believed that a larger party, aided by a ladder, would be able to go higher. As quickly as possible he descended to Breuil to secure the ladder and again enlist the services of Carrel.

His plans, however, were doomed to frustration, for during his absence on the mountain Professor John Tyndall and his famous guide, Bennen, had arrived in the village. The conqueror of the Weisshorn had made an attempt on the Matterhorn in 1860 and departed with the conviction that it was unclimbable. Two years, however, had apparently changed his mind, for Whymper found him now prepared for an immediate attack. To make matters even worse, he had a ladder with him and had engaged Carrel and Caesar to accompany him.

In an agony of disappointment and suspense Whymper fretted about Breuil, while his expert and well-equipped rival set out for the mountain. At sunrise of the second day the villagers claimed excitedly that they had seen a flag on the summit. Scanning the peak with his binoculars, Whymper determined that this was not so, but what he did see gave him little comfort: the climbers had passed his own highest point and even as he watched were disappearing over the great shoulder of the upper mountain. With sinking heart he resigned himself to the belief that his prize had been snatched from his grasp.

But the Matterhorn played no favourites. At sunset of that day Tyndall and his men returned to Breuil with "no spring in their step." They had gone to a height of almost 14,000 feet—less than 800 from the summit—but there they too had been turned back, defeated. Tyndall was completely discouraged. "Have nothing more to do with this awful mountain," was his parting word to Whymper.

As it turned out, Whymper did not have anything more to do with it that year, but a few days later his work called him back to England. But, unlike Tyndall, he was to return—and return again. For the Matterhorn was still there—the unconquered Matterhorn; *his* Matterhorn.

The following year, however, he made only one attack on the mountain—his sixth—and it met with speedy repulse. His party, which included Carrel, Caesar, little Meynet and two other porters, was the strongest he had ever had, and in addition he was supplied with a ladder and other important equipment he had not had before. The chance of success seemed bright, but it was not to be.

The ascent of the glacier, the Col du Lion and the lower southward ridge were made easily and in perfect sunny weather. At the foot of the Great Tower, however, they felt a sudden warning rush of cold air and in a matter of seconds the sky had blackened and a storm descended upon them. Somehow they succeeded in pitching their tent and for twenty-six hours lay huddled under its frail protection while a gale-borne blizzard screamed against the mountain walls and thunder and lightning raged above their heads.

It was the most ferocious Alpine storm any of them had encountered, and it required all their remaining strength, when at last it blew away, to make the descent to Breuil. The weather was beautiful there, and the villagers looked sceptical when they heard the climbers' story.

"We have had no snow here," said the innkeeper. "It has been fine all the time. There has been only that small cloud upon the mountain."

Small cloud or raging tempest, that night of terror put an end to Whymper's 1863 campaign on the Matterhorn. Again he returned to England, defeated and disconsolate. "But like a gambler," he said, "who loses each throw, I was only the more eager to have another try—to see if the luck would change."

A change of luck he was to have in full measure, but not only the change for which he hoped.

In 1864 Whymper, already one of the most famous mountaineers of his generation, made many notable ascents in the Alps but it was not until a year later that he returned to his greatest struggle. This time he brought with him not only all his old skill, courage and determination, but a new, revolutionary plan.

Throughout his earlier attempts he had concurred in the general opinion that the Matterhorn could be conquered, if at all, only from the south-west. Now, however, he determined to turn his back on the great ridge, up which he had struggled so often in vain, and attack the mountain from the east. His decision was based not on mere whim, but on careful observation and reasoning. For one thing, he had noted in his many crossings of the Theodule Pass that the east face appeared much less steep when seen in profile than it did head-on from the valley of Zermatt. For another, he had observed that the rock strata of the peak sloped from north-east to south-west. This meant, he reasoned, that, whereas the rocks on the south-west sloped outward and down, those on the north-east must be tilted inward and up. As a seasoned mountaineer he knew that a narrow ledge or hold that sloped upward was easier and safer than a far wider one that sloped down; if his suppositions were correct, the east face of the mountain should be, in effect, a huge natural staircase.

A thorough reconnaissance in June of 1865 only served to strengthen his new convictions, and a few days later he was ready to launch his first attack by a new route. His companions on this venture were Michel-Auguste Croz, a famous Chamonix guide with whom he had made many difficult ascents, two other noted guides named Christian Almer and Franz Biener and—sole veteran of his previous attempts—faithful Meynet, the hunchback.

Following the plan which had been carefully worked out by Whymper and Croz, these five approached the mountain from the Mont Cervin Glacier and began the ascent of a steep gully which led to the Furggen, or south-east, ridge above. It was Whymper's theory that once they gained this ridge they could cross over onto the east face and continue up and to the right until they reached the north-east shoulder, just below the summit. The great danger, he realized, was that they might encounter avalanches in the gully, but he believed that they could minimize it by keeping well out on the gully walls and avoiding the centre trough, which would be a natural chute for falling stones.

He was not long in being proved wrong. Pausing for lunch at a point about halfway to the ridge, their attention was suddenly drawn to an ominous trickle of small rocks skimming down the mountainside. An instant later there was a roaring on the heights above, and they looked up to see a huge welter of boulders and stones hurtling down upon them at a mile-a-minute speed. Worse yet, they saw that the avalanche was not confined to the centre of the gully, but was raking its sides as well, bounding from wall to wall in the wildest confusion. Dropping their food, the men dashed for cover, hiding under defending rocks while the cannonade of death crashed past them. Almost by a miracle none of them was struck, but, white-faced and shaken, they all agreed they had had enough of the gully. To have advanced further in it would have been tantamount to sauntering toward the muzzle of a firing cannon.

Whymper, hoping against hope, clambered out of the gully and tried to reach the ridge by scaling the neighbouring cliffs. Of his companions only Meynet followed him, a grin on his homely face, the tent slung across his gnarled back. "Come down, come down!" shouted Croz from below. "It is useless!" Even Whymper, the eternal optimist, could see that the guide was right, and after a few minutes' fruitless struggling he turned back. His seventh assault on the mountain had, like all the others, ended in failure.

Now at last began the strange and complicated sequence of events by which fate set the stage and selected the characters for the last act of the drama of the Matterhorn. No playwright has ever devised a more triumphant and tragic final curtain.

Whymper had resolved to make his next attempt by the east face and north-east, or Zermatt, ridge, and his companions of the gully were ready to accompany him. A storm, however, delayed them, and before they could make a start the guide Croz was called back to Chamonix by a previous engagement. The artist accompanied him and, while Croz was occupied elsewhere, made a notable first ascent of the Aiguille Verte, in the Mont Blanc range, with Almer and Biener. But the Matterhorn was in his blood. Too impatient to wait longer for Croz, he returned to Breuil with the other two guides, only to have them back down on him at the last moment.

"Anything but the Matterhorn," they implored him. "*Anything* but that!"

Whymper was not unduly upset by their change of heart. Carrel was available and eager for another go at the great peak, and of all the men the Englishman had ever climbed with he respected this proud, self-confident guide the most. After considerable argument Carrel agreed to attempt the east face; Caesar and another helper enlisted for the venture, and it was agreed the assualt would be made on the first fine day.

As it turned out, however, the first fine day brought no setting-out for Whymper, but only anger and frustration. A few days previously a large and well-equipped party of Italians had arrived in Breuil, with the avowed intention of scaling the Matterhorn by the south-west ridge. Now the artist was to suffer the ordeal of standing helplessly by while Carrel pleaded "a previous engagement" and joined forces with his rivals. Whymper knew that the previous engagement was a fiction and that the real reasons for the guide's act lay deep in his proud and stubborn character. An Italian himself, he felt that his first duty was to his fellow-countrymen, and although he had reluctantly agreed to try the east face, his heart was set on conquering the peak from the side of his native valley. But whatever Carrel's motives, the important thing to Whymper was that his treachery was an accomplished fact. Again, as on the day of Tyndall's attempt, he saw himself about to be cheated of his great prize. He had to act and act fast.

This was easier decided than done. Carrel apparently was not the only Italian patriot in the Val Tournanche, for not a man could be found who would agree to climb with him, or even to act as his porter across the pass to Zermatt. The crowning blow came when Luk Meynet turned him down; the little hunchback claimed to be in the thick of some cheese-making operations which it was impossible for him to leave. Whymper was desperate. The Italians, he knew, were burdened with ponderous equipment and were moving on the mountain very slowly. But he could not move at all.

In that dark moment fate intervened in the persons of two young men who came swinging down into Breuil from the Theodule Pass. One of them was a strong and adventuresome young Englishman, Lord Francis Douglas, who had recently distinguished himself by several difficult Alpine ascents; the other was his porter, young Peter Taugwalder, son of one of the foremost guides of Zermatt. Whymper told Douglas his plight, and Douglas, for his part, said that he would like nothing better than a try at the famous Matterhorn. Furthermore, he declared that the elder Taugwalder, who had heard of Whymper's plans, agreed that the eastern face might be climbed and could undoubtedly be persuaded to accompany them. With high hopes the two Englishmen, with young Taugwalder as porter, raced over the pass to Zermatt. At the zero hour the fight for the Matterhorn had become an international rivalry.

But fate had yet stranger twists in store. Who should walk into the hotel in Zermatt that same night but Michel-Auguste Croz! He explained to Whymper that his employer in Chamonix had returned home earlier than expected and that he had subsequently been engaged by another climber—the distinguished clergyman-mountaineer, Charles Hudson. Hudson, with Croz and a young travelling companion named Hadow, had now come to Zermatt for the express purpose of attempting the Matterhorn. Whymper and the clergyman met after dinner that night and promptly decided to join forces.

It was therefore a party of seven men who set out for the mountain the following morning. Whymper and Hudson shared the leadership; Douglas and Hadow, both of whom were only nineteen, were what might be called the junior climbers; Croz and the elder Taugwalder were the guides:

the younger Taugwalder the porter. Of the seven only Whymper and Croz had ever been on the Matterhorn before and Croz had been there only once, on the short-lived venture in the gully. But the others were all strong, able men, and Whymper was satisfied with them—and full of hope.

Ascending steadily, they reached the foot of the north-east ridge before noon of the first day and a few hours later made camp on a ledge at about 11,000 feet on the east face. The route thus far had been incredibly easy. During the afternoon, while the others rested, Croz and young Taugwalder made a scouting trip high on the cliffs above and returned in a state of great excitement. "Not a difficulty," they reported. "Not a single difficulty!" It was a lighthearted group of mountaineers that huddled that night on their dizzy perch. "Long after dusk," wrote Whymper, "the cliffs above echoed with our laughter and with the songs of the guides, for we were happy and feared no evil."

Seven times in five years Edward Whymper had risked life and limb in futile battle against the Matterhorn. Now—by a supreme irony—he was to go to the top with almost ridiculous ease. The morning of July 14, 1865, dawned clear and still, and as soon as it was light enough to see, the seven adventurers began the ascent. The appalling precipices of the east face towered above them 3,000 feet into the sky, but, as Croz and young Taugwalder had reported, there were no formidable obstacles. Whymper had been right. This side of the mountain was not so steep as it appeared from the valley, and the upward slope of the rocks made it a giant staircase.

They gained altitude rapidly. Twice they struck the northeast ridge and followed it for a little distance, but both times they soon worked back onto the face, where the rock was firmer. Hadow, the least experienced climber among them, encountered some difficulty on the steeper pitches; a helping hand, however, was all that was needed to get him over them, and for the greater part of the way it was not even necessary to take the precaution of roping up. At 6.30 they had reached the height of 12,900 feet and at ten they were at 14,000.

Above the point at which they now stood the last few

hundred feet of the east face shot up in an almost vertical wall. It was obviously unclimbable. Bearing to the right, they again worked over to the ridge, crossed it, and crept out and upward onto the northern face. Here, for the first time, the climbing was such as to call for all their mountaineering skill. The north wall of the mountain was less precipitous than the east, but the rocks were covered with a thin film of ice and at their backs was nothing but blue air and the Matterhorn Glacier four thousand feet below. Using the rope, they advanced one by one, Croz, Whymper and Hudson leading and bracing themselves against a possible slip by their less experienced companions.

This difficult section was of no great extent. They bore almost horizontally across the face for some 400 feet, ascended directly toward the summit for another sixty, then doubled back to the north-east ridge. One last obstacle remained—a shoulder of rock that jutted out into space at the uppermost extremity of the ridge. Carefully they edged around it: two or three short sidling steps—one long step over the abyss. An upward glance, and their hearts were suddenly pounding with wild excitement. Above them was only a gentle snow slope and beyond it the empty blue dome of the sky.

Whymper and Croz raced for the top and made it together. The Matterhorn was conquered.

But one great fear was still in all their minds: Were they the first? Or had Carrel and the Italians, after all, beaten them to their prize? Whymper almost ran along the narrow snow-ridge that formed the summit of the mountain, searching for footprints. There were none. Then from the extreme southern end, staring down, he saw a cluster of tiny moving dots on the ridge far below. Up went Whymper's arms in triumph. He and his companions shouted until they were hoarse; they rolled rocks down the mountainside; and at last the defeated Italians paused and gazed upward at the victors. A few minutes later they turned and began the descent of the mountain. Whymper and his men were alone in their triumph.

Yet even in that most exalted moment of his life the conqueror of the Matterhorn felt a pang of regret. "Still," he wrote later, "I would that the leader of that party might have stood with us at that moment, for our victorious shouts conveyed to him the disappointment of the ambition of a life-time. Carrel was *the* man, of all who attempted the ascent of the Matterhorn, who most deserved to be the first upon its summit. It was the aim of his life to make the ascent from the side of Italy, for the honour of his native valley. For a time he had the game in his hands, he played it as he thought best; but he made a false move and he lost it."[1]

Secure in their victory, Whymper and his companions remained on the summit for an hour. They shouted and pummelled each other and danced for joy. Croz produced a tent pole, which he had carried on his back the whole way up, set it in the snow and tied his shirt to it as a flag. It was seen in Zermatt, in the Val Tournanche, in the valleys and towns of the Alps for miles around. At Breuil it was taken as a sign that the Italians had conquered, and there was great jubilation, only to be followed by bitter disappointment when their defeated champions returned. At Zermatt the excited villagers poured into the streets, staring upward at the tiny scrap of cloth that flapped triumphantly in the sky, speaking with awe of the heroes who had done the impossible. Everywhere men knew and rejoiced that the Matterhorn had been conquered at last.

Even nature itself seemed to be taking part in the celebration. The sun shone brilliantly above; not a cloud or wisp of mist veiled the horizon; and from their perch in the sky the seven conquerors looked out upon a vast, glittering panorama of summits, snowfields and valleys. "Not one of the principal peaks of the Alps was hidden," wrote Whymper. The gigantic shining dome of Mont Blanc loomed on the horizon to the west. The great crests of the Pennines and the Oberland tiered away endlessly to the east and north—Monte Rosa, the Mischabel, the Weisshorn, the Finsteraarhorn and hosts of others—incredibly white and vivid against the blue immensity of sky. They could even see Monte Viso, a hundred miles away, clear and gleaming in the crystal light. Their shouts stilled,

[1] Carrel reached the summit by the southwest ridge only three days later. But for all the joy it gave him it might as well have been a hundred years.

they gazed out upon the gorgeous pageant, too moved for words. More than seventy-five years have passed since that magic summer afternoon when they stood, the first of all men, on the summit of the Matterhorn, but it is doubtful if in the whole subsequenct history of mountaineering men have ever again been granted so glorious an hour of triumph. Certainly it was the most glorious of their own lives.

For four of them it was also the last.

They had reached the summit at 1.40. At exactly 2.40 they began the descent. In a moment or two they had come down the snow slope and reached the beginning of the short "difficult section" on the north face. Here they paused to rope up, and Whymper and Hudson worked out the order of descent. Croz went first and Hadow second. Then came Hudson and after him Douglas. Old Taugwalder, Whymper and young Taugwalder brought up the rear, in that order. In such a sequence the stronger members of the party were in a position to help the weaker—Hadow and Douglas—if they should encounter any difficulties. Or so they thought.

They rounded the jutting shoulder of rock and worked cautiously down the steep slabs on the other side. Only one man was moving at a time. A moment later——

"Croz had laid aside his axe, and in order to give Mr. Hadow greater security was absolutely taking hold of his legs and putting his feet, one by one, into their proper positions. As far as I know, no one was actually descending. The two leading men were partially hidden from my sight by an intervening mass of rock, but it is my belief, from the movements of their shoulders, that Croz, having done as I said, was in the act of turning around to go down a step or two himself. At this moment Mr. Hadow slipped, fell against him, and knocked him over."

There was a sharp, choked-off cry from Croz, and he and Hadow went flying downward. In an instant Hudson was dragged violently from his steps and Douglas after him. Whymper and the two Taugwalders braced themselves, clinging to the rocks. The rope spun out between Douglas and the elder Taugwalder, went taut with a violent jerk——

And broke.

"For a few seconds we saw our unfortunate companions sliding downwards on their backs, and spreading out their hands, endeavouring to save themselves. They passed from our sight uninjured, disappeared one by one and fell from precipice to precipice on to the Matterhorngletscher below, a distance of nearly 4,000 feet in height."

Thus the Matterhorn adventure ended—in victory and appalling tragedy. The last great unconquered peak in the Alps had succumbed at last to the skill and courage and perseverance of man, but in the very hour of conquest it had exacted a frightful vengeance.

Whymper's descent of the mountain with the two Taugwalders was a waking nightmare such as few men have ever been called upon to endure. Even worse was the ordeal that awaited him below. It was presently disclosed that at the time of the accident the climbers had been using an old, frayed rope, although they had plenty of sound rope with them; and for weeks the surrounding countryside resounded with recriminations and accusations. It was even whispered that Whymper and the Taugwalders had deliberately cut the rope, consigning their companions to death to save their own skins. What, a few short hours before, had been a joyous, magnificent triumph ended in a sordid, miserable epilogue.

Croz, Hudson and Hadow were discovered lying on the great glacier and were buried in the churchyard in Zermatt. The body of Lord Francis Douglas was never found. As for Whymper, except for a second ascent of the Matterhorn nine years later, he never climbed again in Europe. His subsequent mountaineering exploits, as we shall see, took him to the far places of the earth—to Greenland, to the Andes of South America, to the Canadian Rockies. But the spell the Alps had cast upon him was never altogether broken, and almost half a century later we find him, an old and dying man, returning to the scene of his early adventures to pass his last days among the great mountains he loved the best of all.

In the years since Whymper the Matterhorn has become one

of the most-climbed mountains in the world. Today it has been ascended by every ridge and every face, its more frequented routes bristle with fixed ropes and ladders, and scarcely a fine summer day passes that its summit does not do service as a picnicking ground for a party of tourists. The "awful mountain" has been tamed.

Yet its magic remains. It is still, as it was three-quarters of a century ago, the most famous peak in the Alps, and it still possesses the power to move all who look upon it with wonder and excitement. For the Matterhorn is more than a mountain. It is a monument and a legend. And as long as men raise their eyes to its heights they will remember the time when Edward Whymper and his companions set out upon their great adventure—and struggled and won and lost.

IV

MOUNTAINEERING COMES OF AGE

1865-1941

WITH THE FALL of the Matterhorn the great period of Alpine first ascents came to an end. A few scattered peaks and peaklets lingered on unclimbed into the late decades of the nineteenth century, but the Golden Age of pioneering was gone. The Alps were known, their mighty summits conquered. And a new era in the history of mountaineering had begun.

One might suppose that the exhaustion of virgin peaks—and on top of that, the widely publicized Matterhorn tragedy—would have caused a decline of interest and activity in climbing. But the effect was exactly the opposite. Whereas in the earliest days mountaineering had been the province of the select and initiated few, its popularity, after 1865, increased to such a phenomenal degree that within a few years it had become one of the foremost sports of Europe. The original Alpine Club of London, at its founding in 1857, had twenty-eight members. By 1875 it boasted ten times that many, and a variety of younger organizations, with less stringent admission requirements, numbered their adherents in the thousands. Nor was the expansion by any means limited to the pioneering English. The lure of the new sport spread with the speed of an epidemic; each summer saw more and more climbers of more and more nationalities swarming over the cliffs and glaciers of the Alps; and in seemingly no time at all Switzerland became in fact what it has always claimed to be in the travel-brochures—"the Playground of Europe." Mountaineering is both by tradition and its inherent nature a non-commercial sport, but its enormous growth in the late years of the last century made it, willy-nilly, the father of one of the most flourishing hotel industries in the world.

The great majority of climbers, in the 'seventies and 'eighties as now, confined themselves to activities in which others had blazed the way. With guide and guide-book they followed the famous routes to the famous summits, and before long ascents which on their first achievement had been considered almost miraculous were known casually as "standard climbs," negotiable by anyone except a cripple or a sufferer from vertigo. In the early days ascents of any of the major peaks had been looked upon as great and desperate adventures, usually preceded by a solemn making out of wills and followed, if successful, by band concerts and torchlight parades. Now lofty summits like Mont Blanc, the Jungfrau and even the "awful" Matterhorn were climbed a hundred or more times a summer, and in fine weather it was a not uncommon occurrence for there to be fifteen or twenty parties on one of them at the same time. A striking example of the change in attitude appears in a well-known story about the noted guide, Père Gaspard. In 1877 Gaspard led the first ascent of the fearsome Meije, in the Dauphiné, in what was universally regarded as one of the most hazardous exploits in Alpine history. But only a few years later we find him approaching an inexperienced tourist with the casual invitation: "Come up the Meije—all you need is an umbrella."

A natural result of the popularization of climbing was a tremendous boom in the profession of guiding. Herdsmen and farmers in scores of Swiss villages turned from their old pursuits to the far more lucrative business of leading sportsmen up Alpine walls, and in the big tourist centres like Chamonix and Grindelwald virtually the whole adult male population were soon earning their living as guides. As in any profession, most were of the journeyman variety, but a remarkable number, both among the veterans of the pioneer days and the younger generation who followed them, were mountain-men of the very first rank. Jean Antoine and Louis Carrel, Jakob and Melchior Anderegg, Alexander Burgener, Christian Almer, Mattias Zurbriggen, Franz Lochmatter, Josef Knubel,

Christian Klucker, Armand Charlet—these are names which will be remembered and honoured as long as the sport of climbing endures. It was men such as these, together with the most illustrious of their employers, who painstakingly raised mountaineering from the realm of haphazard adventure to a science and an art. And it was their skill and pride and sense of responsibility in their profession, often passed on directly from father to son to grandson, that won for Alpine guiding the high standards of performance that it has maintained ever since.

Still it is not to the men who climbed for a living that we must look for the most notable advances in the field, but to the men who climbed because climbing was in their blood. As we have indicated, most amateurs of the late nineteenth century were content to follow where others had led. There remained, however, the skilled and ambitious few for whom routine activity and hand-me-down achievement were not enough and who longed, like the pioneers before them, for the challenge of the unknown and unconquered. The virgin summits were no more; a mountaineer could no longer come out at last upon a soaring rock-fang in the sky and feel his heart pound with exultation, knowing himself to be the first. So the second generation of Alpine climbers did the next-best thing. They set about conquering the old peaks by new routes.

Thus began a new type of mountaineering, which has continued with ever-increasing ramifications to the present time. In the world's great unconquered ranges, to be sure, climbing is still primarily a matter of getting to the top in the quickest and easiest way; but since the 1880's the practice of the sport in the Alps has concerned itself less and less with the mere reaching of summits and more and more with the manner in which the summits are attained. Soon it was no longer "Have you climbed the Matterhorn?" but "Have you climbed the Matterhorn by the Zmutt or the Furggen Ridge?" Not "Have you ascended Mont Blanc?" but "Have you ascended it by the Ancien Passage or the Col de la Brenva?" As the interest in new routes grew it was soon discovered that there was not one, but three or six or a dozen possible ways to most of the great summits and that peaks whose so-called "standard climbs" were an easy walk-up for a duffer might also possess ridges and faces to tax the powers of the most skilful expert. And the experts were not long in answering the challenge. Only a few short years after the Alps had been considered won the winning began all over again. The difference was that the important consideration was now no longer "what," but "how."

One name stands pre-eminent among the pioneers of the reborn sport—that of Mummery. In his everyday, non-climbing life A. F. Mummery was a conventional and phlegmatic English businessman, but once he laced up his nailed boots and felt Alpine rock and Alpine ice beneath them he became mysteriously transformed into the very incarnation of mountaineering skill and daring. For more than twenty years between the 'seventies and 'nineties he ranged indefatigably through the length and breadth of the Alps. A "climber's climber" if ever there was one, he regarded mountains less as a playground than as a laboratory for the development of his craft, welcoming difficulty and hazard for their own stern sake, despising easy successes and the mere gathering of records.

As a result, his name is perhaps less known to the general public than that of many of the other great men of mountaineering. But among climbers themselves, he has grown with the years into an almost legendary figure, and there is no doubt that he did more than any man before or since to raise the standards of Alpine achievement and technique.

Mummery's climbs were legion, and at one time or another during his career he pioneered new routes in almost every district of the Alps. But he was primarily what the old-school Alpinists called a "centrist," rather than an eclectic, and the centre of his mountain world were the *aiguilles* of Chamonix. Here, on the needle-sharp rock spires that rise in the shadow of Mont Blanc, we see Mummery the cragsman, at the peak of his powers—inching up the "impossible" walls of the Charmoz, the Grépon, the Aiguille du Plan, finding finger- and toe-holds where there appeared to be only smooth slabs and green, glaring ice, pushing daringly, relentlessly on into new vertical worlds where no man had ever ventured before. If no known technique was adequate to a problem at hand, he would invent a new one. If a pitch or cliff-face offered no chance of ascent by standard methods he would devise one that was nonstandard. Thus did he conquer the appalling north face of the Grépon by the perpendicular cleft now famous as the Mummery Crack. Finding that hands and feet alone were useless, he wedged as much of his body as he could into a narrow slit in the rock-wall and hoisted himself upward by the strenuous use of knees, shoulders, elbows and back. Today, such manœuvres as this, as well as many others which Mummery devised, are part of the bag of tricks of any experienced climber; but in his day they were sensational innovations.

Although indisputably the foremost figure, Mummery was by no means the only early practitioner of "new-route" mountaineering. Each year more and more adventurous spirits turned from the prosaic pleasures of routine climbs to the limitless field of trail-blazing, and before long virtually every great summit in the Pennines, the Oberland and the Mont Blanc district had been ascended and re-ascended by a great variety of approaches. (Mont Blanc itself, for example, had by the turn of the century been climbed by no less than twenty different routes.) To attempt even to summarize the new ascents of old peaks which were made between 1865 and the outbreak of the First World War would be a hopeless task; they fill literally thousands of pages in every Alpine journal of the time. A few individuals, however, have stood out head and shoulders above the rest—notably the Italian, Guido Rey, the German, Paul Güssfeldt and the Englishmen, A. W. Moore, Douglas Freshfield, Sir William Martin Conway, W. A. B. Coolidge and Geoffrey Winthrop Young.[1] Climbing year after year with ever-increasing skill and daring, these men, with their guides and companions, forged new trails up the ridges and precipices of scores of great peaks. Rey on the Grépon and the Furggen ridge of the Matterhorn, Moore on the fearsome Brenva snow-ridge of Mont Blanc, Young on the Täschhorn, Freshfield and Conway on countless mountain-walls between

[1] Young, among his other accomplishments, is perhaps the best writer on both the practical and spiritual aspects of mountaineering that the sport has produced. (See the Reading List.)

Chamonix and the Tyrol—theirs were exploits of the very first rank, and the ascents which they pioneered have since become the great classic climbs of the Alps.

There was still another important contribution that Mummery and his contemporaries made to the development of mountain craft. This was guideless climbing. Skilled and resourceful though they were, few of the earliest generation of mountaineers would have dreamed of attempting a major summit without the advice and assistance of professional companions; but with the passing of the years expert amateurs tended more and more to break away from the old leading-strings and fare forth on their own. Not that even the greatest of them did not climb more often with guides than without: Mummery with Alexander Burgener, Moore with the Andereggs, Young with "Little Josef" Knubel and Franz Lochmatter are among the most celebrated teams in mountaineering history. In later phases of their careers, however, both Mummery and Young showed an increasing tendency to dispense with professional aid, and many others, following their lead, began also to learn the satisfactions and responsibilities of guideless climbing. By the early years of the twentieth century it had become a widely accepted practice among both the more expert and less affluent visitors to the Alps.

What is generally referred to as "modern" mountaineering dates from the end of the First World War. Its most interesting and important feature, as we shall see, has been the expansion of the climber's domain to include virtually every mountainous region in the world; but Alpine climbing, in the narrower sense, has also undergone great changes. The most significant of these—doubly so because they present an almost exact parallel to trends in the world at large—are specialization and mechanization.

In the old days "specialization" would have been a meaningless word applied to climbing. A mountain was a mountain and a man was a man, and when the two came to grips it was merely a matter of the skill and endurance of one pitted against the size and natural obstacles of the other. Of late years, however, there has been an ever-increasing tendency to break the sport down into its component parts, with individual climbers concentrating on one or a few highly technical aspects. Some are interested only in the most difficult types of rock-climbing—cragsmen, they call themselves, or "rock-engineers." Others specialize in snow and ice work, still others in ski mountaineering, exploratory mountaineering, high-altitude mountaineering. The result, by and large, has been an enormous advance in climbing technique and achievement—ascents are made today which would leave a Whymper, or even a Mummery, aghast—but, as usual, the price of specialization has had to be paid in the decrease of first-class all-around performance.

In the matter of mechanical devices mountaineering has also kept pace with the times. Mechanization, as the term is employed in the sport, means the use of artificial aids to accomplish climbs that would otherwise be impossible, and its practice today is so widespread and highly developed that it may almost be said to constitute a new and separate phase of mountain craft. In the old days rope, ice-axe and the necessary boots and clothing constituted the sum-total of a cragsman's equipment, but in recent years these have been augmented by a variety of new instruments and appliances. Most important of these are the piton and the karabiner. The former is an iron or steel spike that may be hammered into tiny cracks in the rock to afford support to hand, foot or rope; the latter a snap-ring which when attached to a piton makes possible many ingenious manipulations of the rope. Using these devices and a number of more complicated derivatives, modern mountaineers have been able to effect ascents which a quarter of a century ago would have been utterly impossible. Holdless cliff-walls, bulging precipices and overhanging cornices, which could defy unaided climbers to the end of time, have been made to yield to man's mechanical ingenuity, with the result that the limits of the "possible" in rock-scaling have been pushed back until there are scarcely any limits left. Virtually all the sensational new ascents in the Alps during the past decade have been achieved only with benefit of piton, karabiner and the like.

No other aspect of mountaineering has been the subject of

such long and acrimonious argument as that of mechanization. The conservatives of the sport—notably the leaders of the (British) Alpine Club—have fought it relentlessly, claiming that mechanical gadgets have no place on a mountainside and that their use merely debases the art of cragsmanship into a form of spectacular, acrobatic circus. Most German and Italian climbers, on the other hand, have welcomed each new development with enthusiasm, and a whole school of young and daring cragsmen has grown up which scarcely considers any climb worth while if it does not involve intricate equipment and manipulations. At its two extremes the controversy can easily be reduced to absurdity. The conservative viewpoint, carried all the way, would outlaw rope, axe and nailed boots as "artificial aids"; the radicals' programme could be extended to include the use of motor-driven pulleys or even dynamite. Needless to say no one on either side has ever suggested such fantastic measures, but within narrower limits the war rages on bitterly, and the Golden Mean which is the ideal of mountaineering is perhaps harder to find today than at any time in the history of the sport.

Neither specialization nor mechanization, however, is as much to blame for this sorry state of affairs as another new factor which strongly influenced Alpine climbing during the past pre-war decade. This was the rise of nationalism. To be sure, mountaineering has suffered from ugly and senseless rivalries since its earliest days (witness the first ascents of Mont Blanc and the Matterhorn), but the jingoistic fervour which began intruding on the scene in the early 1930's touched new heights of absurdity. As might be expected, the Germans and Italians were the chief offenders in this respect. Imbued with the new hero-philosophy of Nazi-Fascism and egged on by flag-waving tub-thumpers at home, brown and black-shirted young climbers began to vie with each other in what they conceived to be feats of courage and skill. All or nothing was their watchword—victory or death. No risk was too great, no fool-hardiness to be condemned, so long as their exploits brought honour to *Vaterland* or *patria*, as the case might be.

But let us allow the instigators to speak for themselves:

"A climber has fallen. Let a hundred others arise for the morrow. Let other youths strew edelweiss and alpenrose upon the body of the fallen comrade and lay it with trembling devotion under the soft turf. Then up once more to the assault of the summit, to commemorate the fallen one in the highest and most difficult of victories!"

Or again:

"The Medal for Valour in Sport, the highest distinction accorded by the Duce to exceptional athletes who break world records or are victors in international contests, will be awarded to climbers who vanquish mountains by new ascents of the most difficult standard."

And still again:

"Many of our wars will take place in the mountains, and the cult of mountaineering, passionately pursued and spreading more and more among our young men, will contribute to the military preparedness of the young generation."

These are quotations from recent articles in important German and Italian alpine journals. When one considers that in 1935 the largest German mountaineering club, the *Deutsch-Österreichischer Alpenverein*, boasted over half a million members and that various other German and Italian climbing organizations were only slightly smaller, it becomes apparent how widely and deeply the fascist philosophy of mountaineering had spread. Surely there could be no clearer proof of how hysterical and perverted nationalism can infect even the most unpolitical of human activities.

As a result of these many influences at work upon it, Alpine mountaineering in the years immediately preceding the present war presents a picture of which no true sportsman can be very proud. Competition was the watchword—competition literally to the death. Each year saw scores of new attempts at "record climbs," hundreds of reckless youngsters clinging to cliff-faces and precipice-walls which a centipede could scarcely have surmounted, much less a man. And each year, inevitably, the fatalities mounted, until two, three, four hundred lives a season came to be accepted as the usual toll. The Alps had once been looked upon as a playground; then as a laboratory. Now they had become a battlefield. Climbers looked upon themselves not as sportsmen, but as soldiers, and as often as not they reaped the soldier's reward.

Aiding and abetting this suicidal insanity was an elaborate system of grading climbs, which became increasingly popular on the continent during the 'twenties and 'thirties. Ascents of all descriptions were ranked according to their degree of difficulty, beginning with a First Degree for an easy walk-up and culminating in a Sixth, which has been aptly defined as "an ascent recognized as impossible until someone does it without being killed." Inherently, perhaps, there is nothing wrong with such a system: the English have used a variation of it for years, with no untoward results. But mountaineers of other nationalities quickly began carrying it to excess, and before long glory-seeking young Germans and Italians were looking down with contempt on anything less than a certified "Super-Sixth." The Eigerwand, the north wall of the Grandes Jorasses, the north and west faces of the Matterhorn—these, together with various rock pinnacles in the Dolomites, were the celebrated "impossible" climbs of recent Alpine seasons, and it was on them in particular that the new order of soldier-mountaineer concentrated and struggled—and died.

One glimpse of this "all-or-nothing" type of climbing is more than enough—

The time is mid-July of 1936; the scene the mile-high precipice of the Eigerwand—"the Wall of the Ogre"—that rises close by the Jungfrau in the heart of the Bernese Oberland.

For several years the Eigerwand had been famous throughout Europe as one of the few great unclaimed "prizes" of the Alps. Many parties of dare-devil climbers—most of them Germans—had tried to force a way up its appalling pitches of rock and ice; but none had succeeded, and almost every venture had ended in the death of one or more participants. Still the suicidal attempts went on—"victory or annihilation"; "for *Führer* and *Vaterland*."[1] And on the morning of July twentieth crowds of sightseers again thronged the terrace of

[1] Hitler himself announced that gold medals would be awarded to the first scalers of the Eigerwand, in conjunction with the Berlin Olympic Games of 1936.

the Kleine Scheidegg Hotel in the valley below, staring breathlessly upward through the telescopes. For yet another assault was under way.

High up on the mountain wall the figures of the climbers could be seen, clinging to the rock like minute black insects. There were four of them—two Bavarians and two Austrians—all of them young, all with records of many sensational climbs behind them, all resolved to win fame and glory by accomplishing "the most difficult ascent in the Alps." By the time the telescopes picked them up on the morning of the twentieth they had already been on the precipice for two full days. Hour after hour they had inched their way upward, digging fingers and toes into tiny crevices, driving pitons where no crevices existed at all, dangling in space at rope's end as they struggled with vertical cliffs and bulging overhangs. The first night they spent standing upright, lashed to a rock-wall with pitons and rope. On the second a storm swooped down, and the whole mountainside around them was sheathed in a whirling fury of ice and snow. The watchers below gave them up as lost, but at daybreak they were still there alive—still able to move. And the third day began.

Throughout the morning they crept on and by noon were almost within a thousand feet of their goal. There, however, their good luck ended. Storm and cold and the savage, perpendicular wall must at last have taken their toll of the climbers' strength, for they were seen to remain motionless for a long time and then begin to descend. But their downward progress did not last long either, and presently they were motionless again—four infinitesimal specks transfixed against the wall. Apparently they were unable to move either up or down.

A council of war was held in the valley below, and four guides set out as a rescue party. Following the tracks of the Jungfrau Railway, which bores through the rock of the Eiger, they came out on the precipice through an opening in the tunnel wall and began working their way across it toward the point where the climbers were trapped. Soon they were near enough to see the four of them clearly. They were clinging to the merest wrinkles in the ice-coated rock-face, one above the other, tied together and supported by a mass of ropes and pitons. Their clothing was in tatters and their faces scarcely recognizable from the effects of exposure and exhaustion. Above them was a sheer, almost holdless wall, down which they had somehow managed to lower themselves. Below was an overhanging precipice and an abyss of blue space.

Slowly, with infinite deliberation and care, the rescue party drew nearer, but while they were still some distance away the inevitable happened. The uppermost of the four Germans lost his hold and toppled backward into thin air, arms and legs twisting grotesquely. The coils of the rope, spinning down after him, caught the next man around the neck, almost literally wrenching his head from his shoulders, while a third, still lower, was struck with terrific force by the falling body of his companion. Then the rope went taut and snapped. The first man plummeted on for 4,000 feet to the valley below; the second and third stayed motionless where they had fallen, half lying, half hanging from the ropes and pitons. In five seconds it was all over. And one man was left alive.

Still the horrified guides kept on. Hacking their way diagonally across a sixty-degree ice-slope, they at last reached a point only a few yards away from the sole survivor—a Bavarian soldier named Kurz. But before they could begin the delicate work of rescue another storm bore down on the mountain, and they were forced to beat a retreat. Kurz was left to spend his third night on the precipice, his body suspended over space and tied to the corpses of two of his companions.

The next morning, miraculously, he was still alive, but so weak that he was scarcely able to speak or move. Again the guides began the grim work of reaching him and this time succeeded in establishing themselves on a narrow ledge some 100 feet below his position. Farther, however, they could not go. The stretch that still separated them from Kurz was an ice-glazed overhang, and to have ventured so much as a step on to it would have been obvious suicide. They called up to Kurz to cut himself loose from the bodies of his companions. This he did, using the point of his ice-axe; then, summoning his last reserves of strength, he knotted several ropes together and lowered them to the guides. He was so feeble by this time that these two operations took him three hours.

On the ropes dangling from above the guides sent up a specially devised rope sling. As there was no possible way of their reaching him, it was up to Kurz to lower himself on it—if he had the strength left. Slowly and patiently he wrapped the coils about his body, leaned out into space, started down. The men below could hear his hoarse breathing and see his boot-nails scraping weakly against the rock. In a few moments he was so close that one of the guides, balancing on the others' shoulders, could almost touch his feet.

Then suddenly the rope sling jammed and Kurz's downward progress ceased. For a desperate, straining moment he clung with fingers and toes to the ice-smooth bulge of the overhang; but the last of his strength was gone. His ice-axe dropped from his hand and went spinning downward. An instant later he himself swung out from the mountain wall into space. And hanging there at rope's end, he died.

This miserable disaster is only one among many of similar nature that have occurred in the Alps in recent years. The Eigerwand was finally climbed in the summer of 1938, and those other famous "impossibles," the north wall of the Grandes Jorasses and the northern and western faces of the Matterhorn, have also at last yielded to climbers with more good luck than good sense. For each success, however, there were many failures and many lives lost; and, far from being deterred by the endless list of catastrophes, there appeared to be an ever-growing supply of young men eager to devise still more spectacular and gruesome ways of killing themselves. Indeed, it is perhaps a good thing that the Alps today have been blacked out along with the rest of Europe. For we can at least hope that when peace comes again and men's thoughts can turn to such things as sport and adventure, that the faith-and-friction school of storm-trooper heroes will have disappeared and that the mountains will be given back again to those who understand and love them.

The Alps were the cradle of mountaineering and have remained through the years the great international centre of the sport. But the day when they were the sum and circumference of the climber's world has long since passed. Whatever else it may signify to various individuals, the heart and essence of mountaineering is adventure, and adventure, by its very definition, means the pushing back of horizons, the search for the untrodden and unknown. During the "Golden Age" of seventy-five years ago the province of the climber was limited to a few hundred square miles in Switzerland, northern Italy and south-eastern France. Today it is limited only by the boundaries of the earth itself.

The earliest non-Alpine climbing, as might be expected, was confined to regions near the great population centres of western Europe. In this field, again, the British were in the forefront, and by the closing years of the last century every peak and sub-peak from northern Scotland to Land's End had been ascended dozens—in many cases even hundreds—of times. To be sure, the British Isles possess no summits even remotely comparable to those of the Alps. The highest of all —Ben Nevis, in Scotland—rises a mere 4,400 feet above the sea, and the other famous pinnacles—Scawfell, Great Gable and Pillar Rock, in the English Lake District, and Snowdon and Tryfaen, in Wales—can scarcely be called mountains at all. Yet climbing has persistently remained one of the most popular recreations in the country, and the record of achievement has been remarkable.

Because of the low altitudes and the nature of the terrain British stay-at-home mountaineering is limited almost exclusively to work on crags and cliffs. "Getting to the top," as an end in itself means nothing; at the top, as likely as not, the climber will find a sheep pasture, a resort hotel, or even a whole village. It is the matter of routes that is all-important —of climbing for its own sake and its own special problems and techniques. On some of the celebrated summits in the Lake District, for example, there are as many as a dozen recognized ways of ascent up a single rock-face, ranging from simple walk-ups to precipice-routes of the severest difficulty.

Fc

As in unhappily bygone times all good Americans hoped some day to go to Paris, so do all good Englishmen—at least if they are mountaineers—hope some day to go to Switzerland. To that end, and for its own sake, as well, they have, in their native hills, developed rock-climbing to a point of technical perfection that is probably unmatched anywhere in the world. Virtually every British climber who has won a name for himself in the Alps or Andes, Caucasus or Himalayas began his career with a strenuous apprenticeship on the cliffs of Scawfell, Tryfaen or Ben Nevis, and these remain today, as they have been for three-quarters of a century, the unexcelled schoolroom of mountaineering. A hundred-foot hillock can often be as effective as a 20,000-foot icepeak in developing an acquaintance with those three prime elements of the climber's world—hard rock, thin air, a rope.

Western continental Europe abounds in mountain ranges, most of them of far greater height and extent than the English hills, but none approaching the grand scale of the Alps. Most famous, because of their long association with human history, are the Pyrenees, which form the high frontier between France and Spain, and the old, rugged chain of the Italian Apennines. Although ideal for walking tours or casual ascents, neither of these ranges presents first-class climbing problems, and their summits are within easy reach of anyone with a guidebook and a sound pair of legs. The same applies, by and large, to the Harz and Black Forest regions of Germany, the Vosges and Jura of France and the many sprawling ranges of central Spain. Almost all the larger Mediterranean islands are mountainous in character—notably Corsica, Sardinia and Sicily, with its fabled Etna—and offer a great variety of climbs in wild and unspoiled country.

The mountains of Norway and Sweden, though of no great height, cover an area of many thousand square miles and in recent years have become a playground second only to the Alps among the sports centres of Europe. The scenery is almost fantastically lovely. Great rock-masses rise sheer from the deep, winding fiords that indent the coastline, and the landscape alternates endlessly between frozen snowpeaks and the deep green pockets of mountain valleys. Because of the high latitude of the range glaciers and snowfields are found at very low elevations, and in the northern sections conditions become truly arctic. Almost alone among the mountains of Europe, the Scandinavian highlands still offer a large number of first ascents. There is also considerable exploration of a minor nature still to be done in the interior of Lapland, above the Arctic Circle.

The principal mountains of Central Europe are the Carpathians, fringing the borders of what were once Poland, Hungary and Czechoslovakia. For the most part low and wooded, they culminate in one wild and spectacular sub-range, known as the High Tatra, which bristles with granite spires and offers climbing comparable to that on the famous *aiguilles* of Chamonix. The Balkans, to the south-east, hold little for the mountaineer except the likelihood of being shot at, with or without benefit of declared war. On the other hand, the brown, crumpled hills of Greece comprise extremely attractive climbing terrain. Topped by 10,000-foot Olympus, they include also Parnassus, Helicon and a host of other summits whose ascents are made doubly interesting by their ancient fame in history and myth.

Europe is both the most thickly populated continent in the world and the world's centre of mountaineering, yet, strangely enough, its highest mountains are but little known and infrequently visited. These are the Caucasus. Rising in the far south-eastern corner of European Russia, between the Black and Caspian Seas, they are far removed from the familiar trade-routes of the modern world, and climbing expeditions into their wild, ice-locked domain have been few and far between.

Most of the important first ascents in the range were accomplished many years ago. After the conquest of the Matterhorn, Alpine mountaineering, as we have seen, turned largely to new routes, improved techniques and guideless climbing. But there were many accomplished and ambitious men who were not content merely to climb, however skilfully, where others had climbed before and who soon began scanning the horizon for new worlds to conquer. Pre-eminent among these was Douglas Freshfield, one of the greatest of English mountaineer-explorers, who was at that time at the beginning of his long and varied career.[1] In the summer of 1868 Freshfield, in company with A. W. Moore, C. C. Tucker and one Chamonix guide undertook the first important expedition to the Caucasus, explored the great chain from end to end and successfully climbed two of its major summits—Elbruz and Kasbek. The ascent of the former, though not in itself difficult, was nevertheless a significant event in the history of mountaineering. In the first place Elbruz, at 18,465 feet, is the highest summit of Europe. Also it had been famous for centuries, under its ancient name, Strobilus, as the legendary prison of the Greek Titan, Prometheus. And—most important of all in a strictly climbing sense—its conquest marked the beginning of the era of serious mountaineering on a worldwide scale.

The last quarter of the nineteenth century was the great period of climbing in the Caucasus. Freshfield himself returned several times, and many of the other leading alpinists of the period also tried their luck in the newly opened mountain wilderness. Even Mummery tore himself away from his beloved Chamonix *aiguilles* long enough to scale the formidable walls of Dykhtau; and the other great peaks—Shkara, Koshtantau and Ushba—fell one by one to various parties of climbers.

In 1888 and 1889 Koshtantau was the scene of one of the most famous of mountaineering tragedies. Two well-known British climbers, W. Donkin and H. Fox, set out with two Swiss guides in the summer of the former year in an attempt to reach its then unconquered summit and vanished without leaving a trace. Wild rumours began to spread that they had been kidnapped and murdered by bandits, and as the months passed the affair developed almost into a minor

---

[1] Freshfield, whose active climbing career spanned a full half century, was one of the widest-ranging as well as one of the most competent of mountaineers. In addition, he was a talented and prolific writer, and his books on the Caucasus, Himalayas and other great ranges have become classics in their field. (See Reading List.)

international dispute. Then, a year after their disappearance, Freshfield and his climbing-companion Clinton Dent went out to the Caucasus with a small party for the express purpose of trying to clear up the mystery. After weeks of reconnoitring and climbing the detective-mountaineers made a dramatic discovery. High on a desolate ridge of the great peak they stumbled suddenly upon Donkin and Fox's last bivouac. Sleeping bags, rucksacks, cooking utensils, personal belongings of every kind—all were lying there neatly in the heart of that frozen, lifeless world, just as if their owners had left them only a few hours before and would return to them again before sunset. The sorrowful remnants made one thing clear —the lost men had been victims of a mountaineering accident and not of foul play at the hands of other men. Long search by Freshfield and companions, however, yielded no trace of the bodies, and where and how Donkin, Fox and their two guides died remains to this day a mystery.

By 1900 most of the major peaks of the Caucasus had fallen, but their lesser neighbours were largely ignored and there are still scores of summits between 12,000 and 16,000 feet which have yet to feel the bootnails of their conquerors. The majority, it appears likely, will not feel them for some time to come, for the Soviet government is inclined to look askance at the solitary and individualistic ways of mountaineers and in recent years has set up many political obstacles to climbing and exploration in the range.

The conquerors of the great Russian peaks were the pioneers of the era of world-mountaineering. Just as Freshfield and his contemporaries had turned from the Alps to the sterner challenge of the Caucasus, so did these same men and their younger successors soon begin to wander still farther afield, searching for still greater prizes. Nor were they long in finding them. What the late fifteenth and early sixteenth centuries were to the exploration of oceans and continents the half century since 1890 has been to the realm of mountaineering. Scarcely a year has passed in that time that some new peak or range or region has not been brought into the ever-widening field of activity, and the climber's world, once bounded by the Ortler on the east and Mont Blanc on the west, has gradually become synonymous with the world itself. During a few years around the turn of the century the expansion took place on an enormous scale. Climber-explorers like Freshfield, A. F. R. Wollaston and the Duke of the Abruzzi—to name only a few of many—pushed doggedly in toward the mysterious mountain-giants of Africa. Other adventurers, but with Freshfield again among them, undertook the exploration of the huge uplift of the Himalayas, in faraway India, blazing precarious trails toward the summits of the highest peaks in the world. Still others roamed the mountain-wilderness of the New World, and fought their way to the pinnacles of the Andes, the Rockies and the sprawling, ice-sheathed ranges of Alaska. By the outbreak of the First World War, in 1914, there was scarcely a mountainous region left on earth—from Greenland to the Antarctic, from Norway to the South Sea Islands—that had not at least been visited and reconnoitred by the new order of globe-girdling climbers.

As might be expected, the great and famous ranges have drawn the lion's share of attention. But as horizons widened and ever more ambitious mountaineers entered the field, even the most remote and obscure corners of the world have become the scene of large-scale climbing ventures. The vast icecap of Greenland, studded with massive peaks, has been visited by expeditions of many nationalities, beginning as early as 1872, when the indefatigable Edward Whymper made ascents of several west-coast summits, and culminating in 1935 with the conquest of Mount Gunnbjornsfjeld (12,139 feet), the highest known mountain in the Arctic.[1] The ranges of Spitzbergen have been systematically explored, notably by the far-ranging Sir William Martin Conway, who made two remarkable journeys to the island during the 'nineties of the last century. And, at the other end of the earth, even the storm-lashed mountains of Antarctica were not long to go unchallenged. In the course of the Shackleton South Polar

---

[1] Mont Forel (11,100 feet) is Greenland's most famous peak, and until very recently was believed to be the highest Arctic summit. It was climbed in 1938 by a party of Swiss explorers.

expedition of 1906 a small party of men made the ascent of the 13,300-foot active volcano, Mount Erebus, and were rewarded by the matchless sight of its huge crater—a boiling, steaming cauldron rising from the icefields of the coldest region in the world.

Meanwhile, the great uplifts of Central Asia, forgotten since the days of Marco Polo and the Europe-to-Cathay caravans, have again come back into the ken of western explorers. Travellers like Sir Aurel Stein and Sven Hedin have penetrated the trans-Himalayan fastnesses of Tibet, Mongolia and Turkestan and rediscovered vast ranges which rank second only to the Himalayas themselves among the mountains of the earth. The Hindu Kush and the Pamirs; the Nan Shan and Kunlun Mountains; the Altais and Altyn Tags—these are only a few of the dozens of gigantic escarpments which rim the desolate plateaus of inner Asia, and every one of them is a range which, if situated in a more accessible part of the world, would be as famous as the Alps or Rockies. Up to the present time exploration rather than mountaineering has been the goal of the few expeditions to this region; perhaps a dozen peaks, all told, have been ascended in an area larger than the United States. But the location and nature of the ranges are now known, and it is inevitable, in spite of their remoteness and inaccessibility, that their summits will fall, one by one, to the men who stalk great mountains.

In sharp contrast to the Atlantic shores, a large part of the continental coastline and most of the large islands of the Pacific Ocean are ruggedly mountainous in character. This is particularly true of Japan, which is itself the crest of a vast submarine uplift and whose ranges cover no less than three-quarters of the total area of the country. The most celebrated, as well as the loftiest, summit is, of course, the volcano Fujiyama, or Fuji-san, rising in flawless symmetry to a height of 12,400 feet above the nearby ocean. Fuji's fame, however, is not based on any difficulties of ascent, and between foreign sightseers and native pilgrims it has probably been climbed by as many people as any other peak of comparable size in the world. Far more challenging to the skilled mountaineer are many of the summits of the so-called Japanese Alps, farther inland, which are said to bear favourable comparison even with the best of their European namesakes.

A great deal of climbing has been done in Japan in recent years, both by white visitors and the Japanese themselves. Several members of the imperial family—notably Prince Chichibu—are devotees of the sport, and as a result it has become an activity of great repute among their prestige-loving countrymen. Huts and trails abound in most of the highland regions, trained guides are available, and climbing conditions in general resemble those of the Alps rather than those of the huge, wild ranges of Continental Asia. If for nothing else, mountaineers owe the Japanese a debt of gratitude for originating a phrase that, in its simplicity and rightness, is worthy of becoming a universal climber's invocation:

"May our five senses be pure," they request respectfully of their ancestral gods at the beginning of an ascent—"and may the weather on the honourable mountain be fine."

Southward from Japan, the large islands of the East Indies and Melanesia are all at least partly mountainous. The Philippines, Sumatra and Java abound in volcanoes, and Borneo's fabled Kinabalu, "the Mountain of the Dead," is only one of a great host of little-known peaks that rise from the steaming jungles of its interior. New Guinea, too, is traversed by lofty ranges, virtually *terra incognita* to mountaineers, but known to possess summits more than 16,000 feet in height—the loftiest island mountains in the world. Still farther afield, the countless islands of Polynesia are for the most part boldly rugged in contour—notably, of course, the Hawaiian group, with its great volcanic trio of Mauna Kea, Mauna Loa and Kilauea.

Kilauea, one of the most famous volcanoes in the world, is actually not a mountain at all, but simply a huge crater in the side of Mauna Loa. Mauna Kea, on the other hand, is not only one of the greatest of volcanic peaks, but, in a very real sense, the tallest of all mountains in the world. Its height above sea level is only 13,825 feet; its roots, however, spring from the ocean floor at a depth of 18,000 feet, and its seaward flanks rise in one unbroken slope of almost 32,000 feet from base to summit.

Australia, strangely enough, has scarcely any mountains worthy of the name, Mount Kosciusko, the apex of the continent, being only a little more than 7,000 feet high. New Zealand, on the other hand, is practically one continuous chain of ranges, and for many years past its great peaks and glaciers have drawn the attention and admiration of western mountaineers. Among the first on the scene were two celebrated English climbers, the Rev. W. A. Green and Edward FitzGerald, who in 1882 and 1894, respectively, came to New Zealand accompanied by Swiss guides and pioneered a way to the summits of many of the principal peaks. The New Zealanders themselves, however, were not long in learning to appreciate the mountains of their remote homeland. Mount Cook, which, at 12,350 feet, is the highest point of the twin islands, fell to a local party in the very same year as FitzGerald's expedition, and in the half-century since by far the greater part of New Zealand mountaineering has been carried on by residents of the country.

The mountains themselves—designated, with a notable lack of imagination, the Northern and Southern Alps—have long held a reputation as one of the finest climbing-grounds in the world. The peaks are bold and imposing, the glaciers, of which there are many, large and magnificent. Unfortunately, however, all of the New Zealand highland region is cursed with atrocious weather, one day of clear skies to five of fog and storm being the depressing year-in, year-out average. As the result of the heavy precipitation, combined with the islands' low latitude, snow and ice-fields abound, and pure rock-climbing, in the European sense, is almost unknown.

The six continents, the Arctic and Antarctic, the islands of the seas—all have been encompassed in the swift spread of mountaineering to the far corners of the earth. In the space of the few preceding paragraphs it has been possible to give merely the barest sketch of a great and infinitely detailed expansion; and in the chapters that follow the spotlight must perforce be focused on a select aristocracy of the greatest mountains and the greatest climbers. But before leaving the general for the specific, the world of mountains for the mountains of the world, it is important that we fix in our minds a few fundamental and essential facts.

The first is that the sport of climbing is still less than a hundred years old and climbing on a worldwide scale scarcely more than fifty. Although almost all of the major ranges of the earth have been opened up and many of the major peaks climbed, what has already been done does not compare with what still remains to be done.

The second is that the famous mountains and mountain expeditions of which we are about to read—the Everests, McKinleys, Aconcaguas, Ruwenzoris; the Abruzzis, Mallorys, Bauers and Smythes—do not by any means comprise the whole story of twentieth-century climbing. They represent merely the bright, highlighted chapters of a history that is being written every day, all over the world, wherever there are mountains and men to climb them.

The third is that mountaineering is no mere vague term indicating any sort of going-up or going-down on the bumpy surface of the earth. It is a sport, possessed of a great body of history and tradition; and climbing as we know it today would not exist if it were not for the long experience and experimentation of the past. Occasionally, as in the case of the "McKinley sourdoughs," we find great ascents made by men who know nothing more about mountains than that you have to go up to get to the top. But, for the most part, climbers the world over are consciously and proudly members of a craft. They use the same implements, and same techniques, the same rules and standards of conduct, and they are the inheritors of a common body of knowledge and tradition that originated in the Alps in the middle of the nineteenth century and have been painstakingly and lovingly developed ever since.

Mountaineering is more than a matter of individual climbers, individual expeditions, individual peaks. It is a way of acting, thinking and living. It is the fraternity of men who seek high adventure in high places.

PART II

V

"THE GREAT ONE"

THE STORY OF MOUNT MCKINLEY

IN THE FARAWAY, frozen heart of Alaska stands the highest mountain in North America. We know it as Mount McKinley. Men of other races, however, have had other, and better, names for it. To many of the aboriginal Indian tribes of the region it was known as Denali—"The Home of the Sun." Others knew it as Tralaika, still others as Doleyka, and the Russians, when they came, called it Bulshaia Gora. Significantly these three names, in three different tongues, meant the same thing—"The Great One."

For this remote snowpeak in our own north-west is not merely the culminating point of the North American continent; it is also one of the greatest single mountains on earth. The giants of the Himalayas and Andes are higher—22,000 to 29,000 feet, as against McKinley's 20,300—but these figures indicate total heights above sea level, and the mountains usually rise from lofty plateaus that are themselves 10,000 to 15,000 feet high. McKinley, however, has no such head-start. The valley of the Yukon River, from which its northern slopes spring, is a scant 1,500 feet above the sea, and the wilderness of forests and glaciers to the south is only slightly more elevated. The mountain soars up in one gigantic, unbroken sweep of rock and ice to its full height—almost four miles straight up from base to peak.

But the greatness of McKinley is more than a matter of arithmetic. Every traveller who has laid eyes on it, from near or far, has declared it to be one of the most impressive sights in the world. From Cook Inlet on the Pacific, two hundred miles to the south, its snowy crest dominates the northern horizon; from Fairbanks, a hundred and fifty miles north, it appears like a great white giant crouched against the sky. Except for its immediate neighbour, 17,000-foot Mount Foraker, it has not a single rival. Its cloud-hung battlements tower, lone and immense, over 300,000 square miles of central Alaska.

This colossus among mountains has been conquered twice. The records of these two ascents, together with those of the several unsuccessful efforts, made a story that, for achievement and disappointment, tragedy and comedy, heroism and even villainy, are unsurpassed in the annals of mountaineering.

So far as we know, the first white man to look upon McKinley was the English navigator, George Vancouver. While exploring the southern coast of Alaska in 1794 he saw "distant, stupendous snow mountains" to the north. He did not, however, approach any nearer, nor did any other white men, so far as we know, for almost a hundred years. The Russians, who owned and occupied the territory for the first two-thirds of the last century, obviously knew of the peak, since they gave it a name, but there is no record of any exploration in its vicinity. In 1867 the United States purchased Alaska for what then seemed the enormous sum of $7,200,000—the famous "Seward's Folly." During the next twenty years traders and prospectors trickled in, and towns and trading posts were established. But they hugged the coasts. It was not until the 1890's that the interior wilderness began to be opened up, and Americans discovered that they had acquired not only a vast arctic storehouse of gold, fish and fur, but the highest mountain on the continent as well.

Most of the pioneers of central Alaska were men in search of gold. One of these, Frank Densmore, penetrated the McKinley region in 1889 and returned with such glowing descriptions of the mountain that it was known for years among the Yukon prospectors as "Densmore's Peak." Another, W. A. Dickey, followed in 1896, reaching the outer edge of the mountain's great skirt of glaciers. Presumably Dickey was ignorant of the already existing names for the peak—or

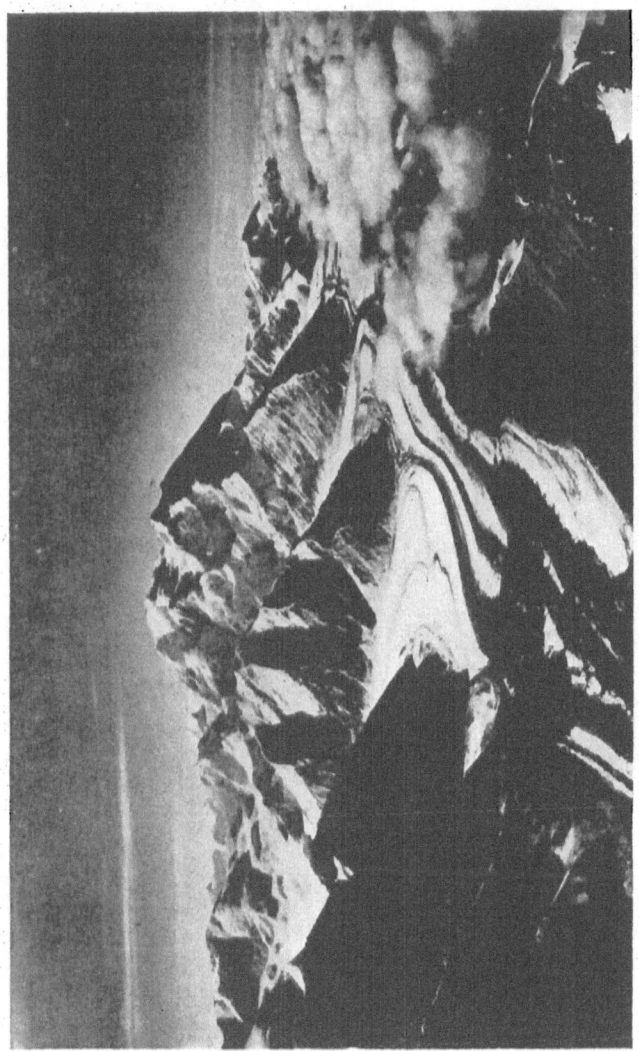

[Photo by Bradford Washburn.

TOP OF THE CONTINENT

Mount McKinley, looking up the Muldrow Glacier. All the parties that have reached the upper mountain have followed the steep arete (Karstens Ridge) which curves up to the snow-basin between the two peaks. The South Peak, on the left, is the true summit of McKinley.

[Photo by A. Pedrett. Courtesy Swiss Federal Railroads.

GIANT'S CAUSEWAY
Hacking steps up the icefall of a great glacier

perhaps he was merely a good Republican. In either case, he named it in honour of William McKinley, who was then candidate for President of the United States. And the name stuck.

In the next ten years several individuals and expeditions approached the mountain, among them George Eldridge and Robert Muldrow, of the U.S. Geological Survey, who measured the mountain by triangulation and fixed its height at 20,300 feet. The first actual attempt at ascent took place in 1903. Under the leadership of Judge Wickersham, one of the foremost citizens of the new boom town of Fairbanks, a party of four men packed into the base of the mountain and began to climb it. They were unfortunate in their choice of route, however, for they were halted almost immediately by unscalable walls of ice, and soon turned back. Thereafter Judge Wickersham was often heard to declare that the summit would never be reached except by an airplane or a balloon. Thereafter, that is, until it was climbed.

The next man to enter the expanding saga of McKinley was one of the strangest figures in the history of exploration and mountaineering. This was Dr. Frederick Cook, who was later to win worldwide notoriety as the bogus "Discoverer of the North Pole." At this time, however, Dr. Cook was concentrating on becoming the equally bogus "Conqueror of Mount McKinley." His first expedition to the mountain was in the same year as Judge Wickersham's, but it was little more than a reconnaissance of the surrounding passes and glaciers. In 1906, however, he returned, and this time plunged energetically into the business of making his own particular brand of history.

Ironically, Cook's companions at the outset of this second venture were two men of complete honour and integrity. They were Herschel Parker and Belmore Browne, whose later battles with McKinley—as we shall see—form one of the brightest, most heroic chapters of mountain history. On this occasion, however, they and Cook bogged down in the great wilderness south of the peak and were forced to withdraw without finding even a way of approach to the heights.

Then began Cook's audacious hoax. With only one companion, a packer named Edward Barrill, he returned to the base of the mountain, was unheard from for a few weeks, and then reappeared with the claim that he had reached the summit. Neither Parker, Browne nor anyone else who knew McKinley well believed him. He had not, for one thing, had enough time for the ascent, and, furthermore, his description of his experiences did not tally with their own observations. But Cook was a fraud who knew his business. Undeterred by suspicions and accusations, he returned to civilization and began systematically to reap the rewards of his "feat." He wrote a book called *To the Top of the Continent*, in which he described his struggles on the ascent and the magnificence of the view from the top. He showed photographs which he said he had taken on the summit. He lectured before great public gatherings and learned societies. As far as the world was concerned, he was what he claimed to be—the conqueror of McKinley.

Seven years passed before the fraud was finally exposed. Parker and Browne could not conclusively prove their suspicions, and it remained for Hudson Stuck and his companions, who in 1913 made the true first ascent, to settle the matter once and for all. Stuck was Archdeacon of the Yukon, a man above suspicion in every way, and his description of McKinley refuted Cook's in countless details. Cook had spoken of "the heaven-scraped granite and frosted rocks" of the summit. Stuck reported that there was no rock of any kind on the peak above 19,000 feet, but only a permanent sheath of snow and ice. Cook devoted pages of his book to vivid descriptions of the view from the top and referred to McKinley as standing utterly alone. Stuck declared that the dominent feature of the view, "bursting on the eye and filling all the middle distance," was the great mass of Mount Foraker. And so on, throughout the account of his ascent.

From this point on the evidence piled up rapidly. Barrill, Cook's packer, after years of silence, signed a sworn statement that his employer's claims were untrue. An insignificant foothill peak was found, which coincided so completely with

Cook's supposed photographs of McKinley's summit that it became obvious they had been made there. Within a short time the "conqueror's" claims were thoroughly discredited. Then, a few years later, came the still more sensational exposure of his faked discovery of the North Pole, and Cook's fantastic career reached its end. He dropped into obscurity—a dishonoured, broken man.

Meanwhile the fight against "The Great One" went on. The bogus conquest had, if nothing else, aroused widespread interest in the greatest American mountain, and the attack was on in full force.

First in the field was a group of men who put even the incredible Dr. Cook to shame. They are known in climbing history as "the sourdough expedition," and no stranger or more haphazard exploit than theirs has ever occurred on any major mountain in the world. By every accepted standard they should not only have made a ridiculous failure of their attempt, but all should have been killed five times over. Instead, they missed immortality by a hairbreadth—or, to be accurate, 300 feet—and, in addition, performed what is undoubtedly one of the greatest exploits in the annals of mountaineering.

The sourdoughs of McKinley were a half dozen prospectors and miners of the vicinity of Fairbanks. None of them had ever been on a mountain in his life, but they were typical Alaskan frontiersmen, with frontiersmen's strength and pride, and when they heard of Cook's claims they snorted in disbelief and decided it was high time they took a hand in the affair themselves. "If McKinley is going to be climbed," they decided in effect, "we're the boys who are going to do it."

And in the spring of 1910, off they went.

The whole venture was organized in a way that would make a good Alpine Club member's hair stand on end. Or, rather, it wasn't organized at all. The $500 which was the bulk of their capital was put up by one Billy McPhee, a public-spirited saloonkeeper of Fairbanks. There was no leader, no prearranged plan of attack, and by the time they reached the base of the mountain half the party had come to blows

Gc

with the other half and left for home. There was no scientific knowledge among them, no proper clothing or equipment, in fact nothing whatever of the things which a mountaineer is supposed to possess—save two. They had pluck and they had luck.

Their first great good fortune was in selecting the Muldrow Glacier as their way of approach. This vast tongue of ice extends from the northern foothills up into the very heart of the McKinley range, and to this day it is the only practicable route that has been found giving access to the upper reaches of the mountain. The sourdoughs obviously did not know this, but their instinct was right. Day after day, week after week, they toiled up the gigantic ice-slope of the Muldrow, hacking steps, bridging crevasses, moving slowly on and up into a silent, frozen world where no living thing had ever moved before.

At last they reached the glacier's head. They were now 11,000 feet above the sea, but barely at the base of the mountain proper, and above them the great white ridges and precipices of McKinley towered almost another two miles into the sky. By this time only three members of the expedition were left —Pete Anderson, Billy Taylor and Charley McGonogol— but these three, as they were soon to prove, were men of herculean strength and determination. For several days they camped at the head of the glacier, studying the vertical wilderness above them and awaiting favourable weather. Then, at two in the morning of April tenth, they started up.

A word is necessary here about the usual methods of scaling great peaks. Climbing itself is only one of the problems involved; more than half the battle is the establishment of high camps and the bringing up of reserve supplies, so that the climbers will not starve or freeze to death in the event of a mishap or a storm. On the great Himalayan peaks, as we shall see, the insurmountable difficulty has always been that of portage. On McKinley, every regular expedition has spent weeks preparing the way for the final assault. Such finicky, tenderfoot precautions, however, were not in the line of the Messrs. Anderson, Taylor and McGonogol. With the food and equipment that an average person might take along for a picnic lunch, they climbed from their glacier camp to within 300 feet of the highest point of North America and back—*all in one day.*[1]

The sourdoughs, unlike most mountaineers, have left no written record of their venture, and the details of their astonishing ascent are very vague. It is known, however, that their route was roughly that followed in all subsequent expeditions: from the head of the Muldrow, up the great ice-spine that was later to be called Karstens Ridge, and into the upper ice-basin near the mountain's summit. It was when they reached this basin—now known as Harper Glacier—that they made a choice that was to cheat them of worldwide fame. McKinley is a mountain of two peaks—the south, or true summit, 20,300 feet high, and the north, a scant 300 feet lower. Standing between them on that day, already at 17,000 feet and with victory in their grasp, the sourdoughs chose the wrong one!

What prompted their choice has never been satisfactorily explained. It may have been that they thought the North Peak was the higher. It may have been the knowledge that half the population of central Alaska was watching through telescopes in Fairbanks, from which the North Peak alone is visible. At all events, the North Peak it was, McGonogol, near collapse, had to turn back within 500 feet of the goal, but Anderson and Taylor struggled on up the fearful ice-slope, in sub-zero cold, until they reached the top. There they unfurled the Stars and Stripes on a fourteen-foot flagstaff they had miraculously carried with them and planted it firmly on the topmost pinnacle. This done, they started down, picked up the exhausted McGonogol, and descended the 9,000 feet to the Muldrow Glacier without a single stop. And in another week or so they were safe and sound in Billy McPhee's Fairbanks saloon, telling all about it to anyone who would buy them a drink.

---

[1] In the Arctic, in spring and summer, the climbing day is limited only by the endurance of the climbers. Instead of darkness, night time brings merely a grey twilight, and it is possible to climb safely at any hour.

Confronted with a performance like this, the usual rules and standards of mountaineering collapse into the wastebasket. Indeed, the whole story of their ascent seemed so fantastic that for several years it was generally disbelieved—those same years, ironically, during which Dr. Cook was still a national hero. It remained again for Archdeacon Stuck to clear things up. In his ascent of the true summit in 1913 he had ample opportunity to view the top of the North Peak, and what he saw completely vindicated the claims of the sourdoughs. The American flag was gone, to be sure, long since torn to shreds in the wild arctic winds; but the flagstaff was still there—"plain, prominent and unmistakable."

The sourdoughs never went back to McKinley. They were prospectors, not mountaineers, and one fling at "The Great One" was enough for them. That they could have reached the true summit had they tried no one who has known them or the mountain has ever doubted. But the fact remains that they didn't. The highest point in the continent still stood, lofty and untrodden, awaiting its next attackers.

They were not long in coming.

Indeed, in the same year as "the sourdough climb" Herschel Parker and Belmore Browne were again in the vicinity of the mountain. As in 1906, they approached it from Cook's inlet, on the south—this time at the head of a party from the Explorer's Club of New York—and again they found that their route lay through almost impassable country. For weeks on end they struggled up icy, raging rivers, through tangled forests and wild boulder-choked gorges until at last they came out on a wide snow-plain at the very foot of the mountain. Through all their long ordeal, however, they had gained only 5,000 feet in altitude, and here at their seventeenth camp, when they were already near exhaustion, McKinley's summit was still 15,000 feet above them.

Worse yet, it was immediately apparent that the southern side of the mountain was unclimbable. Its face rose in a series of ice-hung precipices to which a fly could not have clung—much less a man—and even the two ridges which they discovered ended hopelessly under huge outcropping cliffs and hanging glaciers. As if this were not enough, the whole expanse above them was scoured by avalanches. The south face of McKinley, unlike the north, is exposed to the moist winds from the Pacific, with the result that the snow upon it seldom freezes. There was no surface into which an axe or crampon-spike could bite, but only three vertical miles of roaring, crumbling destruction. Convinced that "The Great One" could never be climbed from that side, the expedition turned away and began the long struggle back to the coast.

But Parker and Browne were not through yet. McKinley had cast its spell upon them, and in 1912, six years after their first attempt, they were back again for their third and last. This, as it was to turn out, was one of the most magnificent, and at the same time, heartbreaking, assaults ever made on a great mountain.

This time, profiting from experience, they approached McKinley from the north, by the same general route that the sourdoughs had used. But there any resemblance between their expedition and that of the doughty pioneers ended. Both of them were thoughtful, highly educated men—Parker a physicist and university professor and Browne a distinguished painter—and their attack was as reasoned and carefully planned as the sourdoughs' had been haphazard. For months in advance they pored over maps, planned their marches and camps, assembled their supplies and equipment. Then, with Merle La Voy and Arthur Aten, two sturdy Alaskans who had been with them in 1910, they set out for their goal.

From late February until late May they mushed in by dog-sled from Seward, on the coast, to the inner fastnesses of the mountain. After much reconnoitring they found a pass through the northern ridge, came out on the Muldrow Glacier and began its steep, laborious ascent. The Muldrow was long and broad, but it could never be mistaken for a paved avenue. It lunged down from the heights like a colossal ski-jump, and its surface was an ice-choked wilderness of humps and hollows. In some places huge seracs, a thousand feet high, had to be surmounted; in others were yawning, seemingly bottomless crevasses that they circumvented. Often the sled-dogs would tumble headlong into them and hang howling by their harnesses until they were pulled out.

Back and forth, back and forth, endlessly, went the men and dogs and sleds, establishing camps and bringing up supplies. But slowly they advanced, and at last, in the first week of June, they reached the head of the glacier. Here, at 11,000 feet the great north-east ridge of McKinley began its skyward climb. Leaving the dogs behind, with Aten to take care of them, Parker, Browne and La Voy set foot at last upon the mountain proper.

Almost immediately they encountered the frightful weather that was to plague them during their whole ordeal on the peak. A blizzard howled down violently, the ice cliffs cracked and groaned, and avalanches roared about them like artillery. For four days the men huddled in their tent, rubbing one another's bodies to keep from freezing to death, clinging to the guy ropes so that they would not be blown into eternity. When the storm had passed they resumed the ascent, undaunted, and for a week crept upward. Uncounted thousands of steps had to be hacked in the glazed snow of the ridge. Backbreaking loads had to be carried in relays to higher camps. At one point their food supply ran so low that they had to descend all the way to the glacier to replenish it. But they pushed on doggedly and at last gained the upper basin, at a height of about 16,000 feet.

Here another savage storm imprisoned them for days, but they bided their time hopefully, for they were confident that the worst of McKinley was beneath them. And, indeed, when the weather finally cleared, the last 4,000 feet of the South Peak appeared as merely a gentle slope into the sky, easy of access and presenting no major difficulties. At six in the morning of June 29 they began the summit dash with high hearts.

Dash, to be sure, is scarcely the word. It was still necessary for them to hack out footholds in the glaring cone of ice and to halt every few steps, gasping, in the thin, freezing air. But they made steady progress and within four hours had gained half the distance. The summit point of North America stood out near and clear above them. "It rose," Browne declared later, "as innocently as a tilted snow-covered tennis court, and as we looked at it we grinned with relief—we *knew* the peak was ours."

Then the last blow fell. With paralysing suddenness the wind sprang up into a howling gale, the sky darkened and the blizzard resumed. By the time they had struggled up another thousand feet they could no longer see one another at five yards through the blinding snow, and the sixty-mile wind threatened to hurl them at any moment from the mountainside. Bent double, frost-crippled, scarcely able to breathe, they still crept on until they reached the limit of human endurance. To have gone another step upward would have been suicide. At a height of 20,000 feet—a mere 300 from their goal—they turned back.

Somehow they succeeded in descending to their highest camp, and two days later they made a second attempt. But again the elements defeated them. A thick, freezing fog closed in about them, in which they could neither see nor breathe, and they were stopped at 19,300 feet. The next day, both their supplies and strength exhausted, they began the descent of the mountain. "I remember," said Browne, "only a feeling of dull despair."

Thus ended one of the most gallant unsuccessful ventures in the story of mountaineering. That it did not end in final and complete tragedy was merely a stroke of the greatest luck. For in that summer of 1912 the volcano Katmai, 400 miles away, was in eruption, and the shock of its explosions was felt throughout the plains and ranges of central Alaska. Only a few days after they had descended to the lowlands, the weary, discouraged men were startled by a vast thunder of sound, so great that it seemed the earth itself were splitting open. And, indeed, it was. Behind them, as they watched, the whole north face and ridges of McKinley, on which they had so recently stood, gave a monstrous shudder, detached themselves from the main mass of the mountain and plunged wildly into the valleys below.

That was their last view of McKinley—roaring defiance at its challengers.

Mountains are not greatly concerned with human concepts of justice. Parker and Browne devoted years of their lives to the exploring and ascent of McKinley, only to meet ultimate defeat. Its next assailants spent a total of two months on its forbidding terrain—and conquered it.

Not that there was anything undeserved in the triumph of Archdeacon Hudson Stuck. He and his companions were mountaineers of the first order; he had made many ascents in the American and Canadian Rockies, and for years past, during his far-flung journeys among the Indians of Alaska, he had seen McKinley from afar and yearned to climb it. When at last he did, he brought to it the same resolution and courage, the same simplicity and integrity of spirit that consistently marked him in his life's work.

In the spring of 1913 Stuck received leave of absence from his churchly duties and set out from the tiny mission station of Nenana to achieve his great ambition. His companions were Harry Karstens, a sturdy sourdough who had come to Alaska in the Klondike gold rush and was later to become superintendent of McKinley National Park; Robert Tatum, a 21-year-old missionary from Tennessee; Walter Harper, a strong, cheerful, young halfbreed, who had been Stuck's dog-driver and interpreter for several years; and two Indian youngsters from the Nenana mission school named Johnny and Esaias.

With dogs and sleds they mushed across the vast white plains of central Alaska, crossed the outer spurs and ridges that guard McKinley and came out at last on the Muldrow Glacier, as the other expeditions had done before them. Here Esaias, having done his bit, was sent back to Nenana, Johnny remaining to take care of the dogs. Slowly and carefully the little party threaded its way up the steep maze of the glacier, probing and zigzagging endlessly to avoid the great crevasses, suffering greatly from cold and snowstorms and the fierce wind that swooped down on them from the frozen heights.

Ironically, though, neither mountain nor elements was responsible for their only serious mishap. Returning one day from a scouting expedition they saw with horror that their camp was afire, and before they could extinguish it a large part of their food and equipment had been burned. The worst loss of all was that of their entire supply of sugar. There is no food more essential than sugar to men struggling in the cold and often close to exhaustion, and in the days to come they were to have ample occasion to bemoan their bad luck.

At last, however, they reached the head of the glacier and, like Parker and Browne and the sourdoughs in earlier years, stood staring upward at the huge white wilderness of the upper mountain. But, as they stared, they realized something was wrong. The great ridge which was to be their route was not at all as the previous expeditions had described it—a thin, clean knife-edge cutting into the sky. What they saw instead was an indescribable chaos of pinnacles and chasms and great tumbled ice-masses piled crazily upon each other as far as the eye could see. And presently they realized what had happened. The great earth tremors of the previous year, from which Parker and Browne had barely escaped with their lives, had indeed blown to bits what had formerly been the northeast ramparts of the mountain. The ridge that the other parties had ascended had completely ceased to be. Instead of following a route which others had pioneered before them, they were faced with the necessity of becoming pioneers themselves.

What Stuck and his companions did then was quite simply this: they cut a three-mile staircase in the ice. With magnificent patience and endurance they hacked and chopped and clawed their way from the 11,000-foot altitude of the Muldrow's head to the 16,000-foot heights of the upper basin. They surmounted ice-blocks as large as three-storey houses, they edged around cornices that hung in space a mile above the glaciers; they struggled up with their supplies on their backs, descended again, struggled up with more. None of them ventured to count the thousands or tens of thousands of steps they cut, but Stuck later estimated that each member of the party, in going back and forth, had climbed at least 60,000 feet—or three times the total height of McKinley.

After days of unrelieved toil the savage earthquake-shattered ridge was at last behind them. On June third they camped at 16,500 feet in the middle of the upper basin, between the twin peaks of the mountain, and three days later at 18,000 feet on the slopes just beneath the summit. And now the blessing that had been so cruelly withheld from Parker and Browne was granted to them: the day of the final assault was clear and fine.

They started at three in the morning and for hour after hour toiled upward through the frozen grey silence of the arctic heights. Sometimes it was still necessary to hack steps with their axes; at other times their crampons sufficed, biting deeply into the hard-crusted slope of snow. At eleven o'clock they passed the point at which Parker and Browne had been turned back by the blizzard. At one they stepped up upon the horse-shoe ridge that forms the summit of the peak. And a few moments later——

"——there still stretched ahead of us," wrote Stuck, "and perhaps one hundred feet above us, another small ridge with a north and south pair of little haycock summits. This is the real top.—With keen excitement we pushed on. Walter Harper, who had been in the lead all day, was the first to scramble up; a native Alaskan, he is the first human being to set foot on the top of Alaska's great mountain, and he had well earned the lifelong distinction. Karstens and Tatum were hard upon his heels, but the last man on the rope had almost to be hauled up the last few feet, and fell unconscious for a moment upon the floor of the little snow basin that occupies the top of the mountain."

Four men stood at last on the summit of North America.

Their first act was to thank God for permitting them to achieve their goal. "This prime duty done," to quote the reverent archdeacon, they set up the instruments that they had carried with them and took thermometer and barometer readings. Then, and not until then, did they let their eyes sweep out over the stupendous panorama that no man had ever seen before—more than 50,000 square miles of Alaska, peaks and ranges, glaciers and valleys, rivers and plains, from the ice-locked arctic interior to the sea.

But it is not alone for the sake of a "view" that men struggle up to the high places of the earth. Let us allow the conqueror of McKinley to describe the mountaineer's reward, for no man has ever described it better:

"Only those who have for long years cherished a great and almost inordinate desire, and have had that desire gratified to the limit of their expectation, can enter into the deep thankfulness and content that filled the heart upon the descent of this mountain. There was no pride of conquest, no trace of that exultation of victory some enjoy upon the first ascent of a lofty peak, no gloating over good fortune that had hoisted us a few hundred feet higher than others who had struggled and been discomfited. Rather was the feeling that a privileged communion with the high places of the earth had been granted; that not only had we been permitted to lift up eager eyes to these summits, secret and solitary since the world began, but to enter boldly upon them, to take place, as it were, domestically in their hithero sealed chambers, to inhabit them, and to cast our eyes down from them, seeing all things as they spread out from the windows of heaven itself."

They constructed a rough cross of birch staves which they had carried with them, thrust it deep into the snow, and, gathering around it, spoke the solemn, joyful words of the Te Deum. Then they started down, the tiredest and happiest of men.

For nineteen years after its conquest no one approached McKinley. Then, in the spring of 1932, two separate expeditions converged upon it at the same time. One was completely successful in every respect. The other culminated tragically in the only deaths that have occurred in the battle for the mountain.

The successful party was composed of Erling Strom, a well-known Norwegian-American skier, Alfred Lindley, a Minneapolis attorney, Harry Liek, superintendent of McKinley

National Park, and Grant Pearson, a park ranger. They reached the upper basin by substantially the same route as the earlier parties—the ridge now named for Harry Karstens—and successfully scaled both north and south peaks, thus becoming the first party to reach both summits of McKinley.

The unusual feature of this expedition was that it was the first to make extensive use of skis in the ascent of a large mountain. This enabled the climbers to save a vast amount of time on reconnaissance trips and in the back-and-forth transportation of supplies, particularly on the Muldrow Glacier and the lower reaches of the ridge. Strom said of one particular stretch that "each ascent took us fully half an hour, but we could return to camp in one minute." In addition, the skis greatly decreased the danger of falling through the innumerable snow-hidden crevasses.

High on Karstens Ridge the Strom-Lindley party discovered a thermometer left by Stuck. It had been the archdeacon's belief that McKinley, in winter, was the coldest place in the world, and on his descent of the mountain he had cached a minimum thermometer at a point where he hoped the next party would find it. The climbers of 1932 proved that he had been right. The indicator of the instrument had dropped past the end of the scale, which was 95° below zero, and was stuck in the bulb, where it could go no farther. It appeared obvious, therefore, that at one time or another during the winters of the intervening years, the temperature had sunk to at least 100° below zero—the greatest natural cold ever recorded anywhere on earth. After this, the discoverers reported, the mere 20° and 25° below temperatures encountered on the heights seemed to them almost balmy!

The second 1932 expedition to McKinley did not arrive on the scene until the first was already high on the mountain. This was the so-called "Cosmic Ray" expedition, which planned to undertake extensive scientific observations at great altitudes and was led by Allan Carpé, one of the most accomplished young American mountaineers. These climbers also brought modern methods to the technique of mountaineering, but, unlike their rivals, their innovation was not skis, but an airplane. On the same day they found Stuck's thermometer on Karstens Ridge, Strom and his companions stared down the face of a precipice to see a plane landing supplies at the head of the Muldrow Glacier, 4,000 feet below. This was the first time in climbing history such a feat had been attempted, much less accomplished.

During the next week, while the first party successfully scaled both the north and south peaks, they saw nothing more of Carpé and his expedition. When at last they descended to the head of the Muldrow, the plane was gone, but two tents were standing near the former site of one of their own camps. And the tents were deserted.

"Immediately," Strom had said, "we felt that something had gone wrong. Inside one tent we found two open sleeping bags and a pot half full of frozen mulligan stew. From the other tent, containing cosmic ray apparatus, we could hear a little mechanism slowly ticking."

From a diary found in one of the sleeping bags they learned that the only occupants of the tents had been Carpé and one companion, Theodore Koven. There being no sign of either man, they pushed on down the glacier, following an almost obliterated track; and it was not long before their worst fears were confirmed. A mile and a half below the camp they spied a tiny dark object against the white immensity of snow. It was Koven's body. One leg had been injured and also the side of his head. He had obviously fallen into a crevasse, but had managed to climb out again, only to collapse and die from exposure.

Carpé's body has never been found.

Thus the story of McKinley, to date, ends in both triumph and tragedy. In 1936 an expedition of the National Geographic and Pan American Societies surveyed the peak from the air, but during the past nine years there has been no further attempt to climb it.

"The Great One" today is not the almost inaccessible mountain it was in the days of the sourdoughs, and of Parker, Browne and Stuck. For the past twenty-three years the country surrounding it has been a National Park. The Alaska Railroad runs within a hundred miles of its summit, and the trail from McKinley Park station is dotted with rangers' cabins nearly to the foot of the Muldrow Glacier. An expedition that formerly required months might be accomplished now in two or three weeks.

Will McKinley be climbed again? To be sure it will. But mountaineers are a strange and hardy breed, and it will be not because of these helping facilities, but in spite of them, that they will come again. And, whatever use they make of trains and planes, of sleds and skis and even tractors, in approaching the mountain, all the marvels of modern science and invention combined will not get them to the top. There is only one key, now as in the past, to the summit of our continent—the endurance and skill and courage of those who seek it.

VI

SNOWPEAKS AND FIREPEAKS

THE ANDES OF SOUTH AMERICA

The continent of South America is built on a vast and simple scale, with three dominant physical features. Its central and north-eastern interior comprises the greatest jungle area on earth—some three million square miles of tropical rain forest in the Amazon and Orinoco basins. Its south-eastern third extends unbroken through horizon after horizon across the flat, open pampas of the Argentine. And on the west is its backbone—the five thousand miles of continuous mountain ranges and chains which, taken all together, are called the Andes.

It is true that, strictly speaking, the Andes are not the only mountains of the continent. The back-country of the Guianas, far to the east, possesses a wild highland region, topped by the mysterious, jungle-clad Mount Roraima; in the uplands of central Brazil there is a little-known range with the fabulous Land-of-Oz name of Serra Roncador—the Snoring Mountains; and the harbour of Rio de Janeiro, to be sure, boasts its fantastic fringe of rocky domes and spires. None of these isolated uplifts, however, is of any great extent or elevation. To all intents and purposes, the mountains of South America are synonymous with the word Andes.

This great range, or series of ranges, forms what is beyond comparison the longest unbroken mountain region in the world. Its northernmost spurs front the Caribbean Sea on the coasts of Colombia and Venezuela, and at Cape Horn, in farthest Tierra del Fuego, its gaunt headlands look south to the Antarctic Ocean. Between these two extremities stretch seventy degrees of latitude—the entire length of the earth's longest continent. In addition to their extent, the Andes are also among the highest of ranges, second only to those of Central Asia. The summit of Aconcagua, capstone of the western hemisphere, towers almost 23,000 feet above the nearby Pacific, and scattered through Peru, Bolivia and Chile are more than twenty-five other peaks exceeding 20,000 feet in height.[1]

Extending from the tropics through the sub-tropics, the south temperate zone and almost to the Antarctic, the Andes vary enormously in formation and terrain, vegetation and climatic conditions. The region of the Atacama Desert, in northern Chile, is among the hottest and driest on earth, and one must ascend to 20,000 feet, or the very tops of the highest mountains, before reaching the level of perpetual snow. In cold and stormy Patagonia, on the other hand, there are places where rain or snow falls on an average of 300 days in the year, and the snow-line dips to a mere 2,500 feet. Throughout Colombia, Venezuela and Ecuador the eastern flanks of the great peaks rise out of the equatorial rain forest of the Amazon and are covered in vegetation up to great heights. In the lake district of southern Chile the terrain and climate are similar to those of the Alps or our own north-west. In the vast central *altiplano* of northern Chile and Bolivia stretch thousands of square miles of peaks and plateaus boasting not so much as a tree, a shrub or a blade of grass. Many of the most important sub-ranges are volcanic in origin, and not a few of their greatest peaks are still active fire-mountains; separating them, however, are extensive areas where there are no volcanoes whatever. In short, the Andes are as various as they are vast. Only one generalization will hold good for them all: they are big.

There is equal variety in their history and their effect on men and civilizations. Many districts of the Andes, notably in the tropical north and the frozen, desolate south, are to this day among the most sparsely inhabited and least-known areas

---

[1] As in the case of many of the world's great mountain ranges, the heights of most Andean peaks have not yet been exactly determined. In this and succeeding chapters the figures given are the most generally accepted estimates.

in the world. The great central highlands of Peru and Bolivia, on the other hand, have been thickly inhabited for uncounted centuries. It was here that Indian America reached its highest development in the remarkable civilization of the Incas, and here too that the Spaniards first established dominion in their bloody conquest of the New World. The brown hills behind Cuzco were veined with trails and pitted with mine-shafts in the days when the Hudson and Mississippi valleys were still untouched, silent wildernesses.

Today, as for the past 400 years, the Andes are economically the most important mountain region in the world. The dry earth and rock of their central ranges are a virtually inexhaustible treasure-house of mineral wealth—gold, silver, iron, tin, copper—and since the days of the Conquistadores mining has been the foremost industry of Chile, Bolivia and Peru. The high peaks are, to be sure, devoid of life, as are all great peaks anywhere in the world; but the plateaus and valleys that lie in their shadow swarm with men and machines. Indeed, this inhabited section of the Andes contains at the present time more than a quarter of the population and produces almost a third of the wealth of all South America.

For the prospector, the miner and the exploiter, the Andes have long been El Dorado. The mountaineer, however, has been slower in coming and has found them less happy hunting grounds. Partly, of course, they have been neglected because they are so far away from Europe, which is the birthplace and home of climbing as a sport. But there are other reasons also. The Andes are vast not only in extent, but in monotony as well. Although terrain and conditions vary greatly from one climatic zone to another, the mountains in any one zone are usually of a dispiriting sameness; the snow-line is apt to be very high, the approaches and lower slopes desolate and uninteresting. Worst of all, even the highest peaks rise from their bases in such gradual, uniform grades that they offer small lure or challenge to the accomplished climber. There is little call for an alpinist's skill on these great, brown sandpaper mountains, but merely for endurance and grim, bulldog determination.

Hc

Nevertheless, the Andes have seen their share of high mountain adventure. With the opening up of new climbing horizons some three-quarters of a century ago, it was inevitable that at least a few wide-ranging mountaineers would set their caps for the loftiest peaks of the New World, and in the years that have passed since, the great summits of Chile and Bolivia, Ecuador and Peru have fallen one by one. As in the case of most of the world's big mountains, scarcely any of the ascents were made by natives of the surrounding country. The high Andes have, for the most part, fallen to Englishmen, Germans,[1] Italians and, in later days, Americans—men from the nations in which the mountaineering instinct has become strongly developed. The great volcanoes of Ecuador were climbed as early as 1880, Illimani, one of the giants of Bolivia, in 1898, and Aconcagua, monarch of them all, in 1897. The 22,350-foot Sahama, in Bolivia, on the other hand, did not fall until 1939, and there remain today literally hundreds of lofty peaks which have not been scaled or, in most cases, even attempted. If there were no other virgin mountains anywhere in the world, the myriad summits of South America would insure climbers an ample supply of "firsts" for many years to come.

The Andes of northern Venezuela and Colombia are little more than outposts of the main range. They converge from four great roots which spread across the northern margin of the continent, the easternmost root being the continuation of the Lesser Antilles and the westernmost the continuation of the Central American chain. For the most part, these are typically tropical mountains, rising out of jungle or semi-jungle country, heavily forested, and with only a very few of the highest summits attaining the levels of perpetual snow. Pre-eminent among these are the peaks of the Sierra Nevada de Santa Marta, at the northernmost tip of Colombia, which, however, are separated from the main cordillera by deep river valleys and are not, strictly speaking, part of the Andes at all. The

---

[1] In the light of current world events, it is perhaps significant to note how large a par Germans have played in the exploration of South America. During the past decade, particularly, virtually all the major mountaineering expeditions to the Andes have been of German origin.

snowcaps of the Santa Martas have been seen by many tourists from the decks of Caribbean cruise ships, but it was not until 1939 that a small American party under the leadership of Walter A. Wood penetrated the surrounding wilderness and climbed several of the highest summits. To the astonishment of the climbers themselves, they found many of the peaks to be between 18,000 and 18,500 feet high—altitudes which rank the Santa Martas among the highest coastal mountains in the world. Great areas of the range are still unvisited and unexplored and, from the descriptions of the Wood party, should prove a rewarding objective for climbers of the future.

Through most of the length of Colombia the Andes proper are considerably lower than the Santa Martas and of far less interest to the mountaineer. Sweeping southward in three separate chains, they are for some 500 miles little more than buttresses of the country's high central plateau, on which are located the principal cities of Bogotá, Medellín and Cali. South-west of Bogotá, however, begins the first of the three great Andean volcanic zones, here known as the Cordillera Central and topped by the 18,700-foot cone of Tolima. This steep and spectacular volcano, believed to be the highest summit north of Ecuador, was ascended in 1926 by a mixed party of Germans and Colombians and is one of the very few climbed peaks in the country.

The ranges of southern Colombia are comparatively low and have been only sketchily explored, but once the Ecuadorian boundary is passed the Andes buckle skyward in their full stature. Here, in a compact area just south of the equator, are clustered some of the loftiest and most impressive volcanoes in the world. More than thirty major peaks, spaced like sentinels, rise from the long rounded ridges of the cordillera, their flanks buried deep in green, primeval jungle, their snowcaps, incredibly white and remote, seeming to hang like great clouds in the blue, tropical sky. High above all their neighbours hang the summits of the two greatest: Chimborazo and Cotopaxi.

These are mountains with a history. Chimborazo—"the Watch-tower of the Universe," the great Bolívar called it—

has been a famous landmark since the earliest days of the Spanish conquest, and the region surrounding its base was well known to travellers and explorers of the Colonial period. Between 1736 and 1744 it was the site of what was probably the first major scientific expedition to any high mountain range—a large and well-equipped party of geographers and naturalists led by the Frenchmen Bouger and La Condamine and the Spaniards Ulloa and Juan Jorge. As a result of their investigations, made long before either the Himalayas or the higher southern Andes were known, Chimborazo was for almost three-quarters of a century ranked as the highest mountain in the world. In 1802, a still more distinguished visitor appeared on the scene in the person of the German naturalist, Alexander von Humboldt. Humboldt and his companions not only occupied themselves with scientific observations, but also made attempts on the actual summits of both Chimborazo and Cotopaxi. Although the ventures were unsuccessful, the subsequent writings of various members of the party served to place the two remote volcanoes among the most famous mountains on earth.

Seventy more years were to pass, however, before either was climbed to the top. Then at last, in 1872, Cotopaxi fell to a German geologist, Wilhelm Reid, and his companion, A. M. Escobar; and in 1880 Chimborazo was conquered by no less an antagonist than Edward Whymper. Still a great mountaineer fifteen years after his epic struggle with the Matterhorn, Whymper was the first top-flight European alpinist to visit the high Andes, and his expedition to Ecuador provided the original impetus to organized climbing in the southern hemisphere. In addition to Chimborazo, which he climbed twice, he reached the top of Cotopaxi—the fifth ascent—and pioneered the way to some half-dozen lesser summits in the surrounding ranges. Ironically, his principal helper and companion on these great climbs was Jean-Antoine Carrel, his brilliant guide and bitter rival of bygone days in the Alps. It is surely not stretching the imagination too far to picture these two old campaigners battling up the last few feet of Chimborazo's icy crest, clasping numbed hands in victory on its lonely, wind-lashed summit, and at that very moment thinking ruefully, each to himself: "It might have been the Matterhorn."

Neither Chimborazo nor Cotopaxi has been climbed often in recent years, and both remain among the most spectacular and difficult ascents in the Andes. Of the two, Chimborazo is the higher—20,500 feet to Cotopaxi's 19,600—but its high base and massive, irregular form detract considerably from its impressiveness. Cotopaxi, on the other hand, is a mountain of almost legendary beauty. Soaring a full 10,000 feet above its green skirt of valleys, its great cone is proportioned in measured symmetry and its summit snowcap looms like a perfect, white triangle against the sky. Also it has the distinction of being a live volcano—the only one in Ecuador and the highest active fire-mountain in the world. When in eruption, molten streams of lava flow down its icy flanks and vast jets of steam swirl like a veil over the whole upper face of the mountain. Camping beside its crater rim while Cotopaxi was quiescent, Whymper reported that even then the black ash was so hot that it scorched the ground sheet of his tent.

Beyond the great volcanoes of Ecuador, the Andes fall away into a comparatively low zone of several hundred miles. In central Peru, however, they rise again in an enormous and lofty massif known as the Cordillera Blanca. This chain of ice and granite peaks is non-volcanic in origin, abounds in rock-spires, precipices and glaciers, and more closely resembles the great ranges of the Alps and Himalayas than any other mountain district in South America. The chain bristles with scores of steep and jagged peaks, topped by 22,200-foot Huascaran, the highest summit in Peru and generally recognized as the fourth highest in the Americas.

Huascaran holds an interesting place in mountaineering history as being one of the very few major peaks anywhere in the world to be first ascended by a woman. Its conqueror was Miss Annie S. Peck, a remarkable and indefatigable lady from Providence, Rhode Island, who for nine months of the year taught Latin at Smith College and Purdue University and during the other three went big-mountain hunting among the far-flung ranges of Europe, Mexico and South America. In

1904 Miss Peck reached a height of 20,500 feet on Sorata, in Bolivia. In 1908, at the age of over fifty, she visited the Andes again and this time fought her way successfully to the northernmost of Huascaran's formidable twin peaks.

Very little other climbing was done in the Cordillera Blanca until 1932, when a large party of German climbers, under the auspices of the *Deutsch-Österreichischer Alpenverein*, conducted an exhaustive exploration of the region. Besides re-ascending Huascaran, they climbed some twenty virgin peaks between 16,000 and 21,000 feet in height and established the highest astronomical observatory in the world at 20,000 feet on the summit ridge of the snowpeak Hualcan. In 1939 there was a second German expedition to the region, during which Huascaran was climbed once more, as well as several other major peaks of the range. Three members of the party were killed in an avalanche while engaged in cartographical work on the journey home.

Southward from the Cordillera Blanca, the Andes of Peru present a vast conglomeration of peaks and ranges, crisscrossing one another in an inextricable tangle of so-called *nudos*, or knots. Near the great mining centre of Cerro de Pasco rises a massive chain called the Cordillera de Huayhuash, of which almost nothing is known, except that it contains at least one summit, Carnicero, which is almost 22,000 feet high. In the region directly east of Lima there are no notable individual peaks, but the central plateaus, or *punas*, which form the backbone of the range are of enormous extent and elevation. This is an almost rainless world—brown, desolate and forbidding—yet among the most populous zones of the Andes, because it is the heart of the Peruvian mining district. The barren hills surrounding Cerro de Pasco, Oroya and Huancayo have for centuries been one of the principal sources of the world's supply of copper and silver. The Central Railroad of Peru, crossing the continental divide between Lima and Oroya at 16,500 feet, was regarded as one of the wonders of the world when it was opened in 1893 and remains today the highest standard-gauge railway line ever constructed.

The main range of the Andes is narrower in this region than

at any other point between the Caribbean and southern Chile, scarcely 150 miles separating Lima, on the Pacific, from the jungle tributaries of the Amazon to the east of the divide. Farther south, however, the highlands spread again, and the vast central *puna* is contained between two widely separated sub-ranges.

The western sub-range, known as the Cordillera Occidental, sweeps almost due south, becoming more and more desolate as it merges into the Atacama Desert of northern Chile. Here begins the second of the great Andean volcanic belts, but, with few exceptions, the towering, massive cones have long been extinct. Dominating the region is the huge, truncated mass of Coropuna, 21,700 feet high, which rises in lonely grandeur from as bleak and savage a country as exists anywhere in the world. Coropuna was first climbed in 1911 by a small party led by Hiram Bingham, then a professor at Yale University and later United States Senator from Connecticut. As in the case of many South American peaks, the ascent required little skill in the technical mountaineering sense, but it appears to have been as punishing and exhausting a grind as mountaineers have ever undertaken.

Other great extinct volcanoes of south-eastern Peru include Ampato, more than 21,000 feet high, which, so far as is known, has not yet been climbed, and El Misti, the presiding deity of the city of Arequipa. El Misti was first ascended as long ago as 1878, and for many years there was an observatory on its summit ridge, maintained by astronomers from Harvard University. Although 20,000 feet in altitude, the snow-line is so high that the summit can be reached on the back of a mule—provided, of course, that the mule is in the mood. In the black, ashy crater of another volcano near Arequipa archæologists have unearthed ruined temples dating back to prehistoric times.

Of considerably more interest to the mountaineer is the Cordillera Oriental of southern Peru, rising out of the rugged country around Cuzco and the famous ruins of Macchu Pichu. This region was once the heart of the greatest Indian civilization in the New World, and the lower slopes of the mountains abound in terraces and trails and the remnants of watch-towers, centuries old. Higher up, however, is an almost untouched world of rock and snow. The exquisite Salanctay (20,500 feet) was climbed by Bingham and his companions in 1914 but scores of other peaks remain unclimbed and, to date, unchallenged.

South-east of Cuzco, on the frontier of Peru and Bolivia, lies Lake Titicaca, which, at 12,500 feet, is the highest large body of water in the world. Beyond it, extending for hundreds of miles to the east, south and west, is the vast Bolivian plateau, or *altiplano*—the core of the Andes. Here, between the latitudes of 15° and 20° south, the range attains its greatest breadth, spreading in far-flung chains of peaks across an area of more than 75,000 square miles. The plateau itself, the site of almost all Bolivia's larger cities and of its important tin and copper mining industries, is one of the highest inhabited districts on earth. And from its enclosing rim of ranges rise some of the noblest peaks of the continent.

Some of these have long been familiar to mountaineers—particularly the great snow-mountains of the Cordillera Real, which hem in the *altiplano* on the north-east. The famous Illimani, towering above the capital city of La Paz, was attempted as early as 1877 and, after several other unsuccessful ventures, fell at last in 1898 to the noted English explorer and climber, Sir William Martin Conway. Its 21,200-foot south peak—the true summit—has since been reached on several other occasions, but the slightly lower north peak was not gained until 1928 and the central peak is believed to be still unclimbed. In the same range as Illimani, though considerably to the north, is the gigantic massif of Sorata, culminating in the twin peaks of Ancohuma and Illampu. No two authorities have yet been found who agree on which of these mountains is the higher, but both are in the neighbourhood of 21,500 feet. Ancohuma was climbed in 1915 and Illampu in 1919. During the past twenty-five years there has been considerable mountaineering activity in this region, particularly by German climbers, and today only two or three of the important peaks remain unascended.

On the far side of the *altiplano*, some 250 miles to the southwest, rises the other great chain of the Bolivian Andes. Known as the Cordillera Occidental (there is at least one Cordillera Occidental in every country between Mexico and Cape Horn), it is as grim and forlorn a mountain region as exists on earth. Its gigantic brown flanks tilt upward from treeless, streamless wastes; its desolate summits hang transfixed in a parched sky. Highest in the hordes of great peaks is the snow-clad Sahama, which, at 22,350 feet, is the loftiest mountain in Bolivia. After several unsuccessful attempts Sahama was at last climbed in 1939 by Joseph Prem, a German engineer, and Piero Ghiglione, an Italian, in a gruelling siege involving great hardships and few mountaineering pleasures. There has been comparatively little climbing in other sections of the range.

Equally bleak and forbidding is the country to the southwest. Here the main range of the Bolivian Andes swings over toward the Pacific, merging into the coastal volcanic zone of southern Peru and continuing due south across the wastes of the Atacama Desert. This region of northern Chile, some 800 miles in length, is rivalled only by the Sahara as the driest place on earth. In many localities not one drop of rain falls from one year's end to the next; the scorched, lifeless *puno* is carpeted only with gravel and broken rock; and the peaks, rising in lonely, isolated masses, are merely monstrous heaps of slag and debris, volcanic in origin, but long since extinct. Because of the almost total lack of precipitation, even the highest of these—and there are estimated to be several over 20,000 feet—bear scarcely any snow on their summits.

Unlike the highland regions further north, this great desert area is almost uninhabited—particularly since the decline of the Chilean nitrate industry. Even explorers and climbers have largely avoided it, and vast sections remain today unmapped and unexplored. Only a very few of the principal peaks have been ascended; most are completely unknown in a mountaineering sense, and a great many have not even been named. It is a safe assumption that their desolate summits will be among the last in the world to be climbed. Even mountaineers, with all their reputation for wooing hardship and discomfort, draw the line somewhere.

The Atacama Desert stretches roughly from latitude 18° to latitude 28° south. Beyond it is the beginning of the temperate zone, and the Andes enter a region of more frequent rain and snowfall. The terrain, however, is still savagely barren, and the high peaks, rising along the Argentine-Chilean border, are simply huge pyramids of weathered debris. The unrivalled monarch of this realm is Mercedario, a mountain-mass of enormous extent, which is estimated to be about 22,300 feet high and disputes with Bolivia's Sahama the distinction of being the second ranking summit of the Andes. The first attempt to ascend it occurred in 1933 and fell some 2,000 feet short of the summit. It remains today unclimbed, as do virtually all the lesser peaks of the region.

Fifty miles south of Mercedario, on the high frontier between Chile and the Argentine, stands Aconcagua, the tallest mountain in the western world. In appearance it is a peak worthy of its pre-eminence. Rising from a massive base, its 22,900-foot snow-crest towers a full mile higher than any of its surrounding summits and can be seen from the Pacific, 100 miles away, as a looming white-topped sentinel, gigantic and alone. The great Chilean cities of Santiago and Valparaiso lie almost literally in its shadow, and the famous transcontinental trade-route between Santiago and Buenos Aires crosses the Andes only a few miles to the south. As a result it is not only the greatest, but one of the most familiar and impressive landmarks of the continent.

Aconcagua is of volcanic origin, but is not itself a volcano. Like virtually all the great Andean peaks, it is enormous in extent as well as in height, building itself up in interminable slopes of broken rock and debris and, on its upper reaches, ice and snow. The reports of all the various parties who have battled their way to its summit are unanimous in declaring that, from the point of view of climbing, it is one of the most unattractive mountains imaginable. In the alpine sense there are few, if any difficulties. There is little call for climbing skill

[*Underwood & Underwood.*

HARD ROCK—THIN AIR—A ROPE

CAPSTONE OF THE WESTERN WORLD [*Ewing Galloway.*

The vast mass of Aconcagua, towering above the desolate valleys of the Chili-Argentine frontier.

or generalship. Yet its altitude is so great, its cold so bitter, its storms so frequent and savage, that the ascent ranks among the most gruelling ordeals known to climbers. "An intolerably monotonous slag-pile"; "the dump-heap of South America"—these are merely two of the more printable epithets hurled at it by its battered and exhausted challengers. Indeed, another name for America's highest summit might well be "The Mountaineer's Nightmare."

The first attempt on Aconcagua was made in 1883. The leader of the venture was Paul Güssfeldt, the well-known German alpinist, and the effort was a truly remarkable one, the climbers reaching a point only 1,300 feet below the summit before they were turned back by storms. In the succeeding years a few other attempts were made, but it was not until the winter (or, in the southern hemisphere, the summer) of 1896–97 that the goal was at last attained.

The victorious party was predominantly English. At its head was Edward A. FitzGerald, whose exploits in the Alps and faraway New Zealand had made him one of the best-known mountaineers of his day. With him was a younger, though experienced, British climber, Stuart Vines, a small group of naturalists and a corps of Swiss and Italian helpers headed by the renowned Alpine guide, Mattias Zurbriggen.[1] They formed a strong, and well-equipped group, and it was well that they were. For Aconcagua was to prove one of the most relentless and stubborn antagonists against which mountaineers have ever pitted their strength and will.

Not the least of their problems was finding the mountain in the first place. Although Aconcagua, as seen from the Pacific, stands out bold and unmistakable, its base is almost lost among a vast jumble of lesser peaks, and the FitzGerald party, approaching it from the south and east, spent long weeks

[1] In the first days of high-mountain climbing practically all expeditions—even those to the farthest corners of the earth—took along one or more professional helpers. Whymper, as we have seen, was accompanied by Carrel on his ascents in Ecuador, and Conway's climbs in Bolivia and elsewhere were made in the company of Swiss guides. So too were most of the early ascents in the Caucasus and Himalayas. In later days, however, the tendency has been to dispense with this kind of professional assistance. On most recent expeditions the climbers have acted as their own guides, drawing on the native population for porters and helpers.

searching out a route to its lower slopes. The month was December—the beginning of the southern summer, the sun burned down relentlessly from a rainless sky, and the hot wind, blowing down the desolate valleys, almost overwhelmed them in stinging, choking dust. Luckily, patience, doggedness and endurance were qualities these mountaineer-explorers possessed in full measure. Trying first one way, then another, they came at last into a deep, rock-choked ravine, known as the Horcones Valley, which seemed to twist up toward the very heart of the mountain. Then day followed day, while they laboriously ascended it. There was no shade, no moisture, no vegetation. Men and mules slid and slipped and floundered across interminable slopes of shale and rotting stone. In the parched, petrified world about them only one thing lived and moved—the giant Andean condors wheeling and swooping ominously through the sky.

Finally, a few days before Christmas, the terrible valley was behind them, and they came out at the snout of the Horcones Glacier, near the western base of the great mountain itself. Here, at a height of 14,000 feet, they pitched their advance base-camp. And here their real ordeal was to begin. Above them loomed the 9,000 feet of slanting, crumbling wilderness that formed the mighty cone of Aconcagua.

Elsewhere in this history there are frequent references to "attacks" and "assaults" on mountains, to "rock scrambles" and "summit dashes." None of these spectacular activities, however, have even the remotest applicability to the experiences of FitzGerald and his men on the highest of the Andes. Day by day, hour by hour, yard by yard, they put one foot in front of the other—and, if they were lucky, a little higher; and day by day, hour by hour, yard by yard, the winds grew fiercer and colder, the valleys below receded into more shadowy darkness, and the great plain of the Pacific Ocean swung slowly upward above the horizon. The first ascent of Aconcagua can be described only as a siege. Its conquerors did not so much climb it or surmount it as they wore it down, and in the process they were forever desperately close to being worn down—and out—themselves.

Even at the advance base several of the party began suffering from exhaustion and mountain sickness, and soon only a handful of men were left with enough strength to go on. These included FitzGerald himself, Stuart Vines, Zurbriggen and a sturdy Italian porter-guide called Nicola Lanti. Launching their first great effort, they crept painfully up the decomposed, rotting slopes above the glacier. Their progress was not unlike that of Sisyphus on his hill in Hades, except that that unhappy man's burden had been a huge, rolling stone while theirs were their heavy, swaying packs. Each foot of altitude was won only at the price of parched throats and gasping, burning lungs. For every three upward steps they slipped back two, as the splintering, maddening debris of the mountainside gave way beneath their feet. And the wind, which lower down had been scorchingly hot, now lashed at them with an icy fury that bent them double and chilled them to the bone. Still they kept grinding on. The second day brought them to a broad saddle high up on the western shoulder of the mountain, the third a scant 500 feet higher on the summit ridge.

Here, at about 19,000 feet, FitzGerald, Vines and Lanti reached the end of their endurance. A freezing, sleepless night coughing and choking left them too weak even to eat, and presented them with the grim, unarguable fact—they were unable to go on. Not so the iron-bodied Zurbriggen. Setting out alone, he scouted upward across the wind-lashed slopes and after long hours of climbing reached a point only 1,300 feet below the summit. Here he made an exciting discovery—a man-made pile of stones amid the lifeless desolation. Beneath the stones was a tin box and in the box the card of Paul Güssfeldt, who had made the first attempt on Aconcagua fourteen years before. The cairn marked the highest point that he had reached.

It was Zurbriggen's highest point too—at least for the present. Now close to exhaustion himself, he stumbled down to join his companions, and the next day all hands descended to the Horcones Valley to regain their strength and lay in fresh supplies. So ended their first attempt.

The second carried them no farther. Days of renewed effort brought them again to their high camp at 19,000 feet, and on New Year's Day of 1897 all four went still higher, stumbling up the interminable stretches of broken rock and loose gravel. The westernmost of Aconcagua's twin summits was now clearly visible above them, but long hours of climbing seemed to bring it no nearer. Meanwhile the unrelenting wind grew even colder and fiercer than it had been before, battering them almost to their knees, while at the same time bearing so little oxygen that it was almost impossible for them to breathe. All of them began to suffer from racking headaches, and their throats were bone-dry knots of pain. Finally, to complete their catalogue of woes, Zurbriggen's feet became so badly frozen that he could no longer climb. Turning back at last, it was all the others could do to get him safely down to the high camp.

Once more they descended to the valley to rest and replenish their stores. The fortunes of the expedition were now at their lowest ebb: Aconcagua had twice repulsed them and, in addition, all the high climbers were in poor condition from the effects of altitude and their desperate exertions. Zurbriggen especially seemed to be in a bad way, suffering not only from his frostbitten feet but from a painful shoulder injury sustained in a mishap with a mule. Nevertheless all were resolved on at least one more struggle with their savage antagonist. For the third time they began the long upward push, and on the night of January 12th, FitzGerald, Vines, Zurbriggen and Lanti again found themselves huddled in their 19,000-foot tent, while the winds of space howled through the darkness outside.

That night they were lucky—the temperature dropped to a mere zero. And emerging into the light of early morning they witnessed a spectacle that was ample compensation for all the hardships and miseries they had suffered. The sun was rising. To the north and south, peaks and valleys alike were sparkling in the golden light of full day. But the slanting rays had not yet cleared the summit of Aconcagua, and straight out before them, to the west, the shadow of the great peak was projected over thousands of square miles of land and sea. It fell across the valleys far below, across the western foothills and the coastal plain beyond, finally out across the wastes of the Pacific itself, where the pointed outline of the very summit lay dark and clear on the horizon, almost 200 miles away. Then, as the men watched spellbound, the gigantic image began to move and change. With the rising of the sun behind the peak, the shadow dwindled. Its distant apex rushed toward them across the sprawling distances of sea and land, shortening and shrinking until it was a mere patch of darkness on the mountainside below. Finally it disappeared altogether at their very feet. The sun appeared at last above Aconcagua's summit, and the shadow-mountain was gone.

The real mountain, on the other hand, was still very much there—grim, enormous, implacable—and, with the magic spectacle of sunrise ended, the climbers bent again to their killing toil. To 20,000 feet they went, to 20,500, to 21,000, while the sun disappeared behind grey mists and the savage gales lashed down again across the unprotected slopes of rotting stones. Then FitzGerald broke down. His parched throat was threatening to close and strangle him; his leaden feet would no longer obey his will. Barely clinging to consciousness, he stumbled and staggered down to the camp, with Vines and Lanti doing their feeble best to assist him.

Meanwhile Zurbriggen again went on alone. Detouring and zigzagging to avoid the worst of the loose rock and debris, he fought his way patiently upward, passed his previous highest point at Güssfeldt's cairn, and came at last to a ridge from which he could view the whole summit of the mountain. But what he now saw filled him with dismay. The peak toward which they had striven so long, and which loomed now a scant few hundred feet above him, was not the summit at all. Beyond it, to the east, a jagged saddle of rock swung down, then rose again to a still higher peak beyond—the true pinnacle of Aconcagua. Struggling doggedly toward it, Zurbriggen made the saddle, but his strength would carry him no farther. Defeated, he began the descent, reaching camp after nightfall in a condition little better than FitzGerald's.

Another day, another try. This fourth time, however, all the climbers were soon overcome by dizziness and nausea, and a halt had to be called at 21,000 feet. Men of less heart would surely have descended all the way to the base camp, grateful to be quit at last of that terrible mountain; but these indomitable four simply dug into their high camp for still another freezing, choking night. They had provisions left for one more day—and one more effort.

On the grey morning of January 14th they rested for an hour after breakfast, hoping that this would help their powers of resistance to the dread mountain sickness. Then, once again, they started up—through the crumbling shale; through the numbing cold; through the wind. Apparently the rest had been beneficial, for they made better progress than ever before and by noon, after five hours of climbing, were within a mere 1,000 feet of the eastern, or true, summit. Here they rested again, contrived to build a tiny smudge fire and ate a little food.—It was a disastrous mistake. No sooner had FitzGerald eaten than he was taken violently ill, and all his efforts of body and will could not get him back his strength. Again and again he strove to get to his feet and go on, only to fall back to his knees, gasping and retching. He was done in. With Vines and Lanti once more supporting him, he stumbled blindly, miserably, down the mountain.

But all was not over yet, and that bitter, sunless day was still to end far differently from the others. For the third time, Zurbriggen turned his face to the heights alone, and this time he made mountaineering history. Hour after hour, foot by foot, he went higher, his mind and senses growing numb, his feet thrusting forward like a relentless machine.—Then, suddenly, miraculously, there was no place higher to go. All of the two Americas were beneath him.

Swiss guides are seldom talkative men, and Mattias Zurbriggen was no exception: he has left little record of his thoughts and emotions as he stood at last, the first of all living beings, on the summit of Aconcagua. Joy and exultation must certainly have been his. And a great weariness too. But one cannot escape the conviction that what he must have felt most profoundly of all was utter, terrible loneliness. For, indeed, he was alone as few men have ever been, before or since—alone, half a world away from his native Swiss valleys; alone, with 80,000 square miles of land and ocean spread out beneath him; alone with the rock and the sky and the wind.—What passed in Zurbriggen's mind and heart is, however, merely conjecture. What we know is that he came down from the summit in the fading evening light, leaving there his shining ice-axe, bearing with him a shining victory.

Aconcagua had been won; but the first great Aconcagua adventure was not yet over. FitzGerald, Vines and Lanti still had their hearts set on reaching the top and during the weeks that followed launched two more prodigious efforts above their highest camp. On the first attempt they were overwhelmed by a blizzard, barely escaping with their lives. But on the second, Vines and Lanti plugged on irresistibly and late one February afternoon found themselves beside Zurbriggen's axe on the highest summit of the Andes. Poor FitzGerald alone was denied the ultimate satisfaction of personal victory. The originator and leader of the expedition, whose judgment and courage had been the mainstay of them all throughout the long, heartbreaking siege, he deserved the prize perhaps more than any of them. But on the final try, as on all the others, he collapsed from nausea and exhaustion and could not go on. Turning back for the last time, he descended the mountain—"with feelings," he records, "that I had perhaps better not try to describe." So ended one of the genuinely great campaigns of mountaineering history.

In the years since 1897 Aconcagua had been re-ascended some dozen times. Men of many different nationalities have participated in the ventures, making the highest of the Andes one of the most truly "international" peaks in the world.[1] A mountain climbed is never so formidable as the same mountain unclimbed, and none of these subsequent ascents has had the epic qualities of the first. But let no one assume that the Giant of the South has become an "easy" climb. As against the handful of successful attempts during the past forty years,

---

[1] In 1934 Aconcagua was the scene of something new in mountaineering records. A party of Italian climbers reached the summit accompanied by two dogs, who thereby set a new—and probably—canine altitude mark.

there have been some half a hundred that failed, and not a few luckless climbers have met death from exposure or exhaustion on those interminable, merciless slopes. Aconcagua is still the highest mountain of the western world. It still consists of almost 23,000 feet of slag and snow and ice and cold and wind.—And he who would get to the top must still be—the Chileans have a name for it—*mucho hombre*.

Aconcagua is usually thought of as lying in the far southern Andes, but beyond it the great range sweeps southward for another 1,500 miles. Along this enormous stretch there is, of course, great variety both of climate and terrain. In general, however, the weather is less dry and the mountains less lofty than in the regions farther north.

The hinterland of Santiago de Chile, bordering the transcontinental railway line, is, in a sporting and recreational sense, the most highly developed section in all the Andes. Lodges, inns and resort hotels abound, and both climbing and ski-ing are practised on a scale comparable to that in the Alps or the American North-west. Mountaineers among the large German population of Santiago and Valparaiso have banded together to form a Chilean section of the *Deutsch-Österreichischer Alpenverein*, which has been extremely active throughout this district in recent years. As a result, almost all the important summits have already been ascended many times.

Farther south, the range resumes its usual aspect of uninhabited desolation. Here rises the massive, glacier-clad peak of Tupungato (21,500 feet), first climbed by Vines and Zurbriggen in 1897, a few months after their ascent of Aconcagua. Beyond it begins the third great volcanic zone of the Andes, which extends for more than 500 miles into Patagonia. The major peaks range between 12,000 and 18,000 feet in height and include some of the most active fire-mountains in the world. A surprising amount of climbing has been done in this wilderness region in recent years—almost all of it by Germans resident in Chile or the Argentine.

Suddenly, at about 40° south latitude, the whole range undergoes a sharp, startling change, as it enters the moist climate of the South Chilean Lake District. Described on the travel-folders as "the Switzerland of South America," this region boasts more truly Alpine scenery and climbing conditions than are to be found anywhere else in the Andes. The peaks thrust up sharply in bold relief. Glaciers are numerous and superb. And, most remarkable of all, the surrounding slopes and valleys are carpeted with rolling forests and rich, green meadows. Given ample moisture and a climate neither burningly hot nor arcticly cold, even the barren, brown Andes know how to bloom.

The Lake District, like the section near Santiago, farther north, has in recent years become the site of many flourishing, cosmopolitan resorts. In winter the mountainsides around Valdivia, Osorno and Bariloche swarm with skiers, in summer with climbers of many nations. As an unfortunate result, the region has lately been the scene of much competitive, "do-or-die" mountaineering of the sort that has so marred recent seasons in the Alps. One peak in particular, the spectacular, 11,000-foot El Tronador, enjoyed a decade of notoriety as a sort of Andean Eigerwand or Grandes Jorasses, with numerous parties of Germans and Italians vying to see which could kill themselves off first on its bristling, ice-sheathed precipices. Tronador was finally conquered in the middle thirties, but many fine unscaled summits remain in the outlying areas of the district. In addition, there are scores of peaks which, though no longer virgin, will amply reward anyone to whom mountaineering is something more than a peacetime variation of a blitzkrieg.

The zone of the Chilean lakes is the last outpost of the inhabited Andes. Beyond it lie almost a thousand miles of mountain wilderness, extending through Patagonia to the southernmost tip of the continent. This is a stretch of country as wild and savage as any left in the world today—a region of deep fiords and impenetrable black forests, ceaseless rain and storming winds. Of the hundreds of peaks, few are of great height, but all are remotely inaccessible and girdled with great glaciers and snowfields. Most of them have not yet even been mapped or named, much less climbed.

The Straits of Magellan cut their interoceanic way through ruggedly mountainous terrain. Leaping them, the Andes rise again, to march still farther southward along the jagged western coastline of Tierra del Fuego. Here looms the last great peak of the continent, Mount Sarmiento—not high, compared with the giants farther north, but ranking among the most spectacular mountains in the world in its icy and forlorn grandeur. Almost alone among the southernmost Andes, Sarmiento has been attempted by climbers on several occasions, the first try having been made by Sir William Martin Conway as early as 1890. But its precipitous, storm-lashed slopes have thus far repulsed every challenge, and its 7,000-foot summit remains unconquered.

There is an end to all things—even, though one may sometimes be inclined to doubt it, to the Andes. Some 150 miles south of Sarmiento—and some 5,000 south of the Sierra Nevada de Santa Marta of northern Colombia—the jagged spurs and ridges of Tierra del Fuego fall away to sea-level. Beyond lie only a strip of strait and the bleakly soaring headlands of Cape Horn. Then the longest mountain range on earth disappears at last into the bottom of the Antarctic Ocean.

VII

ICE ON THE EQUATOR

THE MOUNTAINS OF AFRICA

"Darkest africa" is no more. The second largest continent, which for thousands of years was an unknown and unexplored mystery to the western world, has been opened up.

With the exception of tiny Liberia every square mile of its huge area is today owned or controlled by some European nation. It has been penetrated by railroads, girdled by airways, mapped, mined, dammed, cultivated. Schoolboys on the other side of the world know about the Sahara and the Congo, Pygmies and Hottentots, big game and diamonds, Cairo, Capetown and Timbuktu.

But if the dark continent as a whole is dark no longer, there are still sections of it that are imperfectly known and seldom visited, and of which the outside world hears little. To how many of us are the names Kilimanjaro, Kenya, Ruwenzori familiar? These are the three great mountains of Africa—giants among the peaks of the world—and yet they are almost as unknown to us today as when the whole continent was a place of mystery and darkness. To be sure, all three of them have been climbed—as have many of the lesser African peaks—but the expeditions to them have been few and far between, and for the most part they have been left to their remote, inaccessible solitude. There are not many directions in which one may go in Africa today and find himself a pioneer; but there are a few. And one of them is *up*.

There is nothing comparable to the Rockies or the Andes in Africa. Its great peaks do not form one vast, continuous chain, but are widely separated and unconnected, and each mountain region differs greatly from the others in surroundings, structure and climate.

In the extreme north-west of the continent, in Morocco and Algeria, is the extensive uplift known as the Atlas Mountains. Beginning only a few miles from the Straits of Gibraltar and the Mediterranean Sea, the Atlas are more closely connected with Europe, both geologically and historically, than with any of the other ranges of Africa. They came into being millions of years ago in the same great earth-movements that created the Alps, and almost from the beginning of recorded history they have been known to the traders and sailors of southern Europe. Indeed, it was from Greek mythology that they received their name; the ancient navigators of the Mediterranean, marvelling at the great snowpeaks in the desert to the south, associated them with Atlas, the Titan who supported the heavens on his shoulders, and named them for him.

Close as they are to western Europe, the Atlas are seldom visited. The six groups of mountains which form the range rise out of wild, inhospitable country, and for centuries their foothills have been the home of fierce nomadic tribes. In addition, the surrounding plains and valleys—outposts of the Sahara—are among the hottest and driest regions in the world. In recent years, however, most of the high peaks of the Atlas have been climbed, and several English and French expeditions have carefully surveyed the terrain. The loftiest group of the range is the High Atlas, farthest inland from the Mediterranean. The highest single peak is Djebel Toukhal, 13,653 feet above the sea, which is snow-capped for most of the year in spite of the simmering, waterless furnace that spreads around it.

Beyond the Atlas the great deserts of Africa spread endlessly away, and for thousands of miles only sand dunes and low ridges break the parched monotony of the land. To the southeast, almost the entire breadth of the continent intervenes before the earth again buckles upward into the wild, little-known ranges of Ethiopia. To the south, along the west coast, there are five thousand miles, almost to the Cape of Good Hope, without a mountain worthy of the name. The Sahara, the Congo forests and the great grasslands of Central Africa present one of the longest continuous flat stretches to be found anywhere in the world.

South Africa, however, is essentially a mountainous country. Cape Town itself lies in the shadow of the famous Table Mountain, and impressive ranges extend northward from it, along both the Atlantic and Indian Oceans. For many years South Africa has been the most Europeanized region of the continent, and, in addition, a large proportion of its population is English. It is therefore not surprising that there has been considerable mountaineering activity here—more, probably, than in the rest of Africa combined. Cape Town and various of the other important cities have big and well-equipped climbing clubs, and a year seldom goes by that one or more expeditions do not set out into the neighbouring mountains.

Largest and most interesting of these is the Drakensberg range, which extends several hundred miles from south-west to north-east through Natal, the Orange Free State and the Transvaal. The Drakensberge—so named by the Boers—consist of several chains of rugged, rocky peaks, notched by deep valleys and gorges. Most of the principal summits are between ten and eleven thousand feet in height, and the culminating point, the Mont-aux-Sources, rises 11,250 feet above the sea. There is no permanent snow or ice anywhere in the range, and very little at any time; but the far-ranging mountaineer may find literally thousands of rock climbs, of every degree of difficulty. Some sections, notably that surrounding Mont-aux-Sources, have been opened up by the installation of roads and lodgings and are frequently visited. Others, however, are still isolated by miles of wild country, and there are many peaks which have not yet been scaled or even attempted.

The Atlas, the ranges of Ethiopia and the Drakensberge are the most important of the lesser uplifts of Africa. There remain the big three—Kilimanjaro, Kenya and Ruwenzori. These great snow-giants of the tropics rise within a few hundred miles of each other in the section of the continent known as British East Africa. They are, however, not part of one range, but rise as distinct and separate masses, each with its own individual topography, climate and history.

Kilimanjaro, soaring to an altitude of 19,717 feet, is the highest of the three and the loftiest point in Africa. It was also the first of the three to be discovered and climbed. Situated less than two hundred miles inland from the Indian Ocean, its existence was known to white traders and missionaries as early as 1848, and before long adventurous men were pushing in from the coastal villages toward the great white wedge that hung in the sky to the west. The exploration of East Africa was accomplished about equally by England and Germany, and during the 'sixties and 'seventies of the last century expeditions representing both of these nations approached close to the mountain and investigated its approaches and lower slopes. Its topmost summit, known as Kibo, was reached in 1889 by Hans Meyer, a distinguished German scientist and mountaineer, who had devoted many years of study to the mountain and made no less than four visits to it.

Kilimanjaro is one of the most impressive peaks in the world. An extinct volcano, it rises in a magnificent sudden sweep from the flat surrounding wilderness, rivalled only by its own subpeak, Mawenzi, some seven miles to the east. Its base rests in tropical grasslands—the famous big-game country of East Africa, swarming with giraffe, wildebeests, gazelles, hyenas, zebras, ostriches and a hundred varieties of monkeys. Higher up is a belt of dense forest and higher still the thinning, hardier vegetation of a colder climate. At 14,000 feet the lowest reaches of the great glaciers are encountered, and the summit of the mountain rears into the clouds in a vast expanse of gleaming snow. From base to top, in a distance of a few thousand feet, Kilimanjaro presents a panorama of climate and vegetation that would ordinarily embrace thousands of miles—a vertical progression, in effect, from equator to pole.

The mountain has been repeatedly visited by geologists and botanists during the past fifty years, but few expeditions have ascended to the summit crater. Like most volcanoes, it offers no special climbing difficulties, other than those of distance and altitude, and after its various routes had been established and charted it lost much of its attraction for mountaineers. Mawenzi, however, first conquered in 1912, has been climbed on several occasions. It is a jagged rock-peak with tremendous walls and precipices and offers far more challenge to climbers than its larger, more spectacular neighbour.

Mount Kenya, the second highest mountain of Africa (17,040 feet), is situated in Kenya Colony of British East Africa, about two hundred miles due north of Kilimanjaro. It was discovered in 1849, a scant year after its greater rival, and, like it, its approaches were first opened up by missionaries and traders. Attempts to scale it were made in 1887 and 1893, but it was not until 1899 that its summit yielded to an attack by a party of mixed nationalities under the leadership of an Englishman, Sir Halford Mackinder. This expedition not only encountered great climbing difficulties, but was constantly harassed by the savage native tribes of the region. It is probably the only major mountaineering party in history that has had literally to fight its way to its mountain.

Like Kilimanjaro, Kenya is of volcanic origin, but, unlike it, it bristles with crags and precipices. It too has twin peaks—Bation, the highest point, and Nelion—but they are only forty yards apart and the drop between them is a mere two hundred feet. All the routes to the summit, leading over both rock and ice, are extremely difficult, and, although several parties during the early 1900's tried to follow in the footsteps of Mackinder, the second successful ascent was not accomplished until 1929—a full thirty years later.

The third of the three great mountains of Africa was also the third to be conquered. But in every other respect its story and that of its ascent stands first in the annals of African mountaineering. For the whole history of climbing and exploration have few stories more fascinating than that of the discovery and ascent of Ruwenzori, or The Mountains of the Moon.

The Mountain of the Moon! A name to conjure with, to set beside Atlantis and Camelot and the Garden of Eden in the geography of a lost, legendary world. And, indeed, a legend was exactly what they were for upward of two thousand years.

For, although their name has been known to the geographers of Europe since the fifth century B.C., no white man actually laid eyes on them until 1888.

The river Nile was the great waterway of the ancient world, and its lower reaches had since the beginning of history been a crowded highway of men and goods. But its origins were shrouded in darkness—the darkness of the vast, unknown continent of which Egypt was the outpost. All that men knew were the rumours that filtered through to them from far-ranging traders and wandering Arab tribes, and on these, and these alone, they built their theories and fancies. The dramatist Aeschylus wrote of "Egypt nurtured by the snow." Aristotle spoke of the Nile flowing from "a silver mountain," and Herodotus of its rising between "sharp-pointed peaks" in farthest Africa. Ptolemy, the great geographer of the second century A.D., declared that the great river flowed from "The Mountains of the Moon."

This, substantially, was all the ancient world knew. In the Dark Ages that followed even that much was forgotten, and for 1,700 years The Mountains of the Moon were remembered, if at all, only as creations of legend and imagination. Then at last, toward the middle of the nineteenth century, the interior of Africa began to be opened up, and after many centuries the age-old mountains of fiction became suddenly mountains of fact.

The credit for their discovery—or rediscovery—belongs to the explorer, Henry Stanley. Even he was a long time finding them. Time and again during his extensive explorations of Central Africa he passed close to their snow-capped peaks, but although he had heard many reports of their existence months and years went by without his catching so much as a glimpse of them.

The reason for this was that these legendary mountains of antiquity are almost completely hidden by nature from the eyes of men. In contrast to the surrounding lowlands, which have four climatic seasons, two wet and two dry, the uplands of the range have only one—and that is wet. Indeed, the region is now known to be one of the wettest spots in the world, and it has been estimated that rain falls on as many as 350 days a year. Even on the rare occasions when it is not raining the warm air rising from the forests and plains below condenses in heavy mist about the snowpeaks. Once or twice during a year perhaps—and then for only a few hours—the mountains shake loose their cloudy blanket and stand forth, clear and dominant, against the tropical sky. At all other times they are, literally, invisible.

Stanley first visited the interior of Africa in 1871, but it was not until 1888 that he became, so far as is known, the first white man ever to gaze upon The Mountains of the Moon. One day in that year, travelling along the shores of Lake Albert, in eastern Uganda, his eye was caught by what at first he thought to be a fantastically striking cloud formation in the sky to the south-east. "I saw a peculiar-shaped cloud of a most beautiful silver colour," he wrote later, "which assumed the proportions and appearance of a vast mountain covered with snow." Even then he could not quite credit the evidence of his own eyes. The air below the startling white apparition appeared black and menacing, and he believed he was witnessing merely the weird displays of a distant tropical storm. It was not until he had stared into the south-east for hours that he realized he was actually looking at a vast, solid range of mountains.

Stanley gave The Mountains of the Moon a new and appropriate name: Ruwenzori—"The Rain-Maker." Upon his return to civilization he made his discovery known to the world, and the fight for exploration and conquest began.

It was to be a fight lasting many years and involving great struggles, hardships and disappointments. The first actually to penetrate into the unknown terrain was one of Stanley's own men, Lieutenant Stairs, who in 1889 ascended Ruwenzori's mist-hung slopes to a height of over 10,000 feet. During the next decade and a half scattered individuals and expeditions followed in his footsteps—explorers, scientists, missionaries, mountaineers—in the last group several of the most distinguished European climbers. They came, if they were lucky they saw, and they turned back empty-handed. Without exception they bogged down in the steaming wilderness of rain and fog, many of them without even being vouchsafed a single glimpse of the peaks they had journeyed so many thousands of miles to challenge. The Mountains of the Moon were reluctant to give up the remoteness and secrecy which had shrouded them for two thousand years. The problem became not so much to climb them as to reach, or even to find them.

Among those to try their luck was—as might be expected —the indefatigable Douglas Freshfield. In 1905 Freshfield was a man of sixty, but still an active climber-explorer, and early that year we find him setting out for Ruwenzori with his friend and climbing colleague, A. L. Mumm. The two Englishmen penetrated more deeply into the range than had any of their predecessors, reaching as far as the snouts of the great glaciers; but in the end they too were turned away from the heights by the remorseless weather. In 1906 the same fate befell A. F. R. Wollaston and a group of scientists from the British Museum, who were almost literally washed off the range by torrential downpours. Climbers began to despair of ever conquering this will-o'-the-wisp among mountains.— When, suddenly, in the very same year, it was conquered.

Prince Luigi Amadeo of Savoy, Duke of the Abruzzi, was a member of the royal house of Italy and an admiral of the fleet. He was also one of the foremost explorers and mountaineers of his day. In 1897 he had accomplished the first ascent of Mount St. Elias, second highest mountain of Alaska, and two years later had led an arctic expedition that got to within 200 miles of the then undiscovered North Pole. Now, in April of 1906 he set sail from Naples to find, explore and climb the last great unconquered mountain of Africa. In all three objectives he was completely successful.

The Duke's expedition was organized on the grand scale. In addition to a group of mountaineers and sportsmen he took with him a small army of scientists and technicians, writers, photographers, physicians, Alpine guides and porters. Among them were two men who, by virtue of the Ruwenzori exploit and the Duke's later expedition to the Himalayas, were to win enduring fame in their own right: Filippo de Filippi, one of the foremost modern writers on mountains and mountaineering, and Vittorio Sella, who to this day remains the unsurpassed master of mountain photography. There were also many other men distinguished in various fields. What gave the expedition its unique character, however, was not so much the individual talents of its members as the fact that it was organized in a manner new to mountaineering. Theretofore the typical climbing party had been simply a group of friends, with or without professional guides, casually bound together in a common purpose. The Abruzzi venture, on the other hand, was a planned integrated organism, in which every member had his specialized functions and responsibilities. As such, it was to accomplish far more than the conquest of an individual peak: It was to set the style for virtually all ambitious mountaineering expeditions of the future.

The Duke and his men, like the other adventurers before them, pushed in toward Ruwenzori from the east coast of Africa. From Mombassa they travelled by rail to Nairobi and thence to Port Florence on Lake Victoria, passing in turn through the dense coastal jungles, The Taru Desert, home of the death-bearing tsetse fly, and the great grasslands of the Athi Plateau, swarming with lion, giraffe, zebra, antelope and buffalo. The journey across Lake Victoria to Entebbe was made by steamer, and for a day and a night they were out of sight of land on this huge inland sea that ranks second only to Lake Superior among the world's bodies of fresh water. From Entebbe they marched along jungle trails a distance of almost two hundred miles to Fort Portal in Uganda, the last outpost of civilization in the wilderness surrounding Ruwenzori.

During this stage of the journey the expedition became an army in fact. The black tribes of Uganda were at that time among the most savage in Africa, and the British colonial government, concerned for the safety of its royal visitor, supplied him with a troop of native soldiers as escort. These, in addition to the original party and the multitude of porters, guides and camp-followers who had been picked up en route, swelled the total number of men in the expedition to more than four hundred. By day they wound slowly across country in a single file five miles in length; at night they built stockaded encampments that were larger by far than any town or village for hundreds of miles around. The whole journey, indeed, was practically a circus parade in reverse—with the lions, elephants and naked savages of Uganda as pop-eyed spectators and the representatives of western civilization as performers.

Beyond Fort Portal the real work of the expedition began. The mountains which they sought, now less than fifty miles away, were, as usual shrouded in their weaving veil of mist, and only once in their entire journey did they catch a glimpse of shining snowpeaks high in the sky to the south-west. Undaunted, however, they pushed on, following the Mobuku River, which flows down through the labyrinth of Ruwenzori to Lake Albert Edward. This was the route that had been followed by the earlier expeditions, and Freshfield and Mumm had reported the existence of great peaks and glaciers near the head of the Mobuku Valley. As the Duke and his men advanced slowly they could see nothing of what lay ahead, but the gradually rising ground told them that they were at last approaching their goal.

The region into which these climber-explorers now penetrated was one of unimaginable weirdness and savagery—a nightmare-world of jungle, mist and rain. The gorges of the Mobuku were a tangled, choked wilderness of dead and rotting vegetation, through which they had to hack their way, foot by foot. Men and pack-animals floundered to their knees in muck and mould, and through the high foliage of the treetops the rain beat down upon them incessantly. As they gained altitude the temperature fell, but the new coolness was, if anything, more oppressive than the full, glaring heat of the tropical sun. The sweating dampness of the forests pressed in upon them like a physical weight. No wisp of air stirred. It was as if they were moving along the bottom of a stagnant lake—a watery, choking world without light or sound or motion.

Day after day, however, the Duke and his men struggled on, and at last they came to the apex of the valley, at an altitude of about 9,000 feet. Here they laboriously cleared away a few hundred feet of jungle and pitched their base camp on the mire and broken rock. The Europeans in the party were close to exhaustion. The native porters shivered in the unaccustomed cold and huddled in their tents, chanting to keep away the hostile demons of the mountain. They refused to use the warm clothing and blankets which the white men had brought for them, preferring to huddle about the campfires where they could feel the warmth of the flames on their bare skin.

These days and nights at the base camp were the low point of the expedition. The rain never stopped; the mist never lifted; and beyond the radius of the little mud clearing lay an impenetrable veil of ghostly grey. Only two things saved them from defeat then and there. The first was the patience and determination of the Duke. The second was the thoroughness of his organization, that had resulted in there being enough food and supplies on hand to last through even several weeks of delay. A less well-equipped expedition, if it had not been flooded off the mountain, would have been starved off. The Duke and his men were prepared not only to labour, but to wait.

And at last their waiting was rewarded. Days came when there were short intervals between downpours. The mists thinned for an hour or two in the twenty-four, and above them they could see vague, towering battlements of rock and ice. With shouts of relief and joy the men sprang into action. In a few short marches they fought their way through the remaining miles of tangled vegetation and emerged on the upper slopes of the mountain.

Here they came into a world no less strange and fantastic than the jungle below. Between the uppermost trees and the glaciers spread a vast expanse of flowers. They were not, however, the usual tiny flowers of high mountain pastures, but huge dazzling blooms that put to shame the richness of the tropical foliage below. Close under the icefields were vivid banks of colour, countless varieties of plants and shrubs magnified to many times their natural size by the equatorial rains: violets, geraniums and ranunculi, lobelias and senecios twice the height of a man and so densely packed that the guides had to slash their way through them with axes.

Some of the party remained behind to explore and catalogue this marvellous alpine garden. The Duke and his strongest climbers pushed on, ascending a great glacier to its source near the summit of a jagged ridge. From here they were at last able to see the whole vast sweep of the Ruwenzori range—a lifeless, soundless snow-world in the tropical sky on which no men had ever looked before. Directly ahead of them, to the west, was a towering white mass of peaks that glittered through the mist, and they knew at once that these were the pinnacles which they sought.

The conquest of these topmost summits was accomplished by the Duke and three Swiss guides. Packing their tents and provisions on their backs, they worked their way slowly up glaciers and across snowfields to the slopes of the loftiest peak. This, upon closer inspection, proved to consist of two sub-peaks, connected by a long snow-ridge. The climbers established their last camp in the snow some two thousand feet below, spent an almost sleepless night anxiously watching the weather, and began their assault at dawn.

The lesser of the twin peaks seemed to offer the more practicable approach and they climbed it first, encountering no great difficulties on the way. As they reached it, however, great banks of cloud rolled in upon them, and for an hour and a half they were marooned on their lofty perch, straining their eyes for even a glimpse of the higher summit, only a few hundred yards beyond. At last they detected a white glint of snow through the greyness and set out toward it along the icy knife-edge of the connecting ridge.

Step by step they walked a tight rope through the clouds. All they could see was a few yards of the ridge before them; on either side the mountain fell away in sheer precipices, and the gulfs below were wrapped in impenetrable murk. Finally, however, the sharp rising of the ridge told them they had reached the walls of the higher summit. It became necessary to hack footholds in the glazed snow. Only one man moved at a time, the others meanwhile attempting to find a secure stance and paying out the rope that extended between them.

The last fifty feet of the mountain called for climbing skill of the first order. A smooth ice-gully cut vertically to the summit, with no hold of any kind within reach. One man stood at the base of the gully while another climbed to his shoulders, swung his axe into the ice above and pulled himself up by it. From a position on a narrow shelf he was then able to lend a hand to the other three. The process was repeated again—and once more. Then, suddenly, the Duke realized that there was no longer any ice-wall rising above them, but only a billowing wilderness of clouds. He and his companions had reached the topmost summit of The Mountains of the Moon.

They had won out. They had accomplished with complete success what they had set out to do and stood at last atop the legendary mountains of Africa. But the mountains had conquered too. Instead of a vast and majestic panorama spread out beneath them, all they could see were the tiny white knob of snow on which they stood and their own muffled figures outlined in the mist. Nature had permitted another of her great strongholds to yield to the courage and skill of man, but not to his eyes. The Duke had come and he had conquered. But in the moment of his triumph he was lucky if he could see his hand in front of his face.

As has been indicated earlier, the Abruzzi party was an expedition in the best sense of the word. Not content with merely climbing their mountain and rushing down to tell the world about it, they spent weeks in the mysterious tropical arctic which they had discovered. They climbed a half-dozen secondary peaks, made maps, took photographs, collected geological and botanical specimens. The result was that, upon their return to civilization, the world was supplied with as great a body of new information as has ever been brought back from a journey of exploration. Not the least interesting fact was that the ancient geographers had been right—or almost right. The Nile *does* rise in The Mountains of the Moon. Their snow and rains, draining down to the east, pour into the waters of the great lakes, Victoria, Albert and Albert Edward, which are in turn the sources of the famous river of Egypt.

The Duke named the 16,793-feet summit of the range Mount Stanley, in honour of the great explorer. To its two snowpeaks he gave the names of the then reigning queens of Italy and England, Margherita and Alexandra. In the light of recent world events his reasons for so calling them are interesting and sadly ironic. "I have named them thus," he said, "in order that under the auspices of these two royal ladies, the memory of the two nations may be handed down to posterity—of Italy, whose name was the first to resound on these snows in a shout of victory, and of England, which in its marvellous colonial expansion carries civilization to the slopes of these remote mountains." He could scarcely have dreamed that thirty-four years later there would be virtually no other connecting link between these two great nations than his own precarious snow-ridge in the clouds.

Ruwenzori, like the other great African mountains, has been infrequently climbed since its first ascent. Two or three English expeditions have followed in the footsteps of Abruzzi, and in recent years most of the lesser peaks of the range have been ascended and explored. With the gradual opening up of Central Africa, they have become far more accessible—if no less invisible—than formerly, and today there is even a Mountains of the Moon Hotel at what was once the isolated frontier post of Fort Portal.

For the most part, however, the peaks themselves have been left to their solitude of rain and mist. The Duke's successful venture not only brought to a close the period of first ascents in Africa and cleared up an age-old mystery. It also showed the world how great mountains should be attacked. Instructed and encouraged by his example, mountaineers began turning their eyes toward Asia—and the greatest mountains in the world.

VIII

HIGHEST YET

MOUNTAINEERING IN THE HIMALAYAS

"Surely the gods live here. This is no place for men!" So spoke Rudyard Kipling's Kim as he stood on the plains of northern India and raised his eyes to the Himalayas. In the years since, men of many generations and many lands have stood where Kim stood, staring, and all of them, like him, have felt the surge of awe and wonder in their hearts.

For the Himalayas are without rival among the mountain ranges of the earth. Their stupendous white rampart, curved like a bow along the frontier of India and Tibet, is composed of hundreds of peaks higher than the highest summits of Europe, Africa and the Americas; its topmost pinnacles—Everest, K2, Kanchenjunga—soar more than a mile farther into the sky than any other mountains, anywhere. Mount Washington piles upon Aconcagua, Fujiyama upon Ruwenzori, the Matterhorn upon a second Matterhorn would barely match the altitude of these giants of Central Asia. When one considers that most of the passes and glaciers of the range lie at elevations between 15,000 and 20,000 feet above the sea, it becomes literally true that where other mountains leave off is where the Himalayas begin.

The name Himalaya is derived from two Sanskrit words—*hima* and *alaya*—and means The Abode of Snow. Since the beginning of recorded history the range has played a dominating part in the lives of millions of Asiatics. Both the Hindu and Buddhist religions have wrapped it in legend and peopled it with gods and demons, and for centuries the remote Himalayan sources of the great rivers of India—the Ganges, Indus and Brahmaputra—have been the supremely holy places of pilgrimages to men of the Eastern faiths. In a more worldly sense, too, the Himalayas may be said to be almost the determining factor in the whole pattern of civilization in south-eastern Asia. Their crags and snows, peaks and glaciers, have formed an almost impenetrable historic barrier between the Mongolians and Tibetans of the north and the Hindus of the south. The dry, desolate plateau of Tibet and the teeming valley of the Ganges, lying only a few hundred miles apart on either side of the range, are in every other respect as remote from each other as if separated by continents and oceans. Not only the climate, but the history and present civilization of both China and India would be vastly different without the great white wall of mountains that stands between them.

The main range of the Himalayas is some fifteen hundred miles long and between one hundred and one hundred and fifty miles wide. Unlike most of the major mountain chains of the world it runs from east to west; unlike them, too, it is not an isolated and independent uplift, complete in itself, but part of a greater uplift of gigantic proportions. The continent of Asia, roughly speaking, is built on two levels. The lower is composed of a vast margin of almost unbroken lowlands, sweeping through Siberia, on the north, China, on the east, India, on the south, and Turkestan, on the west; the upper consists of the high central plateaux of Mongolia and Tibet. Highlands and lowlands are, for the most part, separated from each other by huge mountain ranges: the Kunlun, the Nan Shan, the Tien Shan, the Altai, the Hindu Kush, the Pamirs, and—greatest of all—the Himalayas. The plains of India, from which the southern slopes of the Himalayas rise, are scarcely five hundred feet above sea level. The plateau of Tibet, a scant two hundred miles to the north, has a mean elevation of 16,000 feet—the veritable "roof of the world." The range may be likened to a prodigious wall supporting that roof and its highest peaks to steeples rimming its southern edge.

One reason why the Himalayas are the highest mountains on earth is that they are the youngest. It was not until comparatively recent geologic times that a great buckling of the earth's crust forced them upward out of the prehistoric ocean that once covered what is now southern Asia, and the slow process of erosion has not yet had time to wear them down. As a result, they are not only the loftiest of mountains, but the most fearsomely jagged and precipitous as well. Peak crowds upon peak in a wild, crumpled confusion of rock and ice. Glaciers snake downward from them into valleys so deep and narrow that they lie in perpetual shadow. And, still lower, the headwaters of great rivers have cut abysmal gorges through the very backbone of the range—their beds a mere four or five thousand feet above the sea, while the snowpeaks on either side tower a full four vertical miles above them into the clouds. The day will come, to be sure, when the patient, endless work of wind and snow and running water will reduce the Himalayas to gently rolling hills; but its coming can be reckoned in millions and tens of millions of years.

The highest peaks of the range are distributed fairly evenly along its 1,500-mile sweep. In the extreme east the Himalaya proper are considered as beginning at the bend of the Brahmaputra—the point where the great river cuts down from Tibet into the plains of India. From here the crest-line runs due west, crossing the semi-independent Indian state of Bhutan in a wilderness of peaks between 20,000 and 25,000 feet in height, of which even today virtually nothing is known. In Sikkim, however, and further west, along the border between Tibet and Nepal, are found the greatest and most famous of all Himalayan giants, among them Everest, Kanchenjunga and Makalu, respectively the first, third and fourth highest mountains in the world. In interior Nepal the chain culminates in Dhaulagiri, probably the sixth-ranking summit, and some three hundred miles further west is the magnificent Garhwal group, topped by Nanda Devi and Kamet. This is the region sacred to Hindus through countless centuries as the source of the River Ganges.

Beyond Garhwal the Himalayas bend gradually to the north-west and sweep across the fabled province of Kashmir. Here, near the northernmost outposts of British India, rise

Nanga Parbat and the colossal sub-range of the Karakorams, whose culminating point, known both as Mount Godwin Austen and K2, is topped only by Everest among all mountains. Actually, the Karakoram uplift rises on the far side of the River Indus, which, like the Brahmaputra on the east, flows down from Tibet into India and is considered to mark the farthermost extremity of the Himalayas. Nevertheless, the Karakorams are usually designated as a sub-division of the greater range and are, next to the Everest-Kanchenjunga uplift, the greatest mountains of the entire Himalayan system.

Northward and westward from the gorges of the Indus, two other great chains of peaks spread out through Russian Turkestan and Afghanistan, but these ranges, known respectively as the Pamirs and the Hindu Kush, are not regarded as parts of the Himalayas.

For centuries the mountain wilderness between India and Tibet was a blank space on the map. Its only inhabitants were scattered herdsmen and small colonies of Buddhist lamas who dwelt in lonely monasteries beneath the sacred snows. Its only visitors from the outside world were occasional caravans, threading up the deep jungle valleys of the south and across the high, wild passes beyond. The great peaks were wrapped in the silence and desolation of the ages, unvisited and unknown.

Then in the early years of the last century, the English conquerors of India began the systematic exploration and surveying of the vast domain which they had acquired. In the beginning, their investigations were principally concerned with the populous regions of the southern plains; but, as time passed, they began also to turn their attention to the great mountain rampart in the north, and gradually the structure and topography of the Himalayas were discovered and made known to the world. By the 1850's most of the important peaks had been named or numbered and their heights determined trigonometrically with a fair degree of accuracy. In 1852 Mount Everest was discovered and recognized as the highest mountain in the world.

The earliest recorded Himalayan ascents were made in the course of these surveys. As early as 1818 two Englishmen named Lloyd and Gerard reached a height of more than 19,000 feet on Leo Pargyal, near Simla—a record climb at the time—and during the succeeding decades hundreds of virgin peaks fell to the surveyors and mapmakers, chiefly in the more accessible regions abutting on the Ganges valley. In 1851 a party of climbers reached the summit of Shilla, a 23,000-foot peak in the same region as Leo Pargyal. This was a particularly notable achievement on two counts: it established an altitude record that was to endure for many years, and it proved that men could live and work at theretofore undreamed-of heights. During the 1860's much further light was shed on high-altitude conditions by a member of the India Survey named Johnstone, who made a remarkable series of climbs above 20,000 feet and even slept for several nights at a height of almost 22,000.

The first purely mountaineering expedition in the Himalayas occurred in 1883, when a party led by W. W. Graham made numerous ascents in Sikkim. Foremost among Graham's exploits was that on Kabru, a 24,000-foot neighbour of the mighty Kanchenjunga. His account of the ascent, however, was so vague and incomplete that many doubted his claim that he had gained the summit, and the controversy has not been settled to this day. If Graham actually did reach the top he performed a truly notable feat, for no loftier summit than Kabru was climbed until 1930, although several expeditions went higher on greater peaks. It is unfortunate that the story of the first major Himalayan ascent, like that of Mont Blanc, a century before, should be marred by argument and suspicion.

Graham's expedition was an isolated, pioneering venture, but with the coming of the 1890's the full tide of Himalayan exploration and climbing was on. The Alps by this time were an old and familiar playground. The Caucasus, the Andes and the ranges of North America and Africa had been opened up. Mountaineering had come of age, and its practitioners began turning their eyes toward Central Asia and the greatest antagonists that the earth had to offer. The great chain of peaks that formed the dazzling backdrop of India has at one time or another during the past fifty years been the goal of virtually every ranking climber in the world.

One of the first on the scene was Sir William Martin Conway, whom we have already glimpsed in Spitzbergen and among the Andes of South America. Conway, at the head of a large scientific expedition from the Royal Geographical Society of London, made a journey to the Karakorams in the summer of 1892—the first time that any large party of Europeans had penetrated into that ice-locked wilderness of the northernmost Himalayas. The purpose of the party was exploration rather than pure mountaineering, but they included among their exploits the ascent of the 22,500-foot Pioneer Peak—the "highest yet" since the climbing of Shilla, if Graham's claims on Kabru are disregarded.

During the next two decades there was much activity in almost all sections of the range. Douglas Freshfield made a difficult and adventurous circuit of Kanchenjunga, bringing back the first close-up description of that third greatest of Himalayan giants. A thousand miles away, in northern Kashmir, the peerless Mummery pioneered the approaches to Nanga Parbat and lost his life in an attempt to scale its lower walls—the first of many great climbers to find his grave in the snows of Central Asia. The Karakorams and adjoining ranges were explored by Dr. and Mrs. William Hunter Workman, a remarkable American couple who became mountaineers in advanced middle age and made no less than six major Himalayan expeditions between 1899 and 1912. Dr. Workman's highest ascent—23,394 feet on Pyramid Peak—was made when he was fifty-six years old, and Mrs. Workman, at forty-seven, set a world's climbing record for women at 23,000 feet, which stood unchallenged for twenty-eight years.

In 1909 the Karakorams were the scene of another expedition —one of the largest and most elaborate which has ever been organized in the field of mountaineering. It was led by the Duke of the Abruzzi, who, encouraged by his recent success on Ruwenzori, marched up the great glaciers of the range and laid siege to the gigantic pinnacle of K2. Although unsuccessful in their principal objective—they barely penetrated the outer defences of the giant—the Duke and his party added greatly to the knowledge of the region, and, before returning to civilization, accomplished the most noteworthy of Himalayan climbs up to that time. This was an attack on Bride Peak, a magnificent snow-mountain of 25,100 feet, rising across the glacial valleys in the shadow of K2. The very summit escaped them, blizzard and fog descending upon them when it seemed almost within their grasp; but before turning back they reached an altitude of 24,600 feet—the highest any climbers were to go until the second Everest expedition of 1922.

Meanwhile other climbers were forging up into the unknown along the entire 1,500-mile rampart of the range. Dr. A. M. Kellas, a London physician and chemist, made hundreds of ascents in Sikkim and Garhwal over a period of many years. Freshfield continued his far-ranging explorations, and other noted British climbers—A. L. Mumm, J. Norman Collie, C. F. Meade, Dr. Thomas Longstaff, C. G. Bruce, to name only a few—climbed and reconnoitred the peaks and passes of the gradually opening wilderness. Some of the expeditions were on the grand scale, as Conway's and Abruzzi's had been. More were comparatively simple affairs, in the fashion of ordinary Alpine climbing. Dr. Longstaff's ascent of the 23,260-foot Trisul, one of the most famous of early Himalayan climbs, was accomplished with the aid of only two Italian guides and required merely one day of actual climbing on the peak.

By 1914 the principal features of most sections of the Himalayas were at least roughly known to mountaineers. True, not one of the scores of summits over 25,000 feet had been conquered, and giants like Everest, Makalu and Dhaulagiri had not even been approached. But the pioneering had been done, the way to the heights opened. After a five-year interim caused by the First World War mountaineers at last felt themselves ready to set their caps for the highest peaks of all.

Before going on to the stories of the great Himalayan climbs of the past twenty years, it is necessary to have at least a general understanding of the unique problems with which the climbers have been confronted. Like all high mountains, the Himalayas present formidable obstacles of rock and ice, precipice and avalanche, enormously magnified, however, by sheer size. Also, as we have seen, they rise from the heart of a remote and inaccessible wilderness, necessitating not only great physical endurance in those who would even approach them, but elaborate arrangements for supply, transportation and communication. Added to all this there is the difficulty of maintaining health and strength on the heights, where the air contains less than one-third the quantity of oxygen which human lungs are accustomed to breathe.

These obvious problems, however, are by no means the whole story. There is also the ever-present question-mark of weather, and Himalayan weather is probably the most changeable and violent on earth. The climates of India and Tibet are almost as unlike as those of equator and pole, with the result that the lofty peaks between are the everlasting battleground of conflicting winds and storms. Central Asia pours down a relentless, icy gale from the west and north, while from India and the tropical seas beyond come the warm, damp air currents that culminate each summer in the monsoon. The monsoon is perhaps the most treacherous and relentless enemy which Himalayan climbers have to face. Every year from June through August, the months which would otherwise be the best for mountaineering, it drenches the northern Indian plains with great rainstorms and turns the heights beyond into vast deathtraps of fog and melting, crumbling snow. In the southern and eastern Himalayas, which catch the monsoon head on, the climbing season is usually limited to a mere few weeks in the late spring and early fall. All winter the peaks are ringed with icy, blizzard-laden storms, all summer by fresh snowbanks and endlessly roaring avalanches. Even in the supposedly "safe" seasons the mountains are often racked by sudden violent storms, which time and again, as we shall see, have meant to climbers the difference between triumph and disaster.

Another great problem in Himalayan climbing has been

the lack of trained guides and reliable porters. Like primitive people everywhere, the vast majority of Hindus and Tibetans have from time immemorial looked upon their mountains with awe and superstitious fear, peopling them with demons and dragons and refusing even to approach their dread domain. Such early explorers as Conway, Freshfield and Abruzzi were therefore compelled to rely largely on Swiss and Italian guides, whom they brought with them all the way from Europe, and were lucky if they could persuade native helpers to advance even as far as the outlying foothills of the peaks. In recent years, however, tremendous progress has been made. As expedition followed expedition, from 1920 on, the history of climbing in the Alps began to repeat itself in the East, and gradually a new and remarkable type of mountaineer has made his appearance—the native Himalayan guide. The word "guide," to be sure, is used qualifiedly, for the day is far distant when tourists will be able to hire a professional to haul them up 25,000-feet peaks *à la* Matterhorn or Jungfrau; but on the great expeditions of the past twenty years these newly developed oriental climbers have proven themselves invaluable. Pre-eminent among them have been the Sherpas, a hardy breed of hillmen of Tibetan origin who dwell in the country around Darjeeling. Though the number of trained climbers among them is still few, they form an elite among Himalayan coolies, and the accomplishments of almost every recent Himalayan climbing party, from Everest on down, have been in no small measure due to their splendid courage, loyalty and endurance.

As if the problems of climbing, distance, altitude, weather, porters and all the rest were not enough, the would-be conqueror of the world's highest peaks is faced with still another obstacle, prosaic but formidable. This is politics. Both Tibet and the two semi-autonomous Indian States of Nepal and Bhutan, which together contain some two-thirds of the whole Himalayan range, have for years been rigidly closed to white men. Special permission must be secured for climbing parties to cross their frontiers, and this permission has been infrequently and reluctantly granted. As a result, the surroundings of many of the great peaks are still known only on the Indian side, and some, which lie beyond the frontiers, have never even been approached at all. It was the restrictions of the Tibetan and Nepalese governments, rather than any natural obstacles, which kept mountaineers away from Everest until as late as 1921, and it has been a rare Himalayan expedition of any kind that has not sooner or later run afoul of the rigid policy of the closed door.

The climbing of great mountains is—and should be—primarily an adventure. But it is adventure wedded to hard work, patient study and experiment, unwavering devotion to an end. Nowhere is the fact better shown than in the history of Himalayan climbing—more than a hundred years old and, yet, in terms of final accomplishment, scarcely begun. In this and the succeeding chapters are related the stories of assaults on various mountains, separated by many miles and many years. At first glance they may appear to be unrelated stories, each complete in itself; but fundamentally they are merely parts in one continuing and unfinished story—a long, slow accretion of knowledge, skill and achievement. Mountaineers today are relentlessly drawing closer to the world's highest peaks only because earlier mountaineers pioneered the way to those peaks, explored and mapped the routes, struggled against precipice and avalanche, altitude and monsoon, suffered exposure and hunger and all manner of hardship, made endless mistakes and learned from them. The final victories, when they inevitably come, will belong not only to those who physically achieve them, but to the gallant ranks of those who went before them—and dared and fought and failed.

The 1920's were a curious period in the history of Himalayan climbing. These were the years of the first great Everest expeditions, and the attendant worldwide publicity had the effect of bringing mountaineering for the first time into the spotlight of public interest. There was, however, comparatively little other activity. The nations of the world were still licking their wounds of battle. Most of the famous climbers of the older generation had reached an age when they could no longer face the rigours of great heights, and the new generation, growing up in the midst of war, had had scarcely any chance to learn the craft of mountaineering. Except for Everest, the great peaks of Asia were left to their immemorial solitude.

The end of the decade, however, saw a resurgence of activity which continued without break until the beginning of the Second World War. This second heyday of Himalayan climbing differed from the first in many respects. Expeditions, for the most part, were larger and more elaborately and scientifically equipped; there was less exploration of unknown terrain and greater concentration on the attainment of summits; and the summits sought were higher than men had dared hope for before. Also, the field was at last wide open in a national sense: in the early days the Himalayas had been almost the exclusive preserve of English climbers; now for the first time they began to attract men of other nations.

Mountaineers—at least most of them—are only human, and it is natural that most of the Himalayan ventures of recent years have been directed at the highest peaks of all. Kanchenjunga, K2 and Nanga Parbat—these three, together with Everest, have been stormed again and again, and the struggles, failures and disasters of their attackers combine to make what are perhaps the most dramatic chapters in the history of mountaineering. Not all Himalayan climbing, however, has been focused on these unconquered giants. Peaks of slightly lesser altitude have been challenged too, and here the record changes from one of spectacular defeat to one of brilliant and hard-earned success. No man has yet gone higher than the 1924 climbers of Everest. No man has yet trod the summit cone of Kanchenjunga, Nanga Parbat or K2. But year by year new peaks of 24,000 and 25,000 feet have been conquered, and the magic figure of "highest yet" creeps skyward.

The year 1928 saw the accomplishment of one of the first great ascents of latter-day mountaineering. This was the climbing of the 23,300-foot Mount Kaufmann[1] by a German party under the leadership of the well-known scientist-explorer,

---

[1] Mount Kaufmann lies in Russian territory and has recently been renamed Pic Lenin by the Soviet government.

W. Rickmer-Rickmers. In the strict geographical sense Mount Kaufmann does not lie in the Himalayas at all, but in the rugged Pamir system to the north-west; but so little climbing has been done in these outlying Asiatic ranges that the rare expeditions to them may be considered as part and parcel of Himalayan mountaineering. The Rickmers venture was notable both because it threw light on a theretofore almost unknown region of Asia and because it marked the first complete ascent of a 23,000-foot peak since Longstaff's climb on Trisul in 1907.

For almost half a century after 1883 no man knew for a certainty which was the loftiest conquered mountain in the world. If Graham's claims were true, Kabru's 24,000 feet marked the record throughout the entire period; if they were not, a whole series of slightly lower peaks had held the distinction at one time or another. In 1930, however, the ghost of Kabru was at last laid to rest and a new and undisputed "highest yet" established. This was the Jonsong Peak, 24,340 feet high, which rises to the north of Kanchenjunga on the border of Sikkim and Nepal.

The climbers of the Jonsong were the members of the Dyhrenfurth Kanchenjunga expedition of 1930.[1] Defeated in their main objective, they longed for one worthy, if lesser, conquest and selected the impressive snow-dome to the north as the highest nearby mountain offering any chance of success. Their undertaking was blessed with both good management and good luck. Although it was already early June when they began the attempt, the dreaded monsoon held off; the Sherpa porters performed splendidly in establishing the high camps; and the long weeks on Kanchenjunga had resulted in all hands being thoroughly acclimatized to great altitudes. The siege was climaxed by two summit dashes, a few days apart, in which no less than six European and two Sherpa climbers reached the top.

Notable though it was, this ascent bore the proud designation of "highest yet" for only one year. Then, in June of 1931, a small but resolute band of climbers won their way to the top

[1] See page 187 ff.

of Kamet, one of the great mountains of British Garhwal, and a new and loftier peak record was established.

Kamet's 25,447-foot summit was a particularly fine mountaineering prize for two reasons: it was over a thousand feet higher than any that had been previously attained; and it was also the first of the more than seventy Himalayan peaks exceeding 25,000 feet on which man had yet to set foot. The climbing party, all English, was composed of Frank S. Smythe, Eric Shipton, Wing-Commander E. B. Beauman, of the Royal Air Force, Captain E. Birnie, of the British army, R. L. Holdsworth and Dr. C. R. Greene. Of these, both Smythe and Shipton had already won a place for themselves among the foremost post-war mountaineers. The former, indeed, had been one of the leading members of the Dyhrenfurth expedition to Kanchenjunga and Jonsong Peak only the year before.

Accompanied by six Sherpa hillmen and a large company of local porters, the climbers approached Kamet along routes pioneered years earlier by Longstaff, Kellas and Meade. Base camp was made at 15,700 feet on the Raikana Glacier, to the east of the mountain, and a chain of higher camps established on the upper glaciers and the slopes of the peak itself. A large part of the ascent was up precipitous ice-walls, under the constant menace of avalanches from above; but after two weeks of strenuous work the fifth and highest camp was finally established within 2100 feet of the summit. From here Smythe, Shipton, Holdsworth and two Sherpas made the first try for the top. Although blessed with fine weather, they found the going underfoot extremely difficult, consisting alternately of sheer ice-slopes, up which they had to chop their way with axes, and huge drifts of powder snow, in which they floundered to their armpits. Halfway to the goal one of the two Sherpas collapsed and had to turn back to Camp V. The others, however, toiled on, hacking and clawing, needing six gasping breaths for every upward step, and after a nine-hour struggle came out at last on the narrow, tilted snow-ridge of Kamet's crest. Lewa, the remaining Sherpa, who had performed magnificently throughout the expedition, was given the honour of being the first actually to set foot on the summit.

Two days later a second group, consisting of Birnie, Greene and one of the Garhwal porters, also reached the top, and in another three days the entire climbing party was safely off the peak and back in their base camp—a battered and exhausted band of conquerors. Ironically it was Lewa, the bright particular hero of the venture, who was to pay the severest price for his triumph. His feet had been so badly frostbitten on the summit dash that he subsequently lost most of his toes—the revenge, so his fellow-Sherpas believed, of the violated snow-gods of the mountain.

Kamet remained for five years the loftiest conquered peak. During this period, however, several noteworthy lesser ascents were accomplished, both in the Himalaya proper and in various neighbouring ranges. Outstanding among the latter was the ascent, in 1932, of the 24,500-foot Minya Konka, in the little-known Amni Machen range of south-eastern Tibet. The climbing party, consisting of Terris Moore, Arthur Emmons and Richard Burdsall, Americans, and Jack Young, an Americanized Chinese, was the first mountaineering expedition from the United States to visit Central Asia in more than twenty years. The attainment of Minya Konka's summit was a remarkable feat in its own right, particularly in that the ascent was made during October, in raging storms and fearful cold. It served, moreover, to whet the interest of other American mountaineers in the great peaks on the other side of the world, with the result that our own climbers were soon to be as active in the Himalayas as those of any other nation. Indeed, as we shall see, they were presently to play an important part in the greatest successful mountain ascent that has yet been accomplished.

Some fifty miles south-east of Kamet, in the heart of Garhwal, stands a beautiful ice-sheathed peak known variously as The Blessed Goddess, The Goddess Nanda and Nanda Devi. It is the holiest mountain in India and the highest lying entirely within the British Empire. It is also, at the present time, the highest in the world that men have climbed to the top.

Nanda Devi's history is straight out of the pages of romance. Its white twin-peaked summit, piercing 25,660 feet into the sky, has been known to the inhabitants of the north Indian plains since the beginnings of recorded history. Uncounted generations of Hindu pilgrims have journeyed into the neighbouring wilderness to worship at the scource of the sacred Ganges, and since the earliest days of British rule in India explorers and mountaineers have striven toward the mountain, longingly. Yet, before 1934, not one human being had ever even reached its base.

The reason for this is that Nanda Devi stands within a unique natural fortress. Around it rises a great ring of mountain walls, seventy miles in circumference, which shut it off from the outside world like the rugged battlements of a medieval castle. Many of the peaks of this barrier tower to a height of 24,000 feet, and, except at one point, there is no gap or pass between them lower than 18,000. But this is only the mountain's outer defence. Within the enclosure of the outer walls there rises a second rampart, equally formidable, cutting the basin straight across from outer wall to outer wall and dividing it into two lesser basins. It is from the second of these, known to mountaineers as the Sanctuary, that Nanda Devi rises—a remote, inaccessible citadel at the heart of its double-walled castle.

Only one break exists in these monstrous fortifications of rock and ice. This occurs to the west where a raging mountain-stream, called the Rishi Ganga, cataracts down from the glaciers and knifes through both inner and outer walls in a series of terrific gorges, on its way to join the Ganges far below. So wild is this torrent, however, and so deep the canyons that contain it, that for years it formed as impassable a barrier as the neighbouring peaks and ridges. Besides, no devout Hindu would even approach it. For among those gloomy caverns and frightful precipices, so the legend went, dwelt the demons who guarded Nanda Devi, the blessed goddess of the secret snows.

Such a fairy-tale mountain as this could not but hold an irresistible lure for men with adventure in their blood. Graham,

Longstaff, Bruce, Hugh Ruttledge, T. H. Somervell—these were only a few of the many noted Himalayan explorers who over a period of fifty years had set their hearts on Nanda Devi and struggled mightily to find the key to its hidden domain. Some had tried to force a way up the fearsome gorges of the Rishi. Others had stormed the barrier walls, and Longstaff, as early as 1905, had reached a point at 19,000 feet from which he had a glimpse—the first granted to any man—of the Promised Land beyond. But none of them had been able to penetrate even the outer of the two unexplored basin valleys. Behind its double curtain of rock and ice the Goddess Nanda remained as mysterious and unapproachable as she had been since the beginning of time.

Then, finally, in the middle of the last decade, there were launched two expeditions to the mountain which were completely successful in every respect. The first broke through both outer and inner guardian walls and carried to the lower slopes of the great peak itself. The second, following after two years, climbed Nanda Devi to the top.

Of the two, the earlier exploit was in many respects the more remarkable, in that it was accomplished by a party of only two mountaineers. These were Eric Shipton, of Kamet fame, who since that ascent had further distinguished himself on the Everest expedition of 1933; and H. W. Tilman, a young Englishman with a notable record for climbs in the Alps and Africa. Accompanied by three Sherpa porters, they left Ranikhet, in Garhwal, in the late spring of 1934, pushed through the wilderness flanking Nanda Devi's western ramparts, and launched an assault on the gorges of the Rishi Ganga. Day after day they crept along a mile-deep gash in the mountain walls. At times their route lay high on the faces of great cliffs, at others deep down beside the bed of the foaming torrent. False trails were followed and abandoned; precipices grew perpendicular, forcing retreat and detours; food and supplies had to be raised and lowered by ropes. But they kept going, and at last came out into the rolling forestland of the outer basin. Here they set up their base camp, near the junction of the Rishi and another roaring glacial stream.

The outer rampart of Nanda Devi was now behind them and they were already in a virgin world where no human being had ever stood before. Their real difficulties, however, had scarcely begun. Ahead, on the far side of the basin, loomed the vast "inner curtain" that guarded the Sanctuary—a second rock wall thousands of feet high and broken only by the deep, jagged slot of the Rishi canyon. Into this second series of gorges the explorers now threaded their way. For hours their route carried along footwide ledges in the cliff-side, a skyscraper's height above the river. Then, presently, the ledges petered out into the smooth vertical walls, and they were compelled to descend to the shadowy, roaring canyon floor. Time and time again they had to battle their way across the Rishi, struggling not to be swept away in the icy torrent, heaving their soaked baggage back and forth on ropes. Then, to add to their woes, it began to snow, and a knife-edged wind beat down into the canyon from the heights above.

Now at last came the greatest obstacle of all—a gigantic buttress of black rock sweeping straight up from the bottom of the gorge to the towering ridges overhead. At first inspection it seemed impassable, but Shipton and Tilman knew that pass it they must, if they were to cherish any further hope of reaching their goal. They named it Pisgah, for they were confident that if it could be surmounted the way to the Promised Land beyond would at last be open.

The explorers went about their labours systematically. While Tilman and one Sherpa investigated the southern cliffs, Shipton and another reconnoitred the northern, climbing high on its sheer black walls, searching patiently for the tiniest shelves and gullies that would take them higher still. Time after time, possible routes seemed to present themselves, but in every case they proved false hopes, and in the end Shipton turned back, defeated. Descending to their camp by the river he waited disconsolately for Tilman to return from his exploration of the far side; but the hours passed and night came on, and still he did not appear. Shipton began to fear that his companion had met not only with disappointment, as he had, but possibly with an accident as well. Then, suddenly, there was an exultant cry in the darkness. Tilman and his Sherpa appeared, struggling across the swirling current of the Rishi —done in, but with their faces shining with excitement. They were shouting that they had found a way.

And they had. The next day the whole party, with all their baggage in tow, began the laborious ascent of the southern cliffs of Pisgah. Gully led to gully, chimney to chimney, ledge to ledge, as men and loads inched upward between the precipices and bulging overhangs of the canyon walls. Late in the afternoon they passed the crest of the great black buttress, and before night fell the angry roaring of the Rishi, which had dinned in their ears for so many days, was only a whisper in the remote depths below. Camping that night among juniper bushes beside a softly bubbling brook, they could scarcely believe what they knew to be the truth: that they had at last passed the great inner curtain of the basin and were in the very Sanctuary of Nanda Devi itself.

The world in which they now found themselves was lovely and serene beyond the dreams of men. On all sides the encircling mountain walls tiered above them like an enormous amphitheatre, their flanks dark with long slopes of fir and spruce. Lower down, the valley floor was a rolling alpine meadow, carpeted with springy turf and great banks of wild-flowers, the grazing-ground of wild herds of sheep and goats. Here and there the green expanse was studded with tiny lakes of the purest cobalt blue, and from the surrounding heights descended the gleaming white fingers of many glaciers. It was a landscape out of a fairy-tale, a lost, secret Eden from the days when the world was young. And in its very centre, incredibly white and majestic, rose the citadel itself—the turrets and cliffs and battlements of the sacred mountain Nanda.

For three weeks Shipton and Tilman explored this virgin paradise. Together with their Sherpas, they traversed the spreading meadows, worked up to the crests of surrounding ridges and studied the great central peak from all sides. Then they threaded their way up the maze of glaciers to the lower slopes of Nanda Devi itself. Their small expedition was not equipped to launch an actual assault on the heights, but they carefully studied the possibilities of routes and campsites, which might be used by future parties, and came to the conclusion that the mountain was by no means unassailable.

It was now late June, and presently the monsoon broke. (Even the hidden Sanctuary of Nanda Devi is not exempt from the rigours of Himalayan weather.) The explorers therefore beat a hasty retreat down the gorges of the Rishi, barely escaping disaster in its now snow-swollen waters, and spent the next several weeks exploring in the lower altitudes of the Garhwal hills. At the end of the monsoon, however, they again returned to Nanda Devi, to reconnoitre further in the Sanctuary and on the crags and ice-fields above. Finally, they found a gap in the precipitous southern walls of the basin, and, crossing it, descended to the outer valleys and the inhabited world, proving that the Rishi canyon was not the only possible key to the mountain.

Thus the secret of Nanda Devi was solved—on two separate occasions and by two different routes. Throughout the following year the mountain was left to its age-old isolation; but there was small chance of climbers long neglecting this alluring and now accessible prize, and in the summer of 1936 a second resolute band of adventurers set out to climb and conquer.

This expedition, far more elaborate than the first, was composed of eight white men—four Englishmen and four Americans. Shipton, a member of that year's Everest party, was not among them, but Tilman was back, eager for the final thrust at the great peak which had become so specially his own. Outstanding among his companions was N. E. Odell, the noted British geologist and mountaineer, who had won world-wide fame as an "Everester" twelve years before. The two other Englishmen were Professor T. G. Brown and Peter Lloyd; the Americans were Dr. Charles Houston, H. A. Carter and W. F. Loomis, all proven young climbers, who were now making their first visit to the Himalayas, and Arthur Emmons, who had been a member of the Minya Konka party of 1932. In addition, there were six experienced Sherpas and fifty-odd locally recruited coolies for the transport work below snow-line.

The observations of Shipton and Tilman had indicated that the best time to attack the mountain proper would be in the late summer, toward the end of the monsoon period. Accordingly, the end of July saw a long cavalcade of men and supplies moving slowly up the roaring gorges of the Rishi. They had, however, scarcely entered this forbidding domain when a severe blow was dealt their chances of success. Thirty-seven Dotial porters, who had been enlisted in Ranikhet, flatly refused to attempt the crossing of the swollen mountain-torrent, dropped their packs on the spot, and returned home en masse. The climbers and their few remaining helpers were now confronted with the task of carrying sixty-two loads, averaging sixty-five pounds each, over the most difficult part of the route. It seemed at first an impossible assignment, but by dogged, backbreaking work it was finally accomplished. Slowly they crept on—clinging precariously to the canyon walls, crossing and recrossing the river—through the gorges of the outer wall, the outer basin, the inner gorges, and, at last, up and over the frowning black bastions of Pisgah. By the end of the first week in August they were established in their base camp in the Sanctuary, at the very foot of Nanda Devi.

From this point the twelve remaining local porters were sent back home, their job well and faithfully accomplished. The party was now stripped to its essential members—eight white men and six Sherpas—and after a few days of rest in the soft, flowering loveliness of the meadows the real work of mountaineering began.

They were not long in discovering that, although Nanda Devi's valleys might be a paradise, the mountainside above them was something quite else again. Hour after hour, day after day, they struggled across endless slanting wastes of ice and mud and broken, sliding boulders, while a bitter wind slashed down at them from the frozen heights. They entered a belt of grey, impenetrable mist. When finally they passed that, it snowed, and soon they were floundering about in drifts up to their thighs. But they kept grimly going, up and down, up and down, back-packing food and supplies; and gradually the chain of high camps began to take form.

The general line of ascent was along the north ridge of the mountain, a great twisting spine of rock and snow that climbed skyward some 8,000 feet above the base camp. In many places, however, the ridge disappeared into smooth snow-covered slopes of ice, tilted at a fearsome angle and necessitating the kicking and hacking of thousands of steps. During this exhausting part of the siege the condition of all the white men held up remarkably—the result, they believed, of their long weeks of acclimatization during the passage of the Rishi gorge. The bad luck with the porters, however, continued. The most dependable of them all, a remarkable Sherpa named Pasang Kikuli, came down with snow-blindness in the early stages of the ascent. Then in turn, the others succumbed to maladies of various kinds, with the result that only one Sherpa of the six ever got higher on the mountain than Camp II. Severest blow of all was the death of one of them, several weeks later from dysentery—the only casualty to mar an otherwise supremely successful venture.

Faced with the necessity of doing all the load-carrying, the climbers made slow progress. Base camp had been established August fifth at 17,000 feet, and it was not until eleven days later that Camp III was pitched at 21,200, less than halfway to the top. But the work went on with systematic doggedness. First, an advance party—usually two men—would reconnoitre upward from the highest camp already established. Their job was to find a feasible higher campsite, dump their loads there and return to the lower camp, all in one day's climbing. The next day they would rest, while a second party went up, carrying more loads; and on the third day, if all went well, the higher camp would be ready for occupation. Then the whole operation was repeated between the new camp and another still higher.

During the expedition's first two weeks on the mountain the weather had been almost freakish in its consistency—still, humid and, in the hours around midday, actually warm. On the night of August twenty-first, however, the long-expected storm caught up with them. Great black monsoon clouds piled up over the south-eastern horizon, the wind rose in a shrieking crescendo, and mountain and men were soon wrapped in the fierce embrace of a blizzard. For the next forty-eight hours all activity was paralysed. The climbers huddled in the various camps, cut off from communication with each other and barely able to restrain their tents from blowing off the mountainside in the fury of the gale. Camp III, the highest occupied at the time, was struck the worst. Snowdrifts were soon piled so heavily upon the two tents that the men inside had to support the canvas roofs with their hands, and on the morning of the third day it required a half hour's strenuous work to dig their way up to light and air.

By dawn on August twenty-fourth the blizzard had at last blown itself out, and a period of glorious weather set in. Nanda Devi's slopes and ridges were now, however, deeply sheathed with fresh, loose snow, and to the endless task of step-cutting was added the exhausting labour of floundering through deep drifts. Kicking and cutting their way, the climbers established Camp IV at 21,500 feet and Camp V, their highest, at 23,500, scarcely more than 2,000 feet below the summit. Set on a tiny, tilting platform above a mile-high chute of ice, this last was so precarious a perch that even an eagle would have eyed it askance. But mountaineers are a more adventuresome breed than eagles, and these were happy that they had been able to find any campsite at all. Their hearts were beating high with excitement and expectation as they camped that first night in the still, frozen world above the clouds. For their goal seemed at last to be within their grasp.

Odell and Houston were selected as the first pair to make a try for the summit. Deciding on a day of reconnoitring before the actual final push, they worked up the ridge to within 1,000 feet of the top, found no obstacles worse than those encountered below and returned to Camp V, confident of success on the morrow. For poor Houston, however, it was not to be. At supper that night he ate from a tin of corned beef that was later found to have been punctured, and the next morning, far from being ready for the summit dash, he was violently ill from ptomaine poisoning. All thoughts of the top had to be temporarily dismissed, while Odell communicated

[Photo by 1936 Nanda Devi expedition. Courtesy Dr. Charles S. Houston.

HIGHEST YET

Nanda Devi from the west, towering 12,000 feet above the meadows of its "sanctuary". The route of the successful expedition of 1936 lay just beyond the righthand skyline ridge.

THE NAKED MOUNTAIN

Nanga Parbat from the so-called "Fairy-tale Meadow," to the north. All the expeditions that have attempted the mountain have ascended diagonally across this face, from the dark moraine hill at lower centre to the white sub-peak (Rakiot Peak) on the skyline at the left; thence along the ridge toward the summit. The highest point visible in the picture is the North Peak (25,550 feet). The top of Nanga Parbat, more than a thousand feet higher, is hidden behind it.

with their companions below and the miserable Houston was helped down to the lower camps.

A council of war followed, and it was decided that Tilman should take the sick man's place. The following day he and Odell moved Camp V some 500 feet higher than its original location and, on the next, set off at six in the morning for the summit. All the members of the party felt that it was now or never, for storm clouds were again appearing to the south and supplies in the upper camps were beginning to run low.

Moving slowly but steadily, Odell and Tilman crept up the mountainside through the long hours of the morning. The way lay first up steep snow-slopes, similar to those below; then along a gently rising rock ridge, sheathed in snow and ice; finally up deep gullies in the face of the summit pyramid. Here great billowing drifts engulfed them to the waist, but they managed to keep going and finally, at mid-afternoon, stepped from a small rock-rib onto a gentle ridge of snow. As they did so, there was a sudden ominous shuddering beneath them, and the drifts below plunged downward in a hissing avalanche. For a terrible, paralysing moment it seemed that the ridge would go too. But it held.—A careful probing with their ice-axes, a few more steps upward, and they stood together upon the flat white summit of Nanda Devi.

How do men feel when they stand victorious atop the highest mountain ever climbed? . . . When it comes to emotions, mountaineers are a traditionally reticent breed, and the report of Odell and Tilman offers small satisfaction to the romantically minded. They were tired; their limbs ached with cold and fatigue, and their breath came in short, hoarse gasps; the world below spread endlessly to the horizon, so remote and unreal that they were no part of it, nor it of them. Then they stood silently, staring. Shouts of victory would have been meaningless—almost blasphemous—in that overwhelming stillness of mountain and sky. And, indeed, in the deepest sense, there was no victory. They had done what they set out to do—that was all. And they had won the mountaineer's reward.—*They were there.*

Except for the unfortunate fatal illness of the one porter,

the descent of Nanda Devi was accomplished as safely and successfully as the ascent. Two climbers had reached the summit. Six others, who had hoped and striven for it as much as they, had not. But it is the very essence of the mountaineering spirit that victory for one is victory for all, and the band of adventurers who, a few days later, turned their backs at last on the sacred mountain consisted of eight supremely weary but happy men.

The natives of the surrounding valleys, however, were not so easily satisfied.

"Was the Goddess Nanda beautiful?" they asked eagerly. "And what did London look like from the top?"

The ascent of Nanda Devi established no altitude records. As we shall see in the next chapter, men had already gone higher on Everest, Kanchenjunga and Nanga Parbat, and within two years they were to go higher on K2. But it remains today the tallest mountain in the world that has been climbed to the summit.

Apart from the record-setting climbs, however, there have been several recent Himalayan expeditions that are worthy of note. A few, on peaks somewhat lower than Nanda Devi, have been successful in reaching their goals; those on higher peaks have not. Siniolchu, a beautiful 22,570-foot snow spire in the Sikkim Himalayas, and its slightly lower neighbour, Simvu, were climbed in 1936 by Paul Bauer and Karl Wien, of Kanchenjunga fame. The following year Siniolchu was climbed again by a second German party, and another famous eastern Himalayan peak, Chomolhari (23,930 feet), yielded to an English mountaineer, F. Spencer Chapman. Gasherbrum (also known as Hidden Peak), a 26,470-foot giant of the Karakorams, was attempted in 1934 by the second Dyhrenfurth Himalayan expedition and again in 1936 by a French party—the latter probably the largest and most elaborately equipped expedition in Himalayan history. Both assaults, however, fell far short of the summit. In 1938 the near-by Masherbrum (25,660 feet), was climbed to within 1,500 feet of its top by a group of English climbers.

Other important expeditions of the late 'thirties were those of the Englishman Marco Pallis in Sikkim and Tibet and of the Swiss team of Arnold Heim and August Gansser in Garhwal. Indeed, Himalayan climbing and exploration reached their peak of activity in the years immediately preceding the present war. As long as the war lasts, to be sure, there will be no further large-scale mountaineering; and Nanda Devi will remain the loftiest summit climbed. But one may be very sure that the time will come when adventurous men will return again to the remote high places of The Abode of Snow—and to new adventures, new conquests, new "highest yets."

IX

"EIGHT-THOUSANDERS"

THE UNCLIMBED HIMALAYAS

FOR EVERY CONQUERED Himalayan peak there are a hundred that are unconquered. And for every Jonsong, Kamet or Nanda Devi, whose ascent has been a bright, successful exploit in the story of mountaineering, there are many mountains still higher which have defied every attempt at ascent or have never been attempted at all. The greatest Himalayas are still the unclimbed Himalayas.

Pre-eminent among them are what the Germans have given the resounding name of *Achttausender*. These are the select aristocracy among mountains—the handful of super-peaks which tower more than eight thousand metres, or roughly 26,200 feet, above the sea. Authorities differ as to exactly how many such giants exist—the count ranged between twelve and twenty-five—and some, in remote districts of the range, remain to this day unnamed and unsurveyed. An outstanding ten, however, are now generally recognized by geographers and known by name and fame to mountaineers the world over. In order of rank, they are: Everest, K2 (Godwin Austen), Kanchenjunga, Makalu, Cho-uyo, Dhaulagiri, Nanga Parbat, Gasherbrum (Hidden Peak), Broad Peak and Gosainthan—the royal family of "Eight-thousanders" and the highest mountains on earth.[1]

---

[1] (1) For years there has been disagreement as to whether K2 or Kanchenjunga is the loftier peak. Currently accepted figures give the former a slight lead.

(2) Until very recently Broad Peak, in the Karakorams, was ranked as the fifth highest mountain. More accurate measurements, made during the past few years, have reduced it to ninth.

(3) Lhotse, the south peak of Everest, is 27,890 feet high, and if counted as a separate summit is fourth in rank. Usually, however, it is considered part of the Everest uplift. For the altitudes of the other "Eight-thousanders" see Appendix II.

Since the beginning of Himalayan exploration, a century ago, each of these ten giants has had a history of its own. Makalu and Cho-uyo, in the shadow of Everest, and Broad Peak, in the remote Karakorams, have on various occasions been studied from their surrounding glaciers, but none of them has ever been attempted by climbers. Gasherbrum, also in the Karakorams, has been challenged twice—by the Dyhrenfurths in 1934 and the French expedition of 1936. Dhaulagiri, in the heart of forbidden Nepal, and Gosainthan, on the Tibetan-Nepalese frontier, have remained the most inviolate of all, no white man, so far as is known, having ever approached within fifty miles of their bases. Everest, on the other hand, has for twenty years been the most sought-after mountaineering prize in the world, while the remaining three —K2, Kanchenjunga and Nanga Parbat—have likewise been subjected to assault after assault.

But not one of the ten greatest mountains has yet felt the tread of boots upon its summit snows.

The mountaineering adventures described in the preceding chapters of this book have been, by and large, success stories. Danger and hardship, injury and even death have beset the climbers, but in the end the summits have been won, the goals attained. The stories now to come will unfortunately have no such happy endings. Instead, they will tell of defeat and disappointment, often of heartbreak and tragedy. The fight for the "Eight-thousanders" presents to date only a record of unrelieved failure.

—But what magnificent failure!

Kanchenjunga is the showpiece of the Himalayas. Everest hides its splendours from the eyes of men behind range after range of lesser peaks. K2 and Nanga Parbat, Nanda Devi and Kamet reveal themselves only to explorers and mountaineers who have toiled through miles of wilderness to reach them. But the third highest mountain stands out proud and bold for all the world to see.

Indeed, "Kanchenjunga from Darjeeling" is one of the celebrated sights of India. Perched on a spur of the Himalayan foothills, 250 miles north of Calcutta, the famous hill-station is a natural observatory facing to the north. Immediately beyond the town the ground falls away, and for more than forty miles the eye can range without obstruction over the wild little border-state of Sikkim, a crumpled world of forested ridges and deep tropical canyons. On the far side of this lowlying green bowl rises the main range of the Himalayas. Peaks without number crowd the horizon in an unbroken hundred-mile sweep: India's dazzling northern battlement, five miles high. Seen from Darjeeling through the intervening mists, it appears less a solid mountain wall of rock and snow than a huge white wave transfixed in the sky.

At the very centre of this gigantic panorama is Kanchenjunga itself. Rising on the border between Sikkim and Nepal, it spreads its ramparts for miles into both countries, a mass of many mountains rather than a single, soaring peak. It culminates in five summits, known to the people of the foothills by the lovely name of "The Five Treasures of the Snow." The highest of all, and the true summit of the mountain, is 28,146 feet high. Beside it, the wilderness of surrounding peaks, themselves higher than any mountain in North America, seem to sink into insignificance.

Favoured by such a spectacular stage-setting, it is small wonder that Kanchenjunga has long worked its lure on adventurous men. As early as 1848 the noted botanist and explorer, Sir Joseph Hooker, pushed northward through the jungles and gorges of Sikkim, to explore its southern approaches. Other expeditions followed, mostly for surveying and map-making, and in 1883 came Graham's climbs on Kabru and other nearby peaks—the first purely mountaineering ventures in the district. It was Douglas Freshfield, however, who was the greatest pioneer on Kanchenjunga. Setting out from Darjeeling in the fall of 1899 with the photographer, Vittorio Sella, and a few other companions, he made a complete circuit of the mountain, thus becoming the first white man to look upon it from any but its southern side. The journey required seven weeks and was fraught with difficulties and hardships of the sternest order; but the investigation of terrain and routes was so thoroughly and accurately carried out that "Freshfield's Circuit" remains today a classic model for mountain exploration. As to the possibility of climbers actually ascending Kanchenjunga, Freshfield was less than optimistic. "It is guarded," he reported, "by the Demon of Inaccessibility."

For thirty years most other mountaineers were disposed to take his word for it. Between 1899 and 1929 more climbing was done in Sikkim than in any other region of the Himalayas—notably by the tireless Dr. A. M. Kellas—but the giant among giants was left to its towering solitude. The sole exception occurred in 1905, when a small, poorly equipped party of Swiss climbers launched a short-lived assault on the summit. They reached a height of about 21,000 feet on the south-west face, but there their luck gave out. The mountain hurled an avalanche down upon them, taking four lives.

The second attempt on Kanchenjunga, twenty-four years later, can scarcely be called an attempt at all. A young American climber, E. F. Farmer, of New Rochelle, N.Y., set out from Darjeeling in May of 1929 and, accompanied only by a handful of native porters, began the ascent of the same south-west face. The porters, realizing the hopelessness of the attempt, soon gave up, but Farmer continued on alone. The next morning the others had a glimpse of him—a tiny moving speck on a snow-slope far above. Then the clouds closed in, and he was never seen again.

Kanchenjunga could brush off efforts like these as a man brushes off flies. Only a few months after Farmer's disappearance, however, the mountain was to be subjected to an assault of far different calibre. This was the first of two attempts by the so-called Bavarian Expedition, led by Paul Bauer of Munich and composed of the most brilliant German climbers of the post-war generation. The giant defeated them in the end, as it had the others, but not until after a siege such as had never been waged before on any mountain. Indeed, the English *Alpine Journal*, which rarely indulges in superlatives, subsequently described the 1929 and 1931 Bavarian attempts on Kanchenjunga as "feats without parallel, perhaps, in all the annals of mountaineering."

The expedition of 1929 had to reconnoitre as well as climb. Setting out from Lachen, in Sikkim, in early August—they had selected the post-monsoon period for their attempt—they approached the mountain from the east and after ten days pitched their advance base camp at about 17,000 feet on the Zemu Glacier. This great river of ice was enclosed by the main north and east ridges of Kanchenjunga, but days of exploration failed to disclose any possible route up their mile-high walls. The only chance seemed to be on an eastern spur of the north ridge, a steep saw-edge of gleaming ice that climbed diagonally across the face of the mountain and joined the north ridge about 2,000 feet below the summit. Freshfield, thirty years earlier, had observed and described this spur, but so formidable had it appeared to him that he had not even mentioned it as a possible way to the heights. Yet it was the way the Bavarians selected.

The next six weeks saw climbing such as had never been attempted on any mountain in the world. There were no rocks anywhere, no base straightaway slopes of ice or snow, such as mountaineers ordinarily encounter on every peak. Instead, the spur climbed skyward for thousands of feet in one unending spine of broken, twisted ice. There were towers piled upon towers, cliff upon cliff, huge vertical columns which tapered like churchspires, and shining curtains, festooned with icicles, hanging down the precipices from cornices above. There were great bulges and chasms, wrenched by the wind and cold into fantastic mushroom shapes and grotesque likenesses of monsters from a nightmare. And, as if all this were not enough, the whole broken, tortured expanse was swept incessantly by avalanches. Gigantic blocks and bergs of solid ice, breaking off high above, swept down the chutes and spirals of the spur in two-mile drops of thundering destruction.

Up through this toppled, frozen world the climbers relentlessly forced their way. To do so they were compelled to improvise, as they went, a totally new technique of mountaineering. Time and again they came to towers and cornices which could not be surmounted by ordinary step-cutting. They bored shafts through them or hacked them away entirely. When they found themselves at the end of a day in a place where it was impossible to pitch the tiniest tent, they slept in caves which they dug in the ice. Up the whole terrible spur there was scarcely a stretch of more than a few yards which did not have to be chopped, tunnelled or excavated before the straining porters could struggle up with their loads.

This almost incredible labour went on not merely for days, but for weeks. Thirteen days alone were required to push a track up from Camp VII, at 20,700 feet, to Camp IX, at 21,700—a distance which on an ordinary mountain usually requires between one and three hours. But slowly they gained altitude, and toward the middle of October the day came at last when the worst seemed to be behind them. Camp X was established in an ice-cave at 23,000 feet, and Bauer and two companions, scouting still higher, reported that the expanse above appeared free of serious obstacles. There were only 3,000 feet remaining to the junction of their spur with the main north ridge; 2,000 more to the summit. There was jubilation among the climbers in the highest ice-cave that night, for victory seemed only a few days away

Kanchenjunga, however, had other plans. For a month and a half it had merely toyed with the intruders—harrying them with precipice and avalanche, but allowing them to creep ever higher toward its inviolate heights. Now, rising in wrath, it struck.

During the afternoon of October sixteenth the sky turned a baleful sea-green colour and wild gusts of wind shrieked down from the summit ridge. By nightfall a blizzard was raging. Digging themselves out of their cave the next morning, the climbers at Camp X saw with horror that the whole mountainside was buried under seven feet of fresh, loose snow. All vestiges of the track below were gone, all communication with the lower camps wiped out: they were marooned, 23,000 feet up, on a frozen perch in the sky. Another twenty-four hours they waited, while the blizzard howled on. All thoughts of the summit had been abandoned, but to stay longer where they were meant sure starvation. As for getting down, it was a feat that seemed humanly impossible; yet the attempt had to be made.

Mc

All the hardships and dangers which had beset the Bavarians on their long push up Kanchenjunga were as nothing compared to the wild ordeal of their descent. First they had to batter their way through snowdrifts so deep that the furrow they cut was more than a man's height in depth. Then they came to steeper slopes, which peeled off in avalanches under their feet. At one point disaster was averted only by the miraculously quick action of one climber. A sudden downrush of snow caught the first three men on one of the ropes and hurled them off the side of a ridge. The fourth man, realizing that in a split second he and the others on the rope would follow them, leapt off the ridge in the opposite direction and, by acting as a human counterweight, stopped the fall of his companions.

That night they reached Camp IX and dug their way to the buried cave entrance through seven feet of snow. But the days that followed were even worse than the first. There were more avalanches, more slips and falls, more driving wind and bitter, bone-clenching cold. New stairways had to be cut in the hanging ice-curtains and new tunnels and shafts in the great cornices and towers. One pitch was so appallingly steep that half the packs had to be thrown over the precipice before the porters could move a step. And—most terrible ordeal of all—the whole of the third night had to be spent on the open ridge without shelter of any kind.

By this time several of the men were so severely frostbitten that they could no longer walk. The others, themselves exhausted, took turns carrying them, sometimes on their backs, sometimes on rudely improvised stretchers, and at last they came out upon the Zemu Glacier, at the mountain's base, with every man still alive. Even here, however, Kanchenjunga was not done with them. A second storm now burst down, as violent as the first; snow and rain lashed the lower camps for three successive days; and landslides and mud-avalanches roared across their path. Not until they reached the village of Lachen, twenty miles away, were the battered, crippled climbers finally safe from the fury of the mountain.

So ended the first Bavarian attempt on Kanchenjunga—not merely in defeat, but in rout. It was a rout, however, in which the feats achieved outranked those of any successful climbs theretofore accomplished, and in which there were established new mountaineering standards for skill, for doggedness and endurance, and for plain unalloyed courage. Bauer and his companions had been subjected to an ordeal such as few men have ever undergone, anywhere; but every man among them came down from the mountain to tell the tale. More remarkable still, almost all of them would be ready, two years later, to go back for more.

Before the second Bavarian attempt of 1931, however, another group of men were to try their luck on Kanchenjunga. Professor Gunther Dyhrenfurth, a noted Swiss geologist and mountaineer from the University of Zurich, had long had his eye on the third highest of the world's mountains, and in the spring of 1930 he set out for it from Darjeeling at the head of a formidable expedition. The climbers who accompanied him included experts from half the countries of western Europe, including one Englishman, Frank G. Smythe, who was later to win fame on Kamet and Everest. Also in the party was Dr. Dyhrenfurth's wife, an accomplished sportswoman and the first member of her sex to take part in a major Himalayan venture since the American Mrs. Workman many years before.

Having received the rarely granted permission to enter Nepal, the expedition attacked Kanchenjunga from the northwest. On this side the mountain soars up from its skirt of glaciers in three giant steps—successive tiers of ice-cliffs and sloping, snow-choked terraces, piled one on top of another across the whole expanse of a mile-wide face. Above the highest terrace the main north ridge of the peak slopes gently upward toward the summit cone. This was the ridge up whose eastern spur the Bavarians had struggled the previous year, and the 1930 climbers, also believing that it held the key to the mountain, now attempted to reach it from the opposite side.

They fared even worse than their predecessors. After days of arduous and dangerous work they succeeded in hacking out a track up the lowest of the ice-walls and were ready to establish the first of their upper camps on the terrace above. But before they could occupy it, catastrophe struck. One fine May morning, just as a large party of climbers and porters were starting up the cliff, there was a sudden shattering explosion high above, and an instant later what seemed to be the entire upper half of the mountain came toppling down in ruins. It was an avalanche such as no men have ever witnessed before or since. Millions of tons of ice and snow peeled loose from the underlying rock—whole hanging glaciers and bergs as big as houses—plunging, tumbling, roaring thousands of feet down the mountainside, to land on the glacier below with a crash that seemed to split the earth. Even there, the maelstrom did not stop. Carried by its own momentum, a vast tide of snow and iceblocks went careening over the almost level glacier for a full mile before it came to rest at last scarcely 300 feet from the expedition's lower camp.

If the column of climbers had been directly in the avalanche's path they would have been wiped out in a twinkling. By miraculous good fortune, however, all except one were a little to the side of its main line of descent and, though stunned and battered, escaped with their lives. The unlucky one was Chettan, one of the most famous of all Himalayan porters. The last in the column, he was caught beneath a crumbling ice-wall and crushed like an insect.

The Dyhrenfurth climbers were brave men, but they were not would-be suicides. Saddened by the death of Chettan and realizing it was only by the grace of God that any of them were still living, they turned away from the terraces and ice-cliffs of the murderous north-west face and launched an attempt on the ridge which enclosed it to the west. Their luck, however, was little better there, for, with their diminished strength and resources, they found it impossible to get the needed supplies up the steep, rotten rocks. After a few days they gave up the hopeless struggle and marched off to Jonsong Peak and a comforting consolation prize.

The second act of the Kanchenjunga drama had been played out. The third was soon to follow.

Mid-July of 1931 saw Bauer and his fellow-Bavarians again hacking and tunnelling a track up their terrible north-east spur.

The storms of two years had festooned the mountain with new monsters of snow and ice, and, as in 1929, almost every foot of the ascent was a bitter, arduous struggle. Bauer himself, in his subsequent account of the expedition, gives a vivid picture of one day's ordeal on that savage, frozen mountainside. "On the crest of the spur," he wrote, "towered successive mushroom-shaped pinnacles, one above the other. At least five of these, each twenty to thirty feet high, had to be demolished altogether. . . . Every blow had to be carefully struck, each was a real technique in itself. We were poised like wild animals, crouching beneath the cornices, balancing between earth and sky, sometimes on the party's respective heads, to try to avoid a simultaneous fall when the overhang collapsed."

In the midst of this arduous work tragedy struck—as sudden and devastating as lightning out of a blue sky. A group of climbers and porters, roped together, were ascending a steep snow-gully over the lip of a precipice, some 4,000 feet above the Zemu Glacier. Hermann Schaller, one of the strongest members of the party, was in the lead, clearing and enlarging the steps in the tight-packed snow. One of the porters followed immediately after him, while a third stood at the foot of the gully paying out the rope. Suddenly the first porter slipped and shot down the groove. Schaller was jerked violently from his steps and flew over him through the air in a great curve, while clouds of snow poured down the gully. The rope spun downward, went taut—and broke. An instant later both men disappeared into the abyss below.

The shock of the disaster stunned climbers and porters alike. For a week all thought of the summit was abandoned, and the whole party descended to the base of the mountain, heartsick and discouraged. The bodies of Schaller and the porter were found beneath the cliffs and were buried on a rock-islet rising from the glacier.

"But the continuance of the attack on Kanchenjunga," said Bauer, "was for us a foregone conclusion and duty." Again the climbers bent to the struggle against columns and spires and curtains of ice. Again men and supplies began moving up, and at last, on September tenth, almost two months after they had first come to grips with the mountain, they succeeded in establishing Camp X at an altitude of 23,000 feet. This was about equal to their highest point of 1929, and, as they had observed then, the worst part of the mountain now seemed to be behind them. Above them the north-east spur swept upward in a comparatively unobstructed snow-slope to its junction with the main north ridge.

For a while their luck held. In spite of sudden, lashing storms and sub-zero cold, they contrived to pitch an eleventh camp at about 25,000 feet, and a few days later two of their number, Hans Hartmann and Dr. Karl Wien, pushed up the remaining distance to the very summit of the spur. It was a great moment —one of the greatest, surely, that mountaineers anywhere have been privileged to enjoy. The terrible ice-ridge, up which they had struggled so desperately through two long summers, had been conquered at last. They were standing at 26,220 feet— higher than men had ever gone before, except on Everest. And above them was only the gentle slope of the north ridge, rising less than 2,000 feet more to the topmost of Kanchenjunga's five summits.

But the moment of triumph was also the moment of defeat. Between the crest of their spur and the north ridge proper was a steep slope of some 400 feet, sheathed in ice and powdered on its surface with eighteen inches of loose, freshly fallen snow. In many places the snow had already slid off; in others it was clinging merely by the tiniest friction of its particles. Under a man's weight it would inevitably have peeled off altogether and plunged to the glacier 8,000 feet below. Hartmann and Wien returned to Camp XI with heavy hearts to report that they had encountered an impassable obstacle.

Nevertheless, on the following day, Wien and three other companions went up again for a final desperate try. If only they could get by the slope and dig out a final Camp XII on the ridge above, the summit was theirs. But what they found confirmed their worst fears. The steep pitch of snow and ice was the only possible way to the ridge, and to have ventured on it would have meant annihilation. Fresh snow was falling daily; the great storms of the early Himalayan winter would soon be roaring out of the north, and there was no possibility of improvement in the condition of the slope. With victory so close, it was a bitter, crushing blow, but there was nothing for it: they turned back, again defeated.—And none of the feats of endurance, skill and courage which they had performed in their two long battles with the mountain bears more eloquent testimony to their worth as mountaineers than their judgment and honesty in knowing when they were beaten.

The Bavarians left Kanchenjunga behind them in October of 1931. No one has tried to climb it since. That it will be attempted again—men being the strange, stubborn beings they are—goes without saying. Whether its summit will fall on the first or the tenth or the hundredth try nobody knows. Only one thing is certain: when at last it yields it will be only to the very skilled, the very lucky and the very brave.

A thousand miles north-west of Kanchenjunga, in the wild border-country between Kashmir and Turkestan, stands the most murderous mountain in the world. Its name is Nanga Parbat, and almost as many lives have been lost in the attempts to gain its 26,620-foot summit as on all the other great Himalayan peaks combined.

Although some 2,500 feet lower than Everest and 1,500 less than Kanchenjunga, Nanga Parbat is second to neither of them as an individual mountain-mass. Rising in isolated splendour at the far western end of the main Himalayan chain, it has no neighbour-giants to dispute its supremacy, no lofty plateaus or foothills building gradually up to its base. The great bend of the River Indus, only a few miles away, is a scant 3,000 feet above the sea. From the hot, dry plains through which it flows the northern ramparts of the peak soar upward in an almost unbroken sweep of four and a half miles—the highest single mountain face on earth. A world in itself is this white colossus, a frozen, lonely world above the clouds, without life, without warmth, without mercy. The Kashmir tribes, gazing up at it with awe and fear, gave to it long ago its ominous name: Nanga Parbat—the Naked Mountain.

Nanga Parbat is nothing if not consistent. From the very beginning disaster and tragedy have stalked its would-be conquerors, and the first venture into its forbidding domain resulted in the death of the foremost mountaineer of his time. This was in 1895, when A. F. Mummery, fresh from his triumphs in the Alps and Caucasus, pushed in to the base of the mountain with two English companions and a small group of porters and attempted to find a way up its lower battlements. Meeting with no success on the southern side, the party worked its way around to the north-west. Camp was established close to one of the great glaciers, and a few days later Mummery, accompanied by two of the porters, set off to reconnoitre on the heights above. None of them was ever seen again. Although no clue to their fate has been found, the generally held belief is that they were caught and overwhelmed by an avalanche.

Thirty-seven years passed before men again set foot on Nanga Parbat. Then, in the summer of 1932, came the second challengers, a well-equipped German-American expedition, which included among its members some of the ablest mountaineers of the day. The leader was Willy Merkl, of Munich, and most of his compatriots were also Bavarians—climbers of the same indomitable stamp as Bauer's band on Kanchenjunga. The Americans were Fritz Wiessner, German-born, who ranks today as the foremost mountain climber in the United States; Rand Herron, a young sportsman who had grown up in Europe and made many ascents on mountains all over the world; and Elizabeth Knowlton, of New York, who, although an accomplished climber, served the party principally as camp manager and newspaper correspondent.

This first of the latter-day expeditions to Nanga Parbat was the most successful of all. Perhaps "successful" is scarcely the word. Let us say instead that it paid the least fearful price.

The attack on the mountain, like all the others to follow, was made from the north-east. On this side the main face rose in a series of gigantic ice-sheathed precipices, and a direct frontal assault on the summit was unthinkable. As in the case of Kanchenjunga, however, a long ridge of comparatively gentle gradient—in this case the east ridge—swept down in a great arc from the summit; and the climbers, like the Bavarians on the other mountain, believed that if they could gain it they would hold the key to victory. And gain it they did. Traversing diagonally under the precipices, they worked slowly upward over steep slopes of snow and ice and, some three weeks after leaving their base camp, came out on Nanga Parbat's main east buttress.

They were now at a height of over 23,000 feet, and all but a fraction of the vertical part of the ascent lay behind them. A long, jagged stretch of ridge, however, still separated them from their objective. Pressing toward it, they surmounted Rakiot Peak, one of the minor summits rising from the ridge, and dug out their seventh camp on the icy knife-edge beyond. It was their plan to make this camp a sort of advance base, strongly built and well-stocked with provisions, from which they might set out to pitch the highest bivouacs and make the final dash for the summit. Nanga Parbat's pinnacle seemed near indeed—a mere 3,000 feet above them, a mile and a half away. A matter of three days, at most, if their luck held——

But their luck was over, and in the days that followed nearly every affliction that can plague an expedition descended upon them. One of the German climbers was stricken with appendicitis and was lucky to get off the mountain and back to civilization alive. Another's feet became so badly frostbitten that he could no longer walk. The expected supplies failed to come up from below, and the porters, to a man, fell ill of real and imaginary ailments.[1] Worst of all, the long-dreaded storm blew up in full fury, and for eight days on end snow fell incessantly. Camp VII had to be abandoned, then Camps VI and V; finally the whole expedition found itself back at the foot of the mountain, literally swept off the heights in billows of driving, drifting snow. Two weeks later a second attack was launched, but it bogged down long before even the ridge was gained, and, with their strength and resources exhausted, the climbers were forced to admit defeat.

[1] The 1932 Nanga Parbat expedition used porters from the Hunza tribe of northern Kashmir instead of the usual Darjeeling Sherpas. It was a choice that they had ample cause to regret.

The 1932 party escaped from Nanga Parbat without disaster, but their venture was still to end on an ironically tragic note. Sightseeing in Egypt on the voyage home, Rand Herron slipped while descending the Second Pyramid, fell 300 feet and was instantly killed. It was almost as if the Naked Mountain, regretting its leniency, had belatedly reached across thousands of miles to claim a victim.

Two attempts, four deaths. But the giant of Kashmir had not yet even begun to show its hand. The next two expeditions to Nanga Parbat, in 1934 and 1937, are, as sheer horror stories, unmatched by anything in the history of mountaineering.

Both ventures were by Germans, and on that of 1934 Merkl was again the leader. His companions were all experienced mountaineers: some, like him, veterans of the earlier attempt, others, old hands who had won their spurs on Kanchenjunga and other Himalayan giants. Misfortune was not long in striking, for scarcely had they reached the base of the mountain when one of their number died of pneumonia. The others, however, pushed on, following the general route of the 1932 party, and reached the east ridge, near Rakiot Peak, without untoward difficulty. Camp VII was established on the ridge between Rakiot and the summit and Camp VIII still farther along, at a height of almost 25,000 feet. On July sixth two climbers, Aschenbrenner and Schneider, went on to a point which they estimated to be not more than 800 feet below the summit, and perhaps four hours' climbing away. Returning to Camp VIII, they reported happily that no obstacles intervened. All that remained was one easy day's walk to victory.

Then Nanga Parbat turned on them with malignant wrath.

That very night a violent storm broke over the mountain. For thirty-six hours the men in the highest camp were pinned in their tiny tents, while all the world beyond a ten-foot radius was blotted from sight behind driving walls of snow. A hurricane wind tore at them, snapping the tent-poles and ripping the canvas to shreds. Their portable cookers refused to function. Their meagre supply of cold food dwindled and disappeared.

By the morning of July eighth the storm had shown no sign of abating, and only two alternatives faced them: to attempt to descend or to die where they lay.

Aschenbrenner and Schneider, with three porters, started down first and, exhibiting almost miraculous endurance, covered the entire distance to Camp IV in one day. The others—Merkl, Welzenbach, Wieland and nine porters—were to have no such good fortune. Starting a few hours after the first party, they were able to do little more than creep along through the driving blizzard and monstrous banks of snow. After a few hours one of the porters collapsed from exhaustion and soon after died. The others struggled on, but darkness overtook them halfway between Camps VIII and VII, and they spent the night on the open ridge. In the morning the storm was still raging, and the frozen, enfeebled men were barely able to move. One after another, the porters dropped in their tracks. Toward midday, Wieland sat down in the snow and never got up again. Food and sleeping bags had to be dropped as they staggered on, or were literally blown off their backs by the fury of the wind.

By evening the survivors reached Camp VII, to find it stripped of bags and provisions—scarcely a shelter at all. The following day five of the remaining porters went on, two of them eventually reaching the lower camps and safety, three of them dying of exposure and exhaustion on the way. Merkl, Welzenbach and three men remained in the camp, where, after two days, Welzenbach died. The others lay there for a third day, the fifth since any of them had had a mouthful of food; then they made their last supreme effort to get down. Merkl, however, was so weak that he could go only a little way, and when night fell they dug a hole in the snow and crawled in. When morning came only one of the porters was strong enough to stand. He continued the descent and at last came staggering, less than half alive, into Camp IV. Merkl and the two others crawled on hands and knees as far as their strength would take them; then they lay down in the great drifts and died.

So the 1934 venture ended, in a disaster that shocked the world. Men had at last climbed to within a few hundred feet of

Nanga Parbat's summit. Until that fateful night of July sixth the expedition had promised to be one of the most brilliantly successful in the history of mountaineering. And a week later the record stood: Nanga Parbat still unconquered; eleven brave men dead on its icy flanks.

It almost passes belief that a catastrophe such as this could be followed by another still worse, yet such is the dark history of the Naked Mountain. Terrible though the 1934 disaster was, at least an appreciable number of the climbers escaped with their lives. The expedition of 1937 was literally annihilated.

The leader of this attempt was Dr. Karl Wien, one of the heroes of the 1931 Kanchenjunga epic, and the climbing party was again composed of the pick of German mountaineers. The route of ascent was the same as before: across the great snow-slopes below the north-east face and then on up toward the east ridge. The weather held, the transport arrangements worked smoothly, and within a few weeks the main party found themselves well established in Camp IV, on a fairly level ice-terrace a few hundred feet below Rakiot Peak. The plan was to push on to the ridge at once, but more supplies were needed for the higher camps. Accordingly, Lieutenant Smart, the British liaison officer of the expedition, started down with a group of porters on the morning of June fourteenth, leaving seven of the nine German climbers and nine porters at Camp IV.

He was the last man to see any of them alive.

A few days later Ulrich Luft, one of two Germans who had remained below, went up with a small band of porters to join his companions. Reaching what he knew to be the site of the fourth camp, he was stunned to find the entire terrace buried under an immense avalanche of ice and snow. Not a vestige of human occupancy, or of any living thing, remained.

From the very first there was not the slightest hope that any one of the sixteen men had survived. Luft, Lieutenant Smart and the other surviving German, however, did what they could to find the vanished men, and as soon as news of the tragedy reached civilization a relief party under Paul Bauer flew all the way from Munich to Kashmir to help them. After days of searching and excavating, the remains of the camp were at last discovered, buried ten feet deep in the debris of the avalanche. All the bodies that were found lay in their sleeping bags, showing no sign of struggle or panic. Several diaries were located, all of them complete through June fourteenth. Three watches, crushed with their owners, had all stopped at a few minutes after twelve. From this grim evidence, and that of the mountain itself, it was obvious that the climbers had been overwhelmed as they slept. An enormous hanging glacier had apparently plunged down from Rakiot Peak in the early morning hours of June fifteenth, swept across the terrace in a wild cascade of ruin and blotted the men out before they could so much as budge. Bauer and his companions recovered what equipment and personal belongings they could and dug graves for the victims in the great ice-slopes of the mountainside. Then they turned away with heavy hearts.

The 1934 and 1937 disasters on Nanga Parbat are unparalleled even in so hazardous a field as Himalayan mountaineering; and the question inevitably arises—how and why could such things happen? Partly, to be sure, they happened through the agency of the blind forces of nature, over which men have no control. But no one who has had experience with great mountains and their hazards can escape the conviction that the two unfortunate parties contributed materially to their own destruction. Both expeditions were wholly German; in conformance with the new Nazi philosophy they looked upon their exploits not merely as mountaineering adventures, but as matters of national pride and honour; and, like the young "suicide climbers" on the Eigerwand and Grandes Jorasses, they were prepared to gamble high for victory. It is always easy to point the finger of blame after the event. Yet the fact remains that no English or American climbers would have pushed as high as the 1934 party with such inadequate supplies and lines of communication, or have pitched camp, as did the 1937 party, without a thorough reconnaissance of the slopes above. The Germans were engaged in all-or-nothing assaults. They were after victory, and nothing else mattered. And while feeling sorrow for the brave individuals who lost their lives, one cannot but feel that collectively they met the fate that they deserved.

Blind, mindless force is no more the key to the conquest of a great mountain than to the conquest of the world.

Routed by Nanga Parbat as no climbers had ever been routed on a mountain before, the Germans were still not done with it, and in 1938 we find Bauer himself leading still another expedition up the north-east face to the ridge beyond Rakiot Peak. High on the mountainside, just beneath the ridge, they found the bodies of Willy Merkl and one of his porters, almost perfectly preserved after four years in the ice and snow. Subsequently, the party pushed on to about 23,000 feet, but here they were driven back by a succession of fierce storms. Even in defeat, however, they accomplished what in the light of previous experiences must be considered a remarkable feat: they came down off the mountain with every man still alive.

Again in 1939 a German expedition was in the vicinity of Nanga Parbat. This time, however, the object was not to try for the summit, but to reconnoitre new routes for a subsequent attack in 1940. Needless to say, it was an attack that never came off, and with the world embroiled in war it may well be many years before the next chapter of the Naked Mountain's sombre history is written.

North-east of Nanga Parbat, and separated from it by the hot, low-lying gorges of the Indus valley, looms the colossal Himalayan sub-range of the Karakorams. Spreading across the frontiers of India, Tibet and Chinese Turkestan, in a region uninhabited by men since the beginning of history, this mountain wilderness is perhaps the most desolate and savage in the whole uplift of south-central Asia. Its glaciers are the largest in the world, outside Alaska and the polar ice-caps. Its summits, rising in an inextricable confusion of spires and domes, rock, snow and ice, present a challenge to men that could not possibly be exhausted in a thousand years of mountaineering.

Indeed, the Karakorams contain more peaks of the first magnitude than any area of comparable size on earth. Uncounted hundreds are over 20,000 feet high, and at least thirty exceed 24,000. Scarcely any have been climbed, merely a handful attempted, and only the greatest even named. Among the latter are: the "Eight-thousanders," Gasherbrum (Hidden Peak) and Broad Peak, respectively the eighth and ninth highest known summits in the world; the huge massifs of Masherbrum and the Golden Throne; Bride Peak, Mitre Peak and Queen Mary Peak; the steeple-like pinnacles of the Baltoro Spires; the incredible vertical obelisk of the Mustagh Tower; and greatest of all—a giant among giants and second only to Everest among the world's summits—K2.

For more than three-quarters of a century after its discovery K2, or Mount Godwin Austen,[1] was looked upon as the classic example of an unclimbable peak. Partly, to be sure, this was because of its enormous height of 28,250 feet, and partly because of its almost inaccessible location in the heart of an ice-choked wilderness. But, in addition to these obstacles, the mountain itself seemed to all who gazed at it to be hopelessly unassailable. Everest had its North Col, Kanchenjunga its north-east spur, Nanga Parbat its east ridge; these buttresses, formidable though they were, at least held out a faint possibility of ascent. K2, however, towered 12,000 feet above its glaciers in a sheer, unbroken pyramid of rock and ice. Its ridges appeared little better than cliffs; its gale-scoured faces bristled with precipices and overhangs; along its entire upward sweep the eye could discern no single spot level enough to hold even the tiniest of camps. In the second highest of the earth's elevations nature appeared to have created a masterpiece: a truly invulnerable mountain.

The history of K2, until very recent years, is accordingly one of exploration and investigation rather than of actual mountaineering. Sir William Martin Conway, in 1892, Dr. and Mrs. Workman, between 1899 and 1908, and occasional other expeditions during the late nineteenth and early twentieth century toiled up the vast glaciers and lofty passes into the very heart of the Karakorams; but their climbing was confined to the lesser peaks of the range, and they were content to survey the monarch from the barren stone and ice-fields around

---

[1] Its alternative name was given it in honour of Colonel Godwin Austen, Surveyor-General of India, who, in 1861, was the first European to approach its base.

its base. The only real attempt at ascent, in those early days, was that of the Duke of the Abruzzi in 1909. His elaborate expedition had been organized for the express purpose of besieging K2, and, with the aid of Italian guides and a large corps of native porters, he made two definite assaults on the summit. His first effort carried to 20,000 feet on the southeast ridge, his second some 1,800 feet higher on the north-west. Beyond these levels, however, it proved impossible to pitch camps or carry supplies, and even the indomitable Duke had to admit defeat. Turning away from the mountain, he devoted the rest of the summer to exploration of the surrounding glaciers and his record-setting climb on Bride Peak.

It was twenty-five years before the next major mountaineering expedition to the Karakorams. In 1934, four years after their exploits on Kanchenjunga and Jonsong Peak, Dr. and Mrs. Dyhrenfurth, of Zurich, visited the range at the head of a second large international expedition. The party made many important climbs, among them a first attempt on Gasherbrum and complete ascents of Queen Mary Peak (c. 25,000 feet) and one of the five summits of the Golden Throne. Most notable of all, perhaps, was Mrs. Dyhrenfurth's ascent to the 24,000-foot west summit of Queen Mary Peak—a women's altitude record to this day. Like most of their predecessors, however, the expedition made no attempt on K2 itself. In the middle 1930's, no less than in the 80's and 90's of the previous century, the second highest mountain still proudly flaunted its double designation: "unclimbed and unclimbable."

It does so no longer. True, no man has yet set foot on the topmost pinnacle of the Karakorams, and the day when he does may yet be far distant. But in the summers of 1938 and 1939 the legend of K2's invincibility was destroyed once and for all. As the record stands today, all but 750 of its 28,250 feet have been climbed—the nearest men have come to the summit of any "Eight-thousander."

Most of the great Himalayan peaks have, over the years, acquired what might be called an adopted nationality. None but English mountaineers have ever set foot on Everest. Nanda Devi, Kamet and the surrounding mountains of Garhwal are predominantly "English" too. Both Kanchenjunga and Nanga Parbat, as we have seen, have been attempted mostly by Germans. Even when no political considerations are involved, as they are in the case of the Tibetan and Nepalese peaks, climbers have come to recognize a sort of squatters' rights among themselves, and certain mountains have, in effect, become the almost exclusive province of expeditions of one nationality. By this token, K2 has in the past few years become an "American" mountain. Both the 1938 and 1939 attempts on its summit were organized under the auspices of the American Alpine Club of New York; the climbers who took part were all from the United States; and the results achieved rank with the foremost in the annals of Himalayan mountaineering.

The 1938 party consisted of only five men. Fritz Wiessner had been originally designated as the leader, but he was unable to make the trip, and the command passed to Dr. Charles Houston, veteran of the successful British-American Nanda Devi expedition of 1936. His companions were Richard Burdsall, of the 1932 Minya Konka venture; William House and Robert Bates, accomplished young climbers who had made many notable ascents in the United States, Canada and Alaska; and Paul Petzoldt, a well-known guide and packer in the Teton Mountain region of Wyoming. On its arrival in India the group was augmented by Captain N. R. Streatfeild, assigned by the British army as transport officer, six Sherpa porters, and the usual crew of locally recruited coolies.[1]

Leaving Srinagar, the metropolis of Kashmir, on May thirteenth, the expedition trekked up from the soft, green valleys into the bleak domain of the Karakorams and by early June were established in their base camp, 16,600 feet high, directly beneath the great south face of K2. The weeks that followed were devoted to long, arduous reconnaissance. Splitting into groups of two and three, the climbers surveyed the mountain from all sides and all angles, ascending and descending the endless chain of glaciers, struggling across windswept passes, seeking patiently for a route upward that might

[1] Captain Streatfeild, recalled to England a few months later, was drowned during the British evacuation of Dunkirk in the spring of 1940.

offer at least a gambler's chance of success. For much of this time the upper part of K2 was hidden from them by great billowing masses of clouds. Only occasionally were they able to catch a glimpse of their goal—the brilliant white ice of the summit pyramid gleaming faintly through the mists.

The Americans were not long in learning that their predecessors were right: there was no "natural" way up the peak. Photographs and maps had indicated that the north-west ridge was perhaps the best possibility, but precipitous, snow-powdered ice slopes stopped them when they had climbed a scant few hundred feet above its base. The situation on the north-east ridge was even worse. Reluctantly they decided to attack the south-east, or Abruzzi ridge, on which the Duke and his men had tried so hard and failed. Towering skyward with fearful steepness, armoured with ice and smooth, down-sloping slabs, it presented a thoroughly discouraging prospect. But things had come to the point where it was this or nothing. Camp I was accordingly established near the foot of the ridge, and on July first, after several false starts, the push up the mountain began.

As had been anticipated, the greatest difficulty was in finding spots sufficiently level to be used as camp-sites. Combing the mountain diligently, they were lucky enough to find a tiny snow-pocket that served as an admirable location for Camp II; but above that they encountered no such protected nooks. At every higher bivouac it was necessary to construct platforms of loose rock on which to pitch the tents, and even with these artificial foundations the climbers found themselves each night tilted precariously over black space.

Nevertheless the work went on, and gradually a thousand and then another thousand feet of the mountain dropped away beneath them. Above Camp III the party was split into three teams, in order that the advance might be more rapid and efficient. Houston and Petzoldt, forming one pair, and House and Bates, as another, took turns reconnoitring and bringing up the loads, while Burdsall and Captain Streatfeild descended to Camp I to co-ordinate operations from below. Each team had with it one or more of the Sherpas, the strongest of them being assigned to whichever party was currently highest on the mountain.

Unlike most Himalayan routes, the Abruzzi ridge of K2 presented rock-climbing difficulties of the severest kind. Between Camps II and III the line of ascent was along a rough outcropping of stone, paralleling an almost vertical ice-wall, and so hard was the going that 900 feet of fixed rope had to be rigged up before the porters with their packs were able to make the ascent. Beyond III things were no better: the mountainside bulged out in a series of cliffs and overhangs, requiring both exhausting physical effort and the most delicate technique to surmount them. Also, to make matters worse, the rock itself was rotten, breaking away from walls and ledges at slight pressure and descending in a murderous cannonade on to the exposed camp below.

The hardest stretch of all, however, was encountered just above Camp IV, at a height of about 22,000 feet. Here, according to House, "a vertical wall of yellowish rock stretched completely across the ridge. There seemed to be no way around it, and when we had cut our way up to it over the ice slopes immediately above camp we found the rock worse than we had anticipated. It was nearly vertical, and what had looked like promising ledges from below were in reality tiny sloping platforms. After much trouble Bates curled himself around a projecting tooth of rock and belayed me while I traversed into the bottom of a shallow chimney. It was difficult to stay in, as the walls flared out and the bed was formed of ice, but after a good deal of exertion and not a little swearing I reached the top, gaining about eighty feet."—House's modest account, one is certain, scarcely does justice to his exploit. For those eighty feet had taken him *four full hours*.

It was impossible for men with loads to climb the chimney, and House and Bates therefore spent the next day rigging up a sort of aerial tramway along its side. Meanwhile Houston and Petzoldt came up, and Camp V was pitched near the top of the chimney. All hands were subsequently held there for a day by high winds and driving snow; but the much-dreaded major storm did not materialize, and soon conditions were such that they were able to move still higher. Finding the going here slightly less difficult, they gained altitude rapidly. Within a few days a sixth camp had been established at about 23,300 feet and a seventh at almost 25,000.

At the latter point the ridge was at last beneath them, and they had come out on to an ice plateau that swept like a great terrace across the upper face of the mountain. Beyond the plateau was a gently rising snow-slope, from which emerged, gaunt and black, the 2,500-foot summit pyramid of K2. The snow section presented what was obviously the easiest stretch on the peak, and even the beetling rock above appeared to offer no obstacles worse than those they had encountered below. For the first time in their long struggle the climbers were within striking distance of their goal.

The time had now come, however, when they were faced with a difficult decision. From the outset the expedition had travelled light—not only in personnel, but in provisions—and, with the long reconnaissance and subsequent slow going on the ridge, their food supply was beginning to run low. They were not, to be sure, in any actual distress, nor would they be likely to be, even if they continued on. The margin of safety, however, had become precariously thin, and a great storm, catching them in a high camp and rendering retreat impossible, might well spell disaster for them all. With the summit so close and beckoning, the temptation to take the chance must have been strong indeed, but they managed to resist it and reluctantly conceded that the pinnacle of K2 was not to be theirs that year. Their decision to call a halt at such a time is perhaps even greater proof of their mettle as mountaineers than all their feats of skill and endurance during their long ascent.

Before descending, however, they allowed themselves one final foray toward the heights. With House and Bates established in Camp VI as support, Houston and Petzoldt went up again to VII, spent the night there, and on the next day, July twenty-first, set out up the snow-slope toward the summit cone. There was no thought in their minds of reaching the top —an eighth camp would have had to be established for that even to be considered—but merely of going as high as they could in one day's reconnaissance and rejoining their companions in Camp VI the same night. Accordingly, they reached the base of the summit pyramid at an elevation of 25,600 feet and even scrambled up its lower rocks some 400 feet higher. The pinnacle of K2 loomed huge and clear above them, now only a short day's climb away. But it might as well have been an eternity, as with reluctant steps they began the descent of the mountain.

Assembled at their glacier base-camp a week later, the climbers were a disappointed group of young men. In point of fact, however, they had carried off one of the most brilliant exploits in the history of Himalayan mountaineering. A magnificent job of reconnoitring and climbing had been accomplished; the "unscalable mountain" had been scaled to within 2,200 feet of the top; and—perhaps most remarkable of all—there had been not a single serious mishap or injury during the entire expedition.

The 1939 party came even closer to conquering K2 than had its predecessor—but at a price.

This second attempt was, like the first, sponsored by the American Alpine Club, but none of the climbers of 1938 participated. Fritz Wiessner, who had been unable to go along the previous year, was now the leader. His companions were Jack Durrance, a well-known American skier and climber; Dudley Wolfe and Eaton Cromwell, old hands at mountaineering in many parts of the world; and Chappell Cranmer and George Sheldon, who at the time of the expedition were still undergraduates at Dartmouth. Upon arrival in Kashmir the party was rounded out by the acquisition of the usual British transport officer, plus nine Sherpas and a battalion of local coolies. It was thus a slightly larger group than that of 1938, but still exceedingly small as Himalayan expeditions go.

As before, the long trek into the heart of the Karakorams was accomplished in remarkably short order, and on May thirty-first the site of the old base camp was re-occupied. Several days were spent in searching for a possible new route leading to the heights above; but the climbers soon reached the conclusion that their predecessors had made the only feasible choice, and the assault was therefore launched on the same south-east, or Abruzzi, ridge. Even before they started, however, it became apparent that they were not going to enjoy the unvarying good fortune that had favoured the climbers of 1938. Cranmer, who, at twenty, was the youngest of the party, fell ill at the base camp and was unable to do any climbing during the whole duration of the expedition.

Missing their companion's assistance, and worried about his condition, the others nevertheless began the push upwards, and gradually the long chain of camps began to take form on the savage, ice-sheathed mountainside. In every case the tents were pitched in exactly the same locations as the preceding year, for the simple reason that there were no other possible locations. The only change made was that Camp III, which lay directly in the path of vicious stone-avalanches, was now used only as a cache for supplies and not as a sleeping place. Along the walls and buttresses the climbers found much of the fixed rope which Houston and his companions had rigged up; but the storms of a long Karakoram winter had scarcely improved its condition, and the larger part of it had to be replaced.

On June twenty-second, after three weeks of work, an advance guard of Wiessner, Wolfe, Sheldon and five Sherpas were established at Camp IV, beneath House's formidable chimney. Here, however, they were overtaken by a storm, and for six long days and nights they huddled miserably in their tents, while the snow billowed down upon them and the wind roared against the canvas like machine-gun fire. Fortunately their food supply was ample, and when the storm at last subsided they found themselves cramped and battered, but eager to renew the struggle. On June twenty-ninth Camp V was set up near the top of the chimney, and a few days later they were ready to go higher still.

Nevertheless, it was a badly depleted high-climbing party that began working its way along the upper ridge toward the great ice plateau. Cranmer was still ailing and lay in the base camp under the care of the transport officer, Lieutenant Trench. Cromwell had likewise remained below, to direct the stocking and maintenance of the lower camps. And now both

Photo by V. Sella. Courtesy American Alpine Club.

KING OF THE KARAKORAM

K2, second highest summit in the world, looming through the clouds above the Godwin Austen Glacier. The route of the American expeditions of 1938 and 1939 was along the skyline ridge on the right.

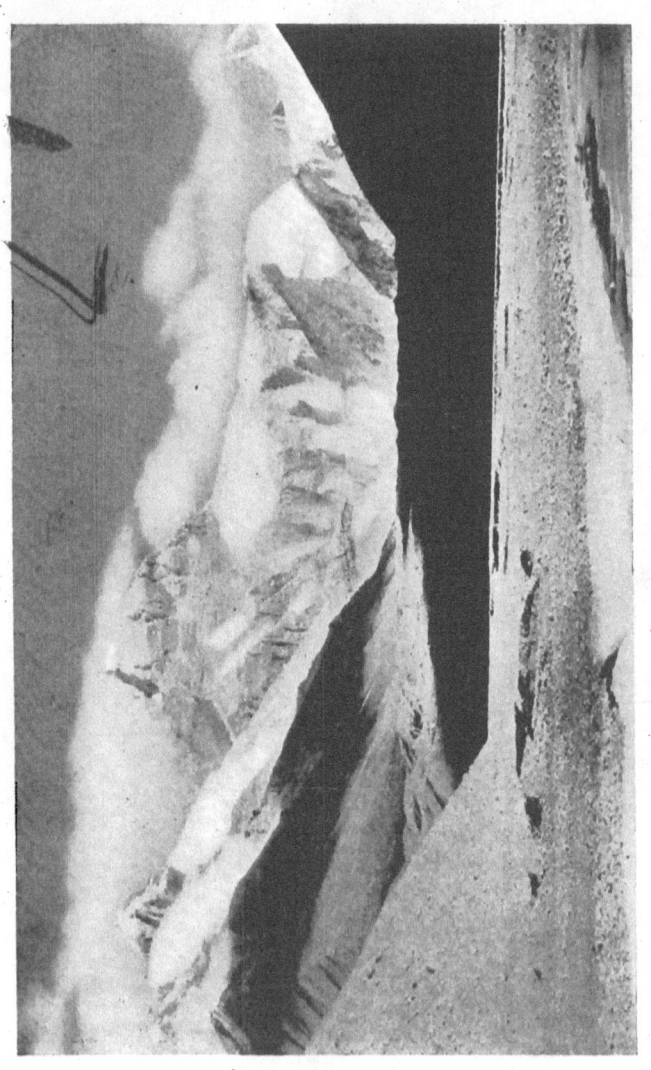

SUMMIT OF THE WORLD [Photo by Capt. J. L. Noel. From Ewing Galloway.

Mount Everest from the Rongbuk Glacier. The mountain is twelve miles distant in a direct line and its summit towers more than 13,000 feet above the glacier.

Sheldon and Durrance were forced to descend—the former with frostbitten toes, the latter because of difficulty in breathing—leaving Wiessner and Wolfe as the only active climbers. The Sherpas, on the other hand, were standing up magnificently under the ordeal. Paced by their headman, Pasang Kikuli, redoubtable veteran of Nanga Parbat, Nanda Devi and the first K2 venture, they toiled up and down, back and forth, along the precipitous ridge, and day by day the straggling column crept higher on the mountainside. The sixth camp was pitched just beneath the crest of the ridge; the seventh on the ice plateau at about 24,700 feet; the eighth, on the snow-slopes above, at almost 25,500—

The bare, frosted rock of the summit pyramid now loomed close above them, and, with luck, it would require only two days' more climbing to reach the top. Storms pinned them in Camp VIII for thirty-six hours, but the morning of July seventeenth dawned clear. While two of the Sherpas descended to the plateau to bring up more supplies, Wiessner, Wolfe and the remaining porter, Pasang Lama, set off to establish a ninth and final camp on the rocks above. Before reaching the base of the summit pyramid, however, they were forced to plough their way through huge drifts of soft, freshly fallen snow. At such an altitude this proved a terribly difficult task, especially for Wolfe, who was much heavier than the others and found himself sinking into the snow up to his armpits. After an hour and more of desperate effort, he was near to exhaustion and had to turn back. Wiessner and Pasang Lama, continuing the struggle, finally got through. That evening they pitched their tent well up on the summit cone's southeast ridge and the next day moved it still farther to a height of 26,050 feet.

On the morning of July nineteenth, in perfect weather, they started for the top. Neither of them, according to Wiessner's subsequent account, was particularly bothered by the altitude. The climbing, however, was of the stiffest order, even necessitating the use of pitons to secure the rope; and their progress was accordingly slow. All morning and all afternoon they toiled on—up cliffs and bristling cornices, through deep ice-coated gullies, along the crests of rotten ridges. They were now so high above the surrounding world that they seemed hardly to be part of it any longer. The glacier, 11,000 feet below, might as well have been a hundred miles; they could see it only as a thin gleaming ribbon between the mountain-masses on either side. Finally, even the pinnacles of Gasherbrum and Broad Peak, themselves far higher than any mountain ever climbed, were swimming below them in the evening light.

A bold plan had taken form in Wiessner's mind. "It was 6 p.m. by then," he wrote in his diary. "I had decided to go to the summit in spite of the late hour and climb through the night. . . . The weather was safe, and we were not exhausted. Night climbing had to be done anyway, as it would take us a long time to descend the difficult route up which we had struggled. Much better to go up the summit slowly, with many stops, and return over the difficult part of the route the next morning."

But it was not to be. Pasang Lama, who had climbed strongly and uncomplainingly through the long hours of the day, suddenly halted when he realized that night was coming on. All Wiessner's arguments could not persuade him to go farther, and when the former made a move to start climbing again he firmly refused to pay out the rope. To have gone on alone—at that height, in the darkness—would have been madness; and in the end Wiessner gave in.

At a height of 27,500 feet—750 below the summit of K2—the two men turned back.

Through eight terrible hours of darkness they descended the cliffs and buttresses of the pyramid—feeling their way with frozen hands and feet, clambering, struggling, swinging at rope's end five miles high in the night. At last, at 2.30 in the morning, they reached their highest camp. There they spent the next day, resting, and on the morning of the twenty-first made their second bid for the summit. The Sherpa, however, had lost his crampons in a mishap during the first attempt and was unable to negotiate the steep ice chimneys that grooved their route. They were turned back without matching their earlier effort.

Now began the long and complex chain of events that was to lead to defeat and tragedy. Wiessner had full intentions of making yet another try for the top, but food at Camp IX was running low, and he and Lama therefore descended to Camp VIII to renew the supply. There they found Wolfe, as they had expected, but there was no sign of the porters who had descended a week before to bring up fresh loads. By this time there were enough provisions at VIII to last for only three or four more days. There was nothing for it but for all of them to descend to Camp VII, the largest and most completely stocked of the high bivouacs.

Arriving there, they had their second shock. The camp was deserted, much of the provisions and fuel had been removed, and they had only one sleeping bag and air mattress for the three of them. After a miserably cold night only one course of action was open: to continue the Camp descent to VI. Both Wiessner and Wolfe, however, were still thinking in terms of another summit attack, and it was therefore decided that only Wiessner and Lama would go down, while Wolfe waited at VII, conserving his strength. The first two, according to the plan, would come back the following day with fresh porters, and the whole party would then re-ascend to the highest camps.

But what was in store for them was something very different indeed. Reaching Camp VI the next day, Wiessner and the porter were stunned to discover that this too had been evacuated. There were no porters, no food, no sleeping bags; everything had been permanently abandoned. Realizing at last that something had gone seriously wrong, the two men continued the descent. Camp V was likewise deserted. So were IV, III and II. At Camp II they spent their second freezing night. They had left their one sleeping bag with Wolfe, and by morning both were badly frostbitten and close to collapse. Nevertheless they stumbled on down and by mid-afternoon reached the base camp—"as truly broken, mentally as well as physically," said Wiessner, "as it is possible for men to be." There their fellow-climbers and porters stared at them as if they were ghosts from another world.

What had happened was that, while Wiessner, Wolfe and Lama were at Camp VIII and higher, the rest of the expedition had broken down below. Cranmer was still sick, and Sheldon, with frostbitten feet, was hobbling about on crutches. Durrance and Cromwell had been unable to hold out for long periods at the altitudes of the higher camps and had been compelled to descend to the base. Meanwhile the Sherpas, who had gone down from VIII to VII for more supplies, had been unable to get back up again. They had waited at VII for several days, and at the end of that time, having seen no sign of life from above, assumed that the summit party had met with an accident and been killed. They had therefore begun the descent and, as conscientious porters, had felt it their duty to clear out the various camps as they went. By the time Wiessner and Lama staggered into base camp their companions had long since given them up as lost and were sorrowfully preparing to start back to civilization.

Now Wolfe was alone, high on the mountain in Camp VII, and it was obvious that heroic measures would be needed to reach him. Wiessner was done in, so weak that he could hardly eat or speak. Durrance, therefore, took over and on July twenty-fifth started up with three Sherpas. But upon reaching the fourth camp he again succumbed to the altitude and two days later returned to the base with one of the porters. The other two had continued on to Camp VI, but needed reinforcements to go still higher. Accordingly two other Sherpas, one of them the head-man, Pasang Kikuli, started up from the base and succeeded in reaching VI in one day's climbing—one of the most remarkable feats of endurance ever performed by men upon a mountain. The next day Kikuli and two others continued on to VII, where they found Wolfe, alive, but apparently badly broken down both physically and mentally. He told them he was too weak to come down that day, but that he would be ready for the effort the next morning.

As there was only one sleeping bag at VII, the Sherpas descended to VI for the night. They were held there the following day—the thirtieth—by a storm, but on the thirty-first three of them, led by Kikuli, went up again. That was the last that anyone saw of them. The fourth Sherpa in the rescue party waited at VI for three days, but no one came down from above, and on August second hunger and cold drove him down to base camp.

One last effort was yet to be made. The following day Wiessner, still very weak, started up from the glacier with two porters, and by dint of great effort got as far as Camp II. His diary tells the sorrowful ending of the story:

"Aug. 5.—It is all grey outside and a fine snow is falling. The south-west wind starts coming up and the Sherpas refuse to go to IV. I have to agree with them; no matter how serious the situation may be, I must not jeopardize my last reserves for the rescue.

"Aug. 6.—Ten inches of snow have fallen during the night, and it storms and snows until noon. The sun comes out for a few hours, but up above Camp III the storm is still raging, making it hopeless for us to go up. It is terrible for us to sit here in the tents at Camp II under the circumstances.

"Aug. 7.—Two feet of new snow outside; the storm above; we must retreat. It is hopeless to get higher this season, and our supplies are running low. The rocks are deeply covered. It is better on the glacier, with the temperature around freezing. Arrive at camp feeling desperately low."

A few days later the expedition started the long homeward journey. High above them great banks of cloud and scudding squalls hid the savage heights of K2—and the bodies of four brave men.

X

SUMMIT OF THE WORLD

THE FIGHT FOR EVEREST

IN THE EARLY afternoon of June 8, 1924, a man stood on a crag in the freezing sub-stratosphere, 26,000 feet above the sea, raised his eyes and stared. On a ridge high overhead he saw two human figures, black and tiny against the sky. Less than 800 feet above them was the snow-plumed summit of the highest mountain on earth.—A minute, two minutes the watcher gazed, while the climbers crept upward. Then clouds swept in upon the mountain-top, blotting them from view.

They were never seen again.

So ended the most splendid and tragic of many attempts to conquer Everest, king of mountains. To this day no one knows whether George Leigh-Mallory and Andrew Irvine reached the top before death overtook them. No one, probably, will ever know. One thing is certain: no man has ever reached the summit and returned to tell the tale.

The story of Mount Everest begins in 1852, when a clerk in the office of the Indian Trigonometrical Survey looked up excitedly from a page of figures and cried to his superior, "Sir, I have discovered the highest mountain in the world!" A careful checking of his calculations proved him right. The remote Himalayan summit listed prosaically on the charts as "Peak XV" was found to be 29,002 feet high—almost a thousand feet higher than its closest rival. Later observers corrected its altitude to 29,141 feet and named it for Sir George Everest, first Surveyor-General of India. But its supremacy remained, and remains today, unchallenged.

What began as an exercise in higher mathematics was to become, as years passed, one of the great adventures of the human spirit.

For a half century after its discovery Everest was a mountain of mystery. Tibet and Nepal, on whose frontiers it rises, were both rigorously closed to outsiders, and, far from climbing it, men of the West were unable even to approach it or learn anything about it. All they knew were the tantalizing figures of the Trigonometrical Survey. All they could see was a remote pinnacle of rock and ice, one of thousands in the great sea of peaks to the north of the Indian plain. The mountain itself—its structure and appearance, its surroundings and approaches—was as unknown as if it stood upon another planet.

Then, in the late 1890's, as we have seen, the full tide of mountaineering interest and activity turned toward the Himalayas. Soon a thin trickle of pioneers began to penetrate into the great passes and gorges where no white man had ever been before; adventurous spirits crossed the frontiers into forbidden Tibet and Nepal, disguised as Hindu or Mohammedan traders; men like Freshfield, Kellas and Longstaff turned their attention from the Sikkim and Garhwal foothills to the greater peaks that lay beyond. Slowly the net closed in about the remote, secret place where rose the highest mountain in the world. Mountaineers had heard the siren call of the mysterious and the unknown, and all the obstacles of man and nature were not going to stop them in their quest.

A lone traveller might slip into Tibet without official sanction; not so a large expedition equipped to tackle Everest. The permission of the Tibetan government was essential, and for long years this permission was not forthcoming. At last, in 1913, it appeared that the way was clear, and an exploring party was about to be organized by Freshfield; but the project was ended before it began by the outbreak of the First World War. It was not until seven years later that men were again able to turn their eyes and thoughts to the greatest mountain.

Early in 1920 the Royal Geographical Society of London and the British Alpine Club joined forces to form the Mount Everest Committee and after prolonged negotiations secured permission for an all-English party to approach and, if possible, ascend the mountain. Preparations were immediately begun on an elaborate scale. It was planned to send out two expeditions, a year apart, the first to explore and reconnoitre, the second to climb. As it eventually turned out, there was a third and it was this final attack that was to end, a scant few hundred feet from triumph, in mystery and tragedy.

But to begin at the beginning:

The 1921 reconnaissance expedition to Everest was composed of the flower of English mountaineers and explorers. The leader was Colonel C. K. Howard-Bury, who had travelled widely in Tibet and knew that mysterious land as well as any white man living. Next in command were Dr. Kellas, and A. F. R. Wollaston, who had won fame on Ruwenzori and many another far-flung mountain range. Others were Harold Raeburn, a veteran Himalayan climber, Dr. A. M. Heron, a geologist, and Major Morshead and Captain Wheeler, army surveyors who had known and travelled among the great Asiatic peaks for years. To these mature and experienced hands were added two younger men with brilliant, if briefer, mountaineering records: G. H. Bullock, of the Consular Service, and George Leigh-Mallory, master at Charterhouse College, Cambridge.

It was Mallory who was to become the foremost of the "Everesters" and the most famous mountaineer of his day. He was the only man to participate in all three of the great expeditions between 1921 and 1924, and although never the official leader (he was only thirty-eight when he died), his marvellous climbing accomplishments and his flaming spirit made him the outstanding figure in every one of them. Everest became *his* mountain, as completely as the Matterhorn, sixty years before, had been Whymper's. His climbing companions, to a man, believed that if any one of them was to achieve conquest of the highest summit on earth Mallory would be the one, and many of them, in later days, clung staunchly to the belief that he attained his goal before death overtook him in the clouds.

There was nothing of the conventional athlete about Mallory.

Slight and slim, with a round boyish face, he was anything but the popular conception of a rugged outdoor man. Again like Whymper, climbing was to him not exercise or amusement, but passionate devotion, and, like all great mountaineers, less a physical than a spiritual adventure. His explanation of why men climb remains today the simplest, and at the same time perhaps the most profound, that has ever been given.

"But *why?*" a friend asked him as he set out for a renewed assault on Everest. "Why do you try to climb this mountain?"

Mallory's answer consisted of four words:

"Because it is there."

"There," however, was a remote, unknown corner of the earth, and it required an arduous journey of many weeks before the Everesters of the 1921 reconnoitring party came even within sight of their goal. Beginning at Darjeeling in the middle of May their march carried them first through the steaming tropical jungles of Sikkim, then up through great mountain passes on to the desolate, windswept wilderness of the Tibetan plateau. In a straight line the distance from Darjeeling to Everest is only a hundred miles, but they had to journey more than three hundred, threading their way among the great peaks and gorges of the eastern Himalayas.

These were days of endless toil and hardship, and they took their toll in sudden and tragic fashion. Dr. Kellas, whose health was no longer robust, strained his heart while crossing the high passes and died in the Tibetan village of Kampa Dzong. Soon after, Raeburn became seriously ill and had to return to India, with Wollaston accompanying him. These two were not able to rejoin the expedition until the middle of the summer. Everest had begun to claim her victims even before they had had so much as a glimpse of her.

The others struggled on, saddened but resolute. There were only six white men now, at the head of a vast cavalcade of Sherpa porters, Tibetan guides and helpers, ponies, donkeys, bullocks and yaks. Day after day they pushed northward and westward across as savage country as exists anywhere on the earth's surface—through sandstorms and raging, glacial torrents, across vast boulder-strewn plains and passes 20,000 feet above the sea. At night they camped under the stars or enjoyed the primitive hospitality of Buddhist monasteries and village headmen. Their passports from the Tibetan authorities in Lhassa assured them kindly and courteous treatment, but the announcement of the purpose of their journey elicited only a dubious shaking of heads and a solemn turning of prayer wheels. To these devout and superstitious orientals, Everest was more than a mountain. Chomolungma, they called it—Goddess-Mother-of-the-World. It was sacrilege, they believed, for mere mortals even to approach it.

At last, late in June, the expedition arrived at the great Rongbuk Monastery, where an isolated colony of priests and hermits dwelt, some twenty miles due north of Everest. And from here, at last, they saw their mountain head on, in its titanic majesty—the first white men ever to have a close-up view of the summit of the world. "We paused," wrote Mallory, "in sheer astonishment. The sight of it banished every thought; we asked no questions and made no comment, but simply looked. . . . At the end of the valley and above the glacier Everest rises, not so much a peak as a prodigious mountain-mass. There is no complication for the eye. The highest of the world's mountains, it seems, has to make but a single gesture of magnificence to be the lord of all, vast in unchallenged and isolated supremacy. To the discerning eye other mountains are visible, giants between 23,000 and 26,000 feet high. Not one of their slenderer heads even reaches their chief's shoulder; beside Everest they escape notice—such is the pre-eminence of the greatest."

The explorers set themselves at once to their tasks, reconnoitring, surveying, studying the colossal rock-and-ice mass that towered before them and probing the possible routes to its summit. They were already at an altitude of 18,000 feet—far higher than the highest summit in the Alps or Rockies—and the slightest exertion set their lungs to heaving and their hearts to pounding. The world around them was a trackless wilderness of peaks, ridges and glaciers, and wind and snow roared down from the heights with hurricane fury. And still there remained two vertical miles of mountain soaring above them into the sky.

Working slowly around its base Mallory and Bullock discovered that Everest was constructed as an almost perfect pyramid, with three great faces and three main ridges sweeping downward from the summit like vast buttresses. The faces were all built up in tiers of precipices which no man could even dream of scaling, and the south and north-west ridges, miles in length and flanked by vertical ice-walls, appeared almost equally hopeless. In addition, the whole southern half of the mountain lay in Nepal and was therefore politically closed to them.

Only on the north-east did Mallory detect any possibilities whatever. Here, bordering the ten-thousand-foot precipice of the north face, a jagged arête descended from a great rocky shoulder near the summit to a high snow saddle on the east of the Rongbuk Glacier. The angle of the arête was steep, but not so steep that experienced mountaineers could not ascend it, and from the shoulder upward the main east ridge and the wedge-like summit pyramid seemed to present no insuperable obstacles. The first great question mark was whether a way could be found to reach the saddle.

A way was found, but the finding required two long months of planning and toil. The saddle—or North Col, as it came to be known—rose from the Rongbuk Glacier as an almost perpendicular ice-wall 4,000 feet high, and even the dauntless Mallory realized that it could never be scaled from that side. His only hope was that the far, or eastern, side might prove more feasible. The next and greatest job was to get there.

The Rongbuk Glacier was a narrow avenue of ice walled in by tremendous mountains in which no break appeared to exist. Actually there was a break, and if Mallory had found it he would have been able to reach the far side of the col in a day or two. But it was so tiny and obscure a passage that he missed it. The result was a circuitous journey of more than a hundred miles, back across the plateaux and passes which they

Oc

had traversed before, and then south and west again toward the base of Everest.

This last stage of their journey took them through a mountain wonderland such as no man had ever been privileged to look upon before. The Kama and Kharta valleys, up which they pushed, were great gashes in the earth, so deep at their lower ends that their floors were covered with lush, tropical vegetation, so lofty at their apexes that the explorers found themselves struggling in snow up to their armpits. At their head loomed the mighty upper slopes of Everest, flanked by the pinnacles of Makalu, Chomolönzo and Lhotse, themselves among the highest summits in the world.

At last, after innumerable delays and hardships, the climbers reached the apex of the Kharta Valley—a wild, blizzard-racked pass known as the Lhakpa La, 22,000 feet above the sea. From here they could see the long-sought eastern approach to the North Col, and it was indeed as Mallory had hoped: the great saddle of snow and ice rose on this side to a height of only 1,500 feet above the glacier floor, as against 4,000 feet on the Rongbuk side. It appeared not impossible to scale. A cheer went up from the lips of the frozen, exhausted men, for they knew they had found the key to the mountain.

By this time it was late August and the brief Himalayan summer was almost over. The work of the expedition, however, would not be done until they had reached the col, and so the three strongest climbers, Mallory, Bullock and Wheeler, pushed on over the Lhakpa La, down its far side and across the glacier below. On their way they made a second important discovery: that there was, after all, a passage from the Rongbuk Glacier to the eastern side of the col. It was of course too late now for it to be of any help to them that year, but the narrow defile was used by all subsequent Everest expeditions.

Once found, the eastern wall of the North Col did not prove a particularly formidable obstacle—at least not in 1921. The outer surface of the wall was composed of frozen avalanche snow, and up it the three climbers hacked their way, slanting carefully to right and left to avoid the gaping blue abysses with which it was scarred. At noon on the twenty-fourth of August they stood upon the top, at an altitude of 23,000 feet—higher than any mountain-top in the world outside of the Himalayas.

The pinnacle of Everest, however, was still 6,000 feet above them and two and a half miles away. Scanning the north-east ridge, the shoulder and the summit pyramid, they saw that Mallory's earlier surmise had been right: the upper mountain slanted upward in a fairly easy gradient of rock and snow, seeming to present neither difficulty nor great danger. The temptation was strong to venture still higher, but they were almost done in from their exertions as it was and realized they could not hope to match their strength against the wild wind and blizzards of the exposed heights. After taking as complete observations as they could they descended from the col, rejoined their companions on the Lhakpa La and began the long return journey to India.

The members of the 1921 expedition had never once actually set foot on Everest itself; their highest point on the North Col was where subsequent expeditions would begin their real work. Yet, except for the untimely death of Dr. Kellas, the venture had been a complete and distinguished success. The trail to the mountain had been blazed, the weakness in its armour found. Everyone was agreed that, as far as actual climbing problems were concerned, the greatest mountain *might* be climbed. That "might" was all the Everesters needed. No sooner had the reconnaissance party returned to England than preparations for the real assault began.

On May 1, 1922, the first Mount Everest climbing expedition pitched its base camp within sight of the great lamasery near the snout of the Rongbuk Glacier. It was composed of thirteen Englishmen, sixty hillmen from Nepal and northern India, a hundred-odd Tibetan helpers and more than three hundred pack animals—a veritable army in miniature. Remote and isolated Tibet had not witnessed such a sight in the thousands of years of its history.

In the preceding year the purpose had been to explore, reconnoitre and learn. Now, however, all else was to be subordinated to one great purpose: to reach the top of Everest.

THE ROUTE TO EVEREST

To this end, the personnel of the party had been almost completely changed, with only Mallory and Morshead remaining from the original group. The new leader was Brigadier-General Charles G. Bruce, a veteran of the British army in India and a far-ranging Himalayan explorer over a period of many years. Colonel E. T. Strutt, another noted mountaineer, was second in command, and Dr. T. E. Longstaff, although now too old for the highest climbing, was on hand to lend the benefit of his wide experience. The others included Lieutenant-Colonel E. F. Norton, Dr. T. Howard Somervell and Dr. Wakefield; Captains Geoffrey Bruce, George Finch and C. G. Morris; C. G. Crawford, of the India Civil Service; and, as official photographer, Captain John Noel. Of these, Norton, Somervell and Finch were climbers in the prime of their careers and were expected, together with Mallory, to make the final bid for the summit.

As we have repeatedly seen, the climbing of a great mountain is far more than a matter of putting one foot in front of the other and moving uphill. Indeed, in the case of a giant like Everest, climbing in itself may be said to be of merely secondary importance. Two-thirds of the 1922 expedition's battles had to be fought before a single man set foot on the mountain proper.

First, there was the all-important problem of weather. No man, to be sure, could hope to prophesy the day-by-day variations of calm and storm in those wild Himalayan uplands, but the observations of the previous year had convinced everyone concerned that Everest was climbable, if at all, only during a very brief period of the year. Until early May the whole region was locked in savage, blizzard-driven winter; after the middle of June the eastern Himalayas received the full brunt of the Indian monsoon and remained through the summer a death-trap of snow and sleet and rotten, melting ice. A period of only some six weeks intervened in which the climbers might hope for reasonably clear skies, a minimum of wind and at least a fighting chance for success. It was therefore not accident, but careful planning, that brought the 1922 expedition to the skirts of Everest on May first. Their next great task was to get on to the mountain itself as quickly as possible. The race with the monsoon was on.

For two long weeks climbers and porters crept back and forth along the vast northern glaciers, transporting food, supplies and equipment. Mallory, in an analysis of the problems of Everest, had likened a climbing expedition to a ladder, in which the higher rungs were useless unless the rungs below were dependable and strong. It was these lower rungs which now had to be fashioned—a chain of camps, not more than an easy day's march apart, extending as high as human strength could take them. Camp I was pitched between the Rongbuk and East Rongbuk Glaciers, in the narrow defile which Mallory had missed the previous year. Camp II was established halfway up the East Rongbuk Glacier, and Camp III near its head, close by the eastern wall of the North Col. The older and less acclimatized members of the party were left behind to staff and maintain communication between these lower stations, while the stronger climbers and porters proceeded to the establishment of Camp IV on top of the col.

This in itself was a feat more difficult than the ascent to the summit of a lesser mountain. Mallory and Somervell led the way, chopping countless steps in the glaring ice-cliffs, edging their way around bottomless, dark crevasses and snow-masses as vast as toppled buildings. The porters followed, straining on the ropes, scarcely more than creeping under their heavy loads. On their return to civilization the Everesters were unanimous in declaring that without these sturdy Sherpas from the hill country of northern India their assault on the mountain would have bogged down before it even began. Unlike the Tibetans, who refused even to set foot on Chomolungma, the haunted mountain, these men climbed doggedly and cheerfully to heights where no men had ever stood before and in 1924 achieved the almost incredible feat of carrying packs and establishing a camp at an altitude of more than 27,000 feet. "Tigers," the Englishmen called them, and they richly deserved the name.

With a huddle of tiny green tents established on the col, the assault on Everest proper was at last at hand. Mallory,

Somervell, Norton and Morshead were selected for the first attempt, and at dawn on May twentieth, accompanied by a group of the strongest porters, they set out for the unknown, untrodden heights. The cold was almost unendurable; the wild west wind roared down upon them like an invisible avalanche; and their goal was still a mile above them, remote and tantalizing in the sky. But their hopes and hearts were high. "No end," wrote Mallory, "was visible or even conceivable to this kingdom of adventure!"

Hour after hour the climbers toiled up the north-east ridge. The going underfoot was not technically difficult, but constant care was necessary to guard against a slip on the steep, ice-coated slabs. The wind tore at them relentlessly, and, worse yet, as they ascended it grew more difficult to breathe. Later expeditions were to learn an important lesson from their ordeal and allow themselves more time for acclimatization before storming the almost oxygen-less heights.

They had hoped to pitch their highest camp close under the north-east shoulder, but at 25,000 feet cold and exhaustion forced a halt. Sending their faithful "tigers" down to Camp IV they pitched their two tiny tents in as sheltered a spot as they could find and crawled into their sleeping bags. All night they lay there, while the wind howled and the mercury in their thermometers dropped to seven degrees below zero.

At first daylight they were moving upward again through thick mist and gusts of windblown snow. After an hour's climbing Morshead reached the limit of his endurance and had to turn back, but Mallory, Somervell and Norton still struggled on. Their progress consisted of fifteen or twenty minutes' slow, painful climbing, a long rest, another period of climbing, another rest. Before long their hands and feet grew numb and their mouths hung wide open, gasping for air. Even their minds and senses, they reported later, were affected by oxygen starvation: ambition, judgment and will disappeared, and they moved forward mechanically, like men in a trance.

By mid-afternoon they had reached a height of 27,000 feet. They had ascended two-thirds of the vertical distance between the North Col and the summit and were a full 2,400 feet higher than any man had ever stood before. Physically they could have gone even farther, but to have done so at that late hour, without food or shelter, would have been suicidal. Too exhausted to feel disappointment, or any other emotion, they turned their backs on their goal and began the descent.

As it was they were lucky to return to their companions alive. At Camp V they found Morshead so crippled by frostbite that he had almost to be carried down to the col. Then, crossing a steep snow-slope lower down, one of them slipped, and the four were carried to the very brink of the precipitous north face before Mallory succeeded in jamming his axe into the snow and holding the rope fast. As a crowning misfortune, night overtook them before they reached the col, and it was past midnight when at last they groped their way into their tents.

The same day that the first attempt ended in heroic failure, the second was launched. The climbers now were Finch, Geoffrey Bruce and Tejbir Bura, a Gurkha corporal who had proved himself a first-class mountaineer. Captain Noel ascended with them to the North Col camp, where he remained in reserve, and twelve porters set up a fifth camp for them at 25,500 feet—a full 500 feet higher than where Mallory and his companions had bivouacked a few nights before. This headstart for the final dash, added to the advantage that they were supplied with tanks of oxygen to aid their breathing, gave the second party high hopes of success.

They were hopes, however, that were to be quickly shattered. No sooner had Finch, Bruce and Tejbir crawled into their tent for the night than a blizzard swooped down upon the mountain. For more than twenty-four hours the wind shrieked, the snow drove down in an almost solid mass, and the climbers struggled desperately with ripping canvas and breaking guyropes. It was little less than a miracle that men, tent and all were not blown bodily off the mountain into the mile-deep gulfs below.

After two nights and a day the weather at last cleared, and

the climbers made their delayed start in a still, frozen dawn. At 26,000 feet Tejbir collapsed and had to return to the tent, Finch and Bruce continuing. The oxygen which they carried spared them the tortures which their predecessors had endured, but this advantage was more than nullified by the thirty pounds of tank and apparatus which each carried on his back. Worse than this, Bruce's apparatus was almost the cause of his death, for without warning, at an altitude of about 26,500 feet, something went wrong with it and the flow of oxygen stopped. Accustomed by then to artificial breathing, Bruce would have been able to live for only a few minutes without it. Finch, however, quickly connected Bruce's mouthpiece to his own tank, and between them they were able to make the necessary repairs.

Hoping to escape the full brunt of the wind, they left the north-east ridge a few hundred feet below the shoulder and headed diagonally upward across the smooth slabs and powdered snow of Everest's north face. They made remarkable progress and by midday had gained a point only half a mile from the summit and a scant 1,900 feet below it. But here they reached the end of their tether. Their bodies and brains were numb; their limbs were ceasing to function and their eyes to focus; each additional foot upward would probably be a foot that they could never return. They turned back defeated, like their companions before them, but in defeat they had set a new world's climbing record of 27,235 feet.

One more attempt the expedition of 1922 was to make. It was doomed to be the most short-lived and disastrous one that has ever been made against the king of mountains.

The dreaded monsoon came early that year, and already in the first days of June dark banks of clouds appeared above the mountains to the south and the snow fell in billowing drifts on the upper slopes of Everest. A final thrust, if it were to be made at all, must be made quickly.

The main base, at which the whole expedition now gathered, resembled a field hospital more than a mountaineers' camp; of the high climbers only Mallory and Somervell were fit for further work. Resolved on a last try, however, they again pushed up the glaciers and, with Crawford, Wakefield and a squad of porters helping, resumed the laborious task of packing supplies up to the North Col. A night of sub-zero temperature had apparently solidified the fresh snow on the great wall, and they had reason to believe the going would be comparatively easy.

Starting early one morning from Camp III, Mallory, Somervell, Crawford and fourteen heavily loaded porters began the ascent. The Englishmen were on one rope, cutting steps and leading the way; three roped groups of porters followed. All went well until they had reached a point some 600 feet below the summit of the col. Then suddenly they were startled by a deep rumbling sound beneath them. An instant later there was a dull, ominous explosion, and the rampart of snow and ice to which they clung seemed to shudder along its entire face. An ocean of soft, billowing snow poured down upon them, knocked them from their feet and swept them away.

By miraculous good fortune, Mallory, Somervell and Crawford were not in the direct path of the avalanche. Caught by its flank, they were carried down a distance of some fifty feet; but by striking out like swimmers they were at last able to struggle to the surface and gain a secure foothold. Not so the unfortunate porters. Struck by the full force of the snow-slide, they were catapulted down the steep slope to the lip of a sheer ice-wall below. A moment before there had been a gaping crevasse beneath the wall; now it was filled by the avalanche. Hurtling over the brink, the porters plunged into the soft, hissing sea of snow, disappearing from sight one by one as thousands of more tons poured down after them.

Grim and heroic work was carried out on the ice-wall that day. Hour after hour the climbers floundered through the great drifts, burrowing, straining at ropes, expending their last reserve of strength to find and rescue the buried porters. One or two they found almost uninjured. A few more, who at first appeared dead from suffocation, they were able to revive. But seven were beyond help. To this day their bodies lie entombed in the snow and ice beneath the North Col, tragic victims of the wrath of the greatest mountain.

So the 1922 attack on Everest ended, not only in defeat but in disaster. Any further attempt on the peak that year was unthinkable, and it was a silent, saddened band of mountaineers who, a few days later, began the long trek across Tibet toward India and home. Behind them the summit of the greatest mountain loomed white and lonely in the sky, its snow-plume streaming in the wild west wind.

The curtain drops for two years on Chomolungma, Goddess-Mother-of-the-World. No expedition was sent out in 1923, but the struggle was by no means at an end. The Mount Everest Committee continued with its work—planning, financing, organizing—and in late March of 1924 a third expedition set out from Darjeeling on the high, wild trail to the heart of the Himalayas. Before it returned it was destined to write the most famous chapter in the history of mountaineering.

Several of the old Everesters were back again in harness: the indefatigable Mallory, of course; Somervell, Norton and Geoffrey Bruce; Noel with his cameras. General Bruce had again been appointed leader, but early in the march through Tibet he was stricken with malaria and had to return to India while Norton carried on as first-in-command. New recruits included N. E. Odell, the geologist, who twelve years later was to reach the top of Nanda Devi; E. O. Shebbeare, of the Indian Forest Service, as transport officer; Major R. W. G. Hingston as physician; Beetham and Hazard, both experienced mountaineers, and Andrew Irvine, young and powerful Oxford oarsman. In addition to these were the usual retinue of native porters and helpers, among them many of the veteran "tigers" from the 1922 attempt. Almost three hundred men, all told, were in the party when at the end of April it set up its base camp beside the great moraines of the now familiar Rongbuk Glacier.

The preliminary moves of the campaign were carried out according to the same plan as before—but more methodically and rapidly. The first three advance camps were established a day's march apart on the glaciers, and within two weeks the advance guard was ready to tackle the North Col. The whole organization was functioning like an oiled machine; there were no accidents or illness, and the weather was fine. According to their schedule they would be on the north-east ridge by the middle of May and have almost a full month for climbing before the arrival of the monsoon. Even the most sceptical among them, staring eagerly at the heights above, could not but believe that Everest at last was theirs.

This time, however, misfortune struck even before they reached the mountain.

Scarcely had Camp III been set up below the col than a blizzard swept down from the north, wrecking everything in its path, turning camps and communication lines into a shambles. The porters, many of them caught unprepared and without adequate clothing or shelter, suffered terribly from exposure and exhaustion. Two of them died. The climbers, who were supposed to be conserving their energies for the great effort higher up, wore themselves out in their efforts to save men and supplies. Two weeks after the vanguard had left the base camp, full of strength and optimism, they were back again where they started, frostbitten, battered and fagged out.

A major blow had been dealt their chances for success, but the Everesters pulled in their belts and went at it again. The porters' drooping spirits were raised by a blessing from the Holy Lama of the Rongbuk Monastery, and a few days later a second assault was begun. At the beginning all went well, and the three glacier camps were re-established and provisioned in short order. But trouble began again on the great ice-wall beneath the North Col. The storms and avalanches of two years had transformed the thousand-foot face into a wild slanting chaos of cliffs and chasms. No vestige of their former route remained.

Then followed days of killing labour. Thousands of steps had to be chopped in the ice and snow. An almost perpendicular chimney, a hundred feet high, had to be negotiated. Ladders and ropes had to be installed so that the porters could come up with their loads. There were many narrow escapes from disaster, notably on one occasion when Mallory, descending the wall alone, plunged through a snow-bridge into a gaping hole beneath. Luckily his ice-axe jammed against the sides of the crevasse after he had fallen only ten feet, for below him was only blue-black space. As it was, his companions were all too far away to hear his shouts for help and he was barely able to claw his way upward to the surface snow and safety.

At last, however, the route up the wall was completed. The body of climbers retired to Camp III, at its foot, for a much-needed rest, leaving Hazard and twelve porters in the newly established camp on the col. During the night the mercury fell to twenty-four below zero and at dawn a heavy snowfall began; but Geoffrey Bruce and Odell nevertheless decided to ascend to the col. They did not get far. Halfway up they encountered Hazard and eight of the porters coming down. They were near collapse after the night of frightful cold and wind on the exposed col. Worse yet, four of the porters were still up above, having absolutely refused to budge downward over the treacherous fresh snow of the chimney.

A sombre council of war ensued at Camp III. Snow and wind were now driving down the mountain in wild blasts, and it was obvious that the marooned men could not survive for long. All plans had to be set aside and every effort devoted to getting them down.

What followed constitutes one of the most remarkable and courageous rescues in mountaineering annals. Mallory, Norton and Somervell, the three outstanding climbers of the expedition, fought their way up the ice-wall and came out at last upon a steep snow-slope a short distance below the top and immediately above a gaping crevasse. At the top of the slope the porters huddled, half-dead from exposure, but afraid to move. The snow between them and the rescuing party was loose and powdery, liable to crumble away at any moment.

At this point Somervell insisted on taking the lead. Roping up, he crept toward the porters along the upper lip of the crevasse, while Mallory and Norton payed out behind him.

But the rope's two hundred feet were not enough; when he had reached its end he was still ten yards short of the men. There was nothing for it but that they must risk the unbridged stretch on their own. After long persuasion two of them began edging across. And made it. Somervell passed them along the rope to Mallory and Norton. Then the other two started over, but at their first step the snow gave way and they began sliding toward the abyss below. Only a patch of solid snow saved them. They brought up at the very edge of the crevasse, gasping, shaken, unable to move an inch.

Now Somervell called into action all his superb talents as a mountaineer. He jammed his ice-axe into the snow and, untying the rope from his waist, passed it around the axe and strained it to its fullest length. Then he lowered himself down the slope until he was clinging to its last strands with one hand. With the other he reached out and, while the snow shuddered ominously underfoot, seized each porter in turn by the scruff of the neck and hauled him up to safety. Within a few hours climbers and porters were back in Camp III, all of them still alive, but little more.

After this harrowing experience a few days' rest at lower altitudes was absolutely necessary, and for the second time in two weeks the Everesters found themselves driven back to the base camp. Their situation could scarcely have been more discouraging. They had planned to be on the north-east ridge by the middle of May, and now it was already June and no man had yet set foot on the mountain proper. In another ten days, at most, the monsoon would blow in and all hope of success would be gone. They must strike hard and strike fast or go down again to defeat.

The next week witnessed climbing such as the world had never seen before.

The plan called for an assault in continuous waves, each climbing party consisting of two men, each attempt to begin the day after the preceding one. The base of operations was to be Camp IV on the North Col. Camp V was to be set up on the ridge, near the site of the 1922 bivouac, and a sixth camp higher yet—as near to the summit as the porters could possibly take it. The climbers believed that the establishment of Camp VI was the key to the ascent; the experiences of the previous expedition had convinced them that the top could be reached only if the final "dash" were reduced to not more than 2,000 feet. In the first fine weather they had experienced in weeks the band of determined men struggled back up the glaciers.

Mallory and Geoffrey Bruce were chosen for the first attack. With Odell, Irvine and nine porters they reached the North Col safely, spent the night there, and the next morning struck out up the ridge, accompanied by eight of the "tigers." Odell, Irvine and one helper remained on the col in support. The climbers made good progress the first day and set up their tents at 25,300 feet—a mere 200 feet lower than the highest camp of 1922. A night of zero cold and shrieking wind, however, was too much for the porters, and the next morning no amount of persuasion would induce them to go higher. Seething with frustration, Mallory and Bruce were forced to descend with them.

Meanwhile the second team of Norton and Somervell, had started up from the col, according to plan. They passed the first party on its way down, reached Camp V and spent the night there. In the morning their porters, too, refused at first to go on, but after four solid hours of urging three of them at last agreed to make a try. The work they subsequently did that day has seldom been matched anywhere for endurance, courage and loyalty. Step by gasping step they struggled upward with their packs—freezing, leaden-footed, choking for air—until at last Camp VI was pitched at the amazing altitude of 26,800 feet. Their task completed, they then descended to the North Col, to be hailed as heroes by all below: Lhakpa, Chede, Napoo Yishay and Semchumbi, greatest of all "tigers."

That night Norton and Somervell slept in a single tiny tent, higher than men had ever slept before. Their hearts now were pounding with more than the mere physical strain of their exertions: the long dreamed-of summit loomed in the darkness only 2,300 feet above them; victory was at last within their reach. Carefully, for the hundredth time, they reviewed their plans for the final day. There were two opinions in the expedition as to the best route to be followed. Mallory and some of the others were in favour of ascending straight to the northeast shoulder and then following the crest of the main east ridge to the base of the summit pyramid. Norton and Somervell, however, believed that by keeping a few hundred feet below the ridge they would not only find easier climbing, but also escape the full fury of the west wind; and it was this route that they now determined to take.

Dawn of the next day broke clear and still. By full sunrise they were on their way, creeping upward and to the west over steeply tilted, snow-powdered slabs. As they had hoped, they were protected from the wind, but the cold was bitter and both men coughed and gasped in the thin, freezing air. They could take only a dozen steps in succession before pausing to rest. While moving, they were forced to take from four to ten breaths for each single step. Yet they kept going for five hours: to 27,000 feet—27,500—28,000——

At noon Somervell succumbed. His throat was a throbbing knot of pain and it was only by the most violent effort that he was able to breathe at all. Another few minutes of the ordeal would have been the end of him. Sinking down on a small ledge in a paroxysm of coughing, he gestured to his companion to go on alone.

With the last ounce of his strength Norton tried. An hour's climbing brought him to a great couloir, or gully, which cuts the upper slopes of Everest between the summit pyramid and the precipices of the north face below. The couloir was filled with soft, loose snow, and a slip would have meant a 10,000-foot plunge to the Rongbuk Glacier. Norton crossed it safely, but, clinging feebly to the ledges on the far side, he knew that the game was up. His head and heart were pounding as if any moment they might literally explode. In addition, he had begun to see double, and his leaden feet would no longer move where his will directed them. In his clouded consciousness he was just able to realize that to climb farther would be to die.

For a few moments Norton stood motionless. He was at an altitude of 28,126 feet—higher than any man had ever stood[7] before; so high that the greatest mountain range on earth, spreading endlessly to the horizon, seemed flattened out beneath him. Only a few yards above him began the culminating pyramid of Everest. To his aching eyes it seemed to present an easy slope—a mere thousand feet of almost snow-free slanting rock beckoning him upward to the shining goal. If only his body possessed the strength of his will; if only he were more than human——

Somehow Norton and Somervell got down the terrible slopes of Everest. By nine-thirty that night they were back in the North Col camp in the ministering hands of their companions, safe, but more dead than alive. Somervell was a seriously sick man. Norton was suffering the tortures of snow-blindness and did not regain his sight for several days. Both had given all they had. That it was not enough is surely no reflection on two of the most determined and courageous mountaineers who ever lived.

Norton and Somervell's assault was the next-to-last in the adventure of 1924. One more was to come—and, with it, mystery and tragedy.

Bitterly chagrined at the failure of his first effort, Mallory was determined to have one last fling before the monsoon struck. Everest was *his* mountain, more than any other man's. He had pioneered the way to it and blazed the trail to its heights; his flaming spirit had been the principal driving force behind each assault; the conquest of the summit was the great dream of his life. His companions, watching him now, realized that he was preparing for his mightiest effort.

Mallory moved with characteristic speed. With young Andrew Irvine as partner he started upward from the col the day after Norton and Somervell had descended. They spent the first night at Camp V and the second at Camp VI, at 26,800 feet. Unlike Norton and Somervell, they planned to use oxygen on the final dash and to follow the crest of the north-east ridge instead of traversing the north face to the couloir. The ridge appeared to present more formidable climbing difficulties than the lower route, particularly near the base of the summit pyramid where it buckled upward in two great rock-towers which the Everesters called the First and Second Steps. Mallory, however, was all for the frontal attack and had frequently expressed the belief that the steps could be surmounted. The last "tigers" descending that night from the highest camp to the col brought word that both climbers were in good condition and full of hope for success.

One man only was to have another glimpse of Mallory and Irvine.

On the morning of June eighth—the day set for the assault on the summit—Odell, the geologist, who had spent the night alone at Camp V, set out for Camp VI with a rucksack of food. The day was as warm and windless as any the expedition had experienced, but a thin grey mist clung to the upper reaches of the mountain, and Odell could see little of what lay above him. Presently, however, he scaled the top of a small crag at about 26,000 feet, and, standing there, he stopped and stared. For a moment the mist cleared. The whole summit ridge and final pyramid of Everest were unveiled, and high above him, on the very crest of the ridge, he saw two tiny figures outlined against the sky. They appeared to be at the base of one of the great steps, not more than seven or eight hundred feet below the final pinnacle. As Odell watched, the figures moved slowly upward. Then, as suddenly as it had parted, the mist closed in again, and they were gone.

The feats of endurance that Odell performed during the next forty-eight hours are unsurpassed by those of any mountaineer. That same day he went to Camp VI with his load of provisions, and then even higher, watching and waiting. But the mountain-top remained veiled in mist and there was no sign of the climbers returning. As night came on, he descended all the way to the col, only to start off again the following dawn. Camp V was empty. He spent a solitary night there in sub-zero cold and the next morning ascended again to Camp VI. It was empty too. With sinking heart he struggled upward for another thousand feet, searching and shouting, to the very limit of human endurance. The only answering sound was the deep moaning of the wind. The great peak above him loomed bleakly in the sky, wrapped in the loneliness and desolation of the ages. All hope was gone. Odell descended to the highest camp and signalled the tidings of tragedy to the watchers far below.

So ended the second attempt on Everest—and, with it, the lives of two brave men. The bodies of George Mallory and Andrew Irvine lie somewhere in the vast wilderness of rock and ice that guards the summit of the world. Where and how death overtook them no one knows. And whether victory came before the end no one knows either. Our last glimpse of them is through Odell's eyes—two tiny specks against the sky, fighting upward.

The rest is mystery.

The story of Everest from 1924 onward continues as it began. The greatest mountain still works its magic on the imaginations of men, and the fight for its conquest goes on. Again and again, through the 'thirties, bands of brave and determined climbers have come to challenge it, struggling through the passes and gorges of the Himalayas, penetrating its inner fastnesses along the great glaciers, storming the North Col, creeping doggedly upward through wind and blizzard and avalanche. Each successive expedition has added something to the store of man's knowledge. Some have performed feats of unexcelled skill and endurance. But every one has failed of its goal. All the determination of the human spirit, all the ingenuity of science, have not yet been able to get a man up the final thousand feet of that gleaming, snow-plumed summit—and down.

For nine years after the 1924 assault no climbers approached Everest. Tibet again closed its gates rigidly to white men, and it was not until 1933 that permission was once more granted for an expedition to try its luck. By this time most of the veterans of the previous attempts were too old for another ordeal on the mountain, but a capable team of younger climbers was assembled by the Mount Everest Committee. The new leader was Hugh Ruttledge, an experienced Himalayan climber. Among the others were Frank S. Smythe, Eric Shipton and Captain Birnie, whom we have met on Kamet, Kanchenjunga and elsewhere; Wyn Harris, L. R. Wager,

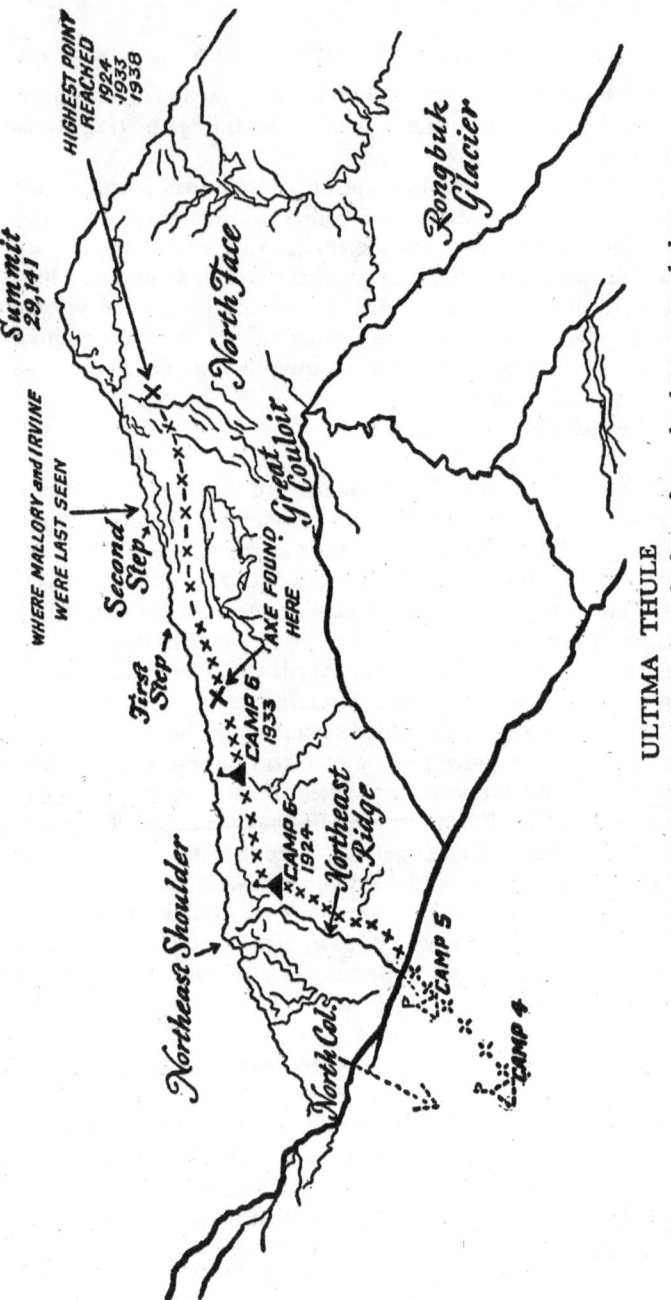

ULTIMA THULE

The upper north face of Everest as seen by telephoto from the base camp below. The routes and camps of the highest climbers are shown in the corresponding diagram.

J. L. Longland and T. A. Brocklebank—most of them still in their twenties, but all among the most capable mountaineers of their generation.

Following the by now traditional route, the 1933 party battled its way along the glaciers, up the ice-wall to the North Col, and established its higher camps close to the north-east ridge. From Camp VI, at 27,400 feet—600 feet above the highest previous bivouac—two successive assaults were made on the summit. The first, by Harris and Wager, carried across the brow of the north face to the far side of the great couloir and ended, with both men near collapse, at almost the identical spot at which Norton had turned back nine years before. The second, by Shipton and Smythe, got no farther. Shipton succumbed to the effects of altitude soon after leaving Camp VI, and was forced to descend, while Smythe, struggling on alone, reached the end of his endurance just beyond the couloir, as had the others before him. It seemed almost as if Everest were ringed by a magic wall a thousand feet beneath the summit, beyond which no man could venture and live.

A dramatic discovery was made by Harris and Wager an hour's climb above Camp VI. On the tilted slabs just below the summit ridge they came suddenly upon a solitary, rusted ice-axe. The name of the Swiss maker, still plainly stamped on its head, left no possibility of doubt as to how it had come there: it was either Mallory's or Irvine's. Some mountaineers have claimed this to be an indication that Mallory and Irvine reached the top. Odell, they argue, saw them at a point much farther along the ridge; neither climber, presumably, would have attempted to go on without his axe, and the logical supposition, therefore, is that it was dropped in an accident on the way down. Others merely shrug their shoulders. Whatever one chooses to believe, there is no proof. The axe is no more than a tantalizing hint at the fate of the lost climbers.

The 1933 Everesters were favoured by no better weather than their predecessors. Immediately after Smythe and Shipton's "all out" attempt, the monsoon struck in a fury of blizzards and all further climbing was out of the question. The expedition had accomplished notable work and suffered not a single fatality or serious accident. But the world's climbing record was still 28,126 feet, and Everest was still 29,141 feet high.

For many years men had looked longingly upward at the summit of the highest mountain. Now, in the same year as the third climbing expedition, men were to look *down* upon it.

Almost since the beginning of aviation airmen had been considering the possibilities of a flight over Everest, and in April of 1933 the first attempt was made. It was completely successful. Under the leadership of the Marquis of Clydesdale (now the Duke of Hamilton) and Air-commodore Fellowes of the Royal Air Force two specially designed planes took off from Purnea, in northern India, and reached the peak in a mere hour. A treacherous down-current of wind almost crashed them against the slopes of the summit pyramid, but at the last moment they succeeded in gaining sufficient altitude to clear it. Then, fortunately, the weather improved, and they spent the next fifteen minutes circling the pinnacle, making observations and taking close-range photographs. In another hour they were safely back at their airport.

A remarkable flying achievement in itself, the flight was of importance to mountaineers chiefly in that it confirmed their belief that the topmost thousand feet of Everest did not present impossible climbing difficulties—provided a human being could reach them with any strength or breath left in his body. The highest pinnacle, viewed from above, was a gentle crest of white, windblown snow. No human relic could be seen.

The year 1934 saw only one short-lived attempt on the mountain—an attempt so foolhardy and hopeless that it appears less an actual climbing venture than an elaborate suicide. The would-be climber was Maurice Wilson, an English aviator who had never been on a high peak in his life. Like the ill-fated Farmer on Kanchenjunga, he smuggled himself into the forbidden regions of the Himalayas, hired a handful of natives to pack his supplies and launched a one-man assault on the mountain. Somehow he succeeded in struggling up the glaciers, but cold and exhaustion caught up with him below the ice-cliffs of the North Col. His body was discovered and buried the following spring.

In 1935 and 1936 the real Everesters returned to the wars. Because of long delays in gaining the sanction of the Tibetan government only a reconnaissance was undertaken the first year,[1] but in late April of '36 a full-fledged climbing party was once more at the Rongbuk base camp, ready for battle. Ruttledge was again the leader, and the climbing personnel was virtually the same as in 1933.

The earlier expeditions had had bad luck with the weather; this one had no luck at all. Wind-storms, blizzards and avalanches thundered down upon them from the first day on, and—crowning blow—the monsoon blew up from the south a full month earlier than expected. After a few hairbreadth escapes on the crumbling death-trap of the North Col, the climbers were forced to withdraw without having even set foot on the mountain itself.

In 1938 came still another expedition—the seventh and, to date, the last. The leadership had passed on to H. W. Tilman, of Nanda Devi fame, but several of the old guard were again on hand—notably Smythe, Shipton and the veteran Odell, now well on into middle age, yet back for another try after fourteen years.

The venture was favoured by slightly better weather than its predecessors. The North Col was reached in short order, the north-east ridge ascended, and Camp VI pitched at 27,000 feet. Beyond it, however, the climbers came up against the same invincible defences that had defeated every previous effort; and with the same result. Two summit assaults were launched —the first by the old team of Smythe and Shipton, the second by Tilman and young Peter Lloyd, who had climbed with him on Nanda Devi. In each case, however, the climbers were turned back short of the final pyramid by exhaustion, oncoming darkness and the slanting, snow-powdered slabs of

---

[1] The 1935 expedition, however, performed many remarkable feats, among them the ascent of more peaks of over 22,000 feet than had ever been climbed before.

the north face. Then, before they could reorganize their forces for still another try, the monsoon struck, putting an end to their hopes.

So stands the fight for Everest up to the present time. Seven great expeditions have come and challenged, struggled and failed. Many brave men, white and brown, have lost their lives. And the summit of the greatest mountain still soars into the sky, untouched and unconquered.

What will happen in the years to come, no man knows. Much has been learned from experience; still many "ifs" and "buts" remain. In general, however, future expeditions will be confronted with the same factors and problems as those of the past. Briefly, these are:

1. *Weather*—Except for a few weeks in the late spring and early fall Everest is unapproachable. Any attempt during a spring in which the monsoon arrives early will be doomed to failure. Some mountaineers believe that an attempt should be made in the fall, after the monsoon and before winter sets in, but this has not yet been tried.

2. *Transport and supplies*—The climbers must obviously be well-fed, sheltered and equipped. This involves the packing of vast quantities of supplies over hundreds of miles of wild, mountainous country, and an elaborate and effective transportation system is essential. It has been suggested that a system of pulleys and conveyors might be established on the ice-wall below the North Col, to hoist loads up this particularly difficult stretch. Most mountaineers, however, are opposed on principle to artificial aids of this sort.

3. *Porters*—The most ingenious system of transport is useless without the proper quantity and quality of man power. Thanks to the earlier expeditions, a corps of first-class, trained "tigers" is now available, and less difficulty should be experienced with porters in the future than has been the case in the past. All Everesters agree that the higher the advanced camps are pitched, the better the chances for success. The establishment of these camps depends almost entirely on the spirit and endurance of the porters.

4. *Climbing personnel*—The conquest of Everest cannot be achieved by any individual, however skilled and daring. An expedition must function harmoniously, as a unit, with the ambitions and wishes of each man subordinated to the welfare of the whole. The party should be neither so large as to be unwieldy, nor so small that the illness or injury of one or two members would ruin the entire undertaking.

5. *Acclimatization*—Experience has shown that men can live and move at a height of more than 28,000 feet. Before they can do this, however, they must have a period for acclimatization, in which their lungs and hearts become accustomed to functioning at increasingly higher altitudes. On the other hand, it has been found that if a man spends too long a period at high altitudes severe bodily deterioration sets in. Individuals vary greatly in the degree and speed of acclimatization.

6. *Oxygen*—Some Everesters have found oxygen a great help to them on the heights; others consider it worse than useless. All agree that no satisfactory apparatus—sufficiently light and yet dependable—has yet been devised. The conquest of the summit will be a more noteworthy triumph if it can be made without artificial aids.

7. *Route*—Every Everest expedition to date has attacked the peak by way of the East Rongbuk Glacier, the North Col and the north-east ridge. On the basis of present knowledge, this still appears to be the only practicable approach. On the upper mountain, most mountaineers favour Norton's route across the north face to the great couloir as against Mallory's route along the summit edge.

8. *Political considerations*—Last but not least, there is the problem of even gaining *permission* to attack Everest. To date, the Tibetan government has granted permission infrequently, and then only to expeditions of all-English personnel. It is to be hoped that in the future these restrictions will be modified, so that climbers of other nations may have their chance at the mountain.

A formidable array of problems and obstacles! Yet, in spite of all of them and a hundred more, the fight for Everest will go on. When and how the mountain will be climbed is the secret of the future, but that it *will* be climbed is sure—as sure as that the oceans have been crossed, the continents spanned, the poles discovered. Perhaps the victory will be won on the next attempt, perhaps not for generations. But still men will come, and more men, and at last the day will come when the weather is right and the mountain is right and the men are right, and those men will get to the top.

Meanwhile, there is something better than victory—something that should make us almost thankful that the summit of the world has not yet been trodden by the foot of man. For until that happens Everest is more than the highest mountain. It is one of the great unfinished adventures of mankind.

PART III

XI

OUR OWN HIGH PLACES

MOUNTAINS AND MOUNTAINEERING IN NORTH AMERICA

MOUNTAINEERING IS SCARCELY an activity for stay-at-homes. The world's great peaks and ranges are scattered over the map with a haughty disregard for the law of supply and demand, and no latter-day Mohammed has had any better luck in moving them than did the original. Man must still go to the mountain, and as often as not it is not only thousands of feet to its summit but thousands of miles to its base.

This is all well and good for the armchair mountaineer. Exploration and adventure are his for the opening of a book, and the pages carry him, as on a magic carpet, to the far and little-known corners of the earth. But what of those of us who want to do more than read? What of those of us who want to *climb ourselves?* A summer's jaunt to Uganda or Peru is not precisely a simple undertaking; an elaborate expedition to Kashmir or Tibet is apt to present a few too many problems. Our climbing, if any, must be done on a more modest scale and nearer home. Fortunately for us, great peaks and ranges are not a monopoly of the other side of the world. "From every mountainside let freedom ring" is not from the national anthem of the Hindus, Nepalese or Tierra del Fuegans: our own country and continent have their mountains too.

And they are mountains of which we may well be proud. True, they are not so high as the Himalayas or Andes, nor so famous in mountaineering history as the Alps, but in extent and variety, sweep and grandeur, they need take second place to none. From the Arctic Ocean to sun-blistered Panama, from Arizona's buttes and mesas to New England's friendly green hills, they march in rank after rank, range after range—a skyline frontier of almost untouched wilderness above our whirring twentieth-century world of men and machines.

It would be a good thing if more Americans raised their eyes to their mountains. Freedom rings from their sides, says the song. Beauty and strength and high adventure are there too, for those who would seek them.

The mountains of western North America are part of the longest continuous highland region on earth. Beginning in far north-west Alaska, almost within sight of the headlands of Siberia, an endless chain of peaks and ranges sweeps south and east down the huge curve of the Pacific Ocean. It covers all of southern and eastern Alaska, vast areas of western Canada, and, broadening as it descends, spreads for a million square miles over the western third of the United States. In north-western Mexico it thins and flattens out, but rises again in the great volcanic highlands of the south and continues, with only a few breaks, through Central America to Panama. There it merges with the northernmost spurs of the Andes, which continue the uplift along the entire length of South America, from Colombia to Cape Horn.

This gigantic highland region is almost 10,000 miles in length —more than three-quarters the distance between pole and pole. It covers approximately twenty per cent of the entire area of two continents. To be sure, it is divided into hundreds of ranges and sub-ranges, each with its own geological structure, its own climate, drainage and configuration; but fundamentally it forms a single connected chain or cordillera. McKinley, in Alaska, and Sarmiento, beyond the Straits of Magellan, are literally half a world apart. Rainier and Aconcagua, the Canadian Rockies and the Sierra Madres of Mexico may seem as remote and disparate from each other as any mountains can well be. But in the most basic sense they are only parts of a greater whole: vertebrae in the enormous rugged spine of the western hemisphere.

The mountains of Alaska, like everything else in that land of superlatives, are on the grand scale. Mount McKinley, as we have seen, is the highest peak in North America. Scores of its neighbours, too, are giants in their own right, and present as formidable obstacles to would-be climbers as any mountains in the world. Some have already been conquered; many more have yet to feel the first bootprint upon their icy flanks. Their heights are defended not only by altitude and cold, but by a remoteness from civilization that makes it a major undertaking even to reach their bases. Food and equipment must be packed in over miles of wilderness; base camps and high camps must be established; vast areas of almost unknown terrain must be explored. Mountaineering here is far more than a matter of mere climbing. It is pioneering and exploration as well.

The Alaskan mountains, whether they lie north or south of the Arctic Circle, are in every sense arctic mountains. Their rocky cores lie buried beneath enormous masses of ice and snow, and the glaciers that spill down from their slopes and fill the valleys between are far and away the largest in the world, outside of the Polar ice-caps. The Malaspina Glacier, which descends to the Pacific near Mount St. Elias, is 1,500 square miles in area; the Hubbard, farther east, is over ninety miles long, and many others such as the Muir, the Childs and the Miles are on a scale so vast as to make the famous glaciers of the Swiss Alps seem miniatures in comparison. Pushing up them toward the inner fastnesses of the mountains, men reckon their journeys not in hours or days, but in weeks.

The peaks themselves comprise eight more or less separate ranges, or groups of ranges, strung out in a tremendous broken arc between the Yukon River, to the north, and the Pacific Ocean, to the south. Proceeding roughly from west to east, they are:

The Aleutian Range—Wholly unlike any of the other Alaskan ranges, in that it is composed almost entirely of active volcanos. Among these is Mount Katmai, whose cataclysmic eruption in 1912 shattered the north wall of McKinley, hundreds of miles away. The area around it, a great steaming terrain of fissures and lava beds, is known as the Valley of Ten Thousand Smokes and has recently been designated as a National Park by the United States Government. Much of the exploration and mountaineering of the noted "glacier priest," Father Hubbard, has been done in this range.

The Alaska Range—The gigantic uplift of south-central Alaska, of which McKinley is king. Closest rival of "The Great One" is Mount Foraker, fourteen miles to the south-west, whose 17,000 feet make it the third highest Alaskan mountain. Other important summits are Mount Hunter (14,900 feet), Mount Hayes (13,750) and the Cathedral Peaks (c. 12,500). The region to the east of McKinley is still little known and contains hundreds of unmapped, unnamed peaks.

The Nutzotin Range—A continuation of the Alaska Range, curving south-east along the basin of the Tanana River. None of the mountains of this group exceed 10,000 feet, but the country is extremely wild and rough. It is as yet little known to mountaineers.

The Chugach Range—A region of tremendous glaciers and snowfields, bordering the coast to the north-east of the Kenai Peninsula. Many of its peaks are believed to be more than 12,000 feet in height, but most of them have been neither climbed nor mapped.

The Wrangell Range—Extending from north-west to south-east between the Nutzotin and Chugach groups, but easier to reach than either of the others, by way of the Copper River. There have been several mountaineering exploits in this range, and its three highest peaks have been ascended.

The St. Elias Range—The mightiest mountain-group in North America—exceeding even the McKinley uplift in everything except the altitude of its topmost summit. Its two greatest peaks are Mount Logan (19,850 feet) and Mount St. Elias (18,024 feet), respectively the second and fourth highest mountains of the continent. The range straddles the international boundary between Alaska and Yukon Territory, its eastern section, including Logan, lying wholly in Canada. The western peaks front on the Pacific and were first seen and described by the earliest explorers of the Alaskan coast. Mount St. Elias, indeed, was named as early as 1778 by the famous British navigator, Captain James Cook; but it was not until a full century later that men penetrated up the great Malaspina Glacier and its tributaries into the hidden, ice-shrouded wilderness surrounding Mount Logan. In addition to Logan and St. Elias, this range contains a host of other great peaks, several of them rising straight up from the coastal bays and fiords. It has been the scene of many of the greatest Alaskan mountaineering exploits.

The Fairweather Range—A southerly continuation of the St. Elias uplift, but lying wholly in Alaska. It is topped by 15,300-foot Mount Fairweather, which has long been one of the famous landmarks of the Alaskan coast.

The Mountains of the Alaskan Panhandle—South of Mount Fairweather the mountains extend in a broken chain along the lower coastal strip of Alaska, becoming lower as they go and gradually merging with the Coast Range of British Columbia. This region contains the historic Chilkoot Pass, over which the great hordes of prospectors struggled in the Klondike gold rush of 1896.

Great mountains, as we have seen repeatedly, are seldom climbed by the men who live near them or by the first pioneers into the regions in which they stand. Such men are usually engaged in too stern a battle with the prime necessities of life—finding food, building shelters, getting to their destination—to go out of their way to seek unnecessary hardship and adventure. This was the case in Alaska, where the early explorers and settlers left the great peaks strictly alone and the nineteenth century had all but passed before the earliest mountaineering ventures were launched. First of the major peaks to be attempted was Mount St. Elias, rising like a great white beacon from the very shores of the Pacific. The approaches to its heights were pioneered in 1890 and 1891 by an American university professor, Dr. Israel Russell; but the summit barely escaped him, and it remained for the Duke of the Abruzzi, at the head of a large and well-equipped expedition from faraway Italy, to carry the campaign to its successful conclusion. St. Elias fell to him in 1897, in one of the outstanding ascents of mountaineering history, and climbers everywhere began turning their eyes to the other lofty snowpeaks of the north-west.

Qa

The result was that during the past forty years Alaska and the neighbouring Yukon Territory of Canada have been the scene of as persistent and successful climbing as any wilderness mountain region in the world. We have already followed the stern battle for McKinley, which fell at last in 1913 to the resolute Archdeacon Stuck and his companions. Five years earlier Mount Wrangell (14,000 feet), an active volcano in the range of the same name, was ascended by Robert Dunn and William Soule, and in 1912 the nearby Mount Blackburn (16,140 feet), also in the Wrangells, was conquered in a remarkable ascent led by a woman, Miss Dora Keen. In the same year as McKinley, Mount Natazhat (13,450 feet), in the St. Elias Range, was climbed by members of the Canadian Boundary Survey, and the following decade witnessed the ascent of several other virgin peaks and the exploration of great areas of theretofore wholly unknown country. Then, in 1925, came one of the truly memorable feats of mountaineering history—the conquest of Mount Logan.

Second only to McKinley in all of North America, this colossus among mountains lies in such wild, inaccessible country that its existence was not even suspected until 1890. Seven years later the Duke of the Abruzzi and his companions gazed at it in awe from the summit of Mount St. Elias, but more than a quarter of a century was still to pass before men even approached its base. Then at last, in 1924, Captain A. H. MacCarthy, a noted Canadian climber, and H. F. Lambart, of the Canadian Boundary Survey, pioneered a way to its lower slopes, and the following year, under MacCarthy's leadership, a strong expedition of Canadian and American mountaineers set out to climb and conquer.

The first step was a remarkable expedition by MacCarthy and a renowned sourdough guide named Andy Taylor, who in the dead of winter, before the arrival of the rest of the party, fought their way up the great glaciers to the base of the mountain and established a long chain of camps and supply depots. This operation alone required seventy days of toil in sub-zero temperatures. In late May the expedition proper began, with nine men participating. In addition to MacCarthy, Lambart and Taylor, they included Colonel W. W. Foster, Norman Read and A. M. Laing, Canadian climbers, and Henry S. Hall, Jr., Robert Morgan and Allan Carpé, Americans.[1]

The ensuing struggle for Mount Logan was fraught with adventure and hardship almost without parallel, even in a field of human activity where such things are taken for granted. The climbers were their own porters, and each man carried a load of seventy pounds on his back, day after day, week after week. From the time they left timberline behind, at a mere three-thousand-foot altitude, they remained on ice and snow for forty-four consecutive days, without once setting foot on rock or earth. Worst of all, they were lashed by relentless blizzards and windstorms. Their undertaking combined the problems and hazards of mountaineering with virtually all the difficulties of polar exploration.

Logan, unlike McKinley, is not a single, isolated peak, but almost a range in itself—more than twenty miles in length along the line of its summit ridge. Starting from the King Glacier, which pours down from the western flank of the mountain, MacCarthy and his companions found a way to this ridge, but once there, at a height of 14,500 feet, they were still separated from their goal not merely by a mile of vertical distance but by a seemingly endless succession of intervening peaks and cols. Over this jagged white skyline they proceeded to fight their way. Day followed day while they hacked steps in the ice and floundered in snowdrifts up to their armpits. Almost each morning brought with it a fresh blizzard; at night the temperature frequently fell to as low as thirty below zero. But slowly they advanced, following the ridge up and down and then up again, and at last succeeded in pitching a tent at an altitude of 18,500 feet. This tiny shelter, known as the Eighteen-Five Camp, is still the highest ever made in North America.

The final dash from here to the summit and back was nothing less than a race with death. At 4.30 in the afternoon of June twenty-third six of the climbers emerged on what they believed to be the highest pinnacle of the ridge, only to behold

[1] It was Carpé whose brilliant climbing career was to end tragically and mysteriously on McKinley in 1932.

a still higher summit three long miles ahead. Night was coming on, and storm clouds were piling up ominously over Mount St. Elias, to the south-west; but the climbers were resolved that nothing would stop them now. For three and a half hours more they crept onward and upward, their hands and feet frozen numb, their lungs burning for want of air. And at last, at eight in the evening, victory was theirs: they were standing, the first of all men, on the 19,850-foot summit of Mount Logan, the highest point of all Canada and the second highest of the continent.

Not one among them, however, had the strength left to feel elation at their triumph, so severe had been their ordeal. And the ordeal had just begun. No sooner had they started the descent than the long-threatened storm closed in, and when darkness fell they were groping blindly in a blizzard. For more than an hour they floundered through the great drifts of the ridge, only to discover at last, to their horror, that they had not been heading toward camp at all, but back again toward the summit. Close to exhaustion and afraid to retrace their steps lest they plunge themselves 10,000 feet to the glacier below, they burrowed into the snow and huddled together through the murky twilight of the arctic night. In the morning the blizzard was still raging, but to remain where they were longer meant quick and certain death. On the ascent Andy Taylor had farsightedly planted a series of willow wands to mark the route, and they were now barely able to struggle from one to another as they descended. Reaching the Eighteen-Five Camp toward evening, they found it a shambles, but were luckily able to salvage some food and supplies. Then they spent a second night in the open.

The third day was again a nightmare of wind, snow and cold. By this time all the men were severely frostbitten, and some of them would have been unable to go on if their stronger companions, notably MacCarthy and Taylor, had not found the strength to help them. The faces and beards of all of them were so coated with ice that they could not recognize one another from a few feet away. Still they groped, floundered and hacked their way along the ridge, passing the ruins of their previous camps, stopping only when exhaustion compelled. This time they kept going not only all day but all the next night, for they knew that if they lay down to sleep again it would be never to awaken. And at last, more dead than alive, they reached their glacier base camp, just as the terrible three-day blizzard was blowing itself out. This camp had been wrecked, like all the others, but they managed to eke some warm food and shelter from the debris and a few days later were strong enough to begin the long trek toward civilization. They had achieved one of the genuinely great feats in mountaineering history. It was not their victory, however, that was in their thoughts as they turned their backs on tempest-crowned Logan; rather was it wonder and thankfulness that they had lived to tell the tale.

Logan climbed is far less alluring, though no less formidable, than Logan unclimbed, and since 1925 no mountaineers have approached it. Throughout the rest of Alaska and the Yukon, however, there has been much activity in recent years, and almost every succeeding summer has seen the conquest of one or more great peaks. Notable first ascents have been made, among others, of the following:

Mount Bona (16,420 feet)—in the St. Elias Range. Climbed in 1930 by Allan Carpé, Andy Taylor and Terris Moore.

Mount Fairweather (15,300 feet)—the famous coastal peak in the range of the same name. Climbed in 1931 by Carpé and Moore, after two previous attempts had failed.

Mount Foraker (17,000 feet)—second peak of the Alaska Range, in the shadow of Mount McKinley. Climbed in 1934 by a mixed party of American and English climbers. Its leader was the young American physician, Dr. Charles Houston, who was later to distinguish himself on Nanda Devi and K2.

Mount Crillon (12,725 feet)—a neighbour of Fairweather, in the coastal chain of south-eastern Alaska. Climbed in 1934, by a Harvard-Dartmouth party, after preliminary reconnaissances in 1932 and 1933. The leader of this expedition was Bradford Washburn, of Boston, whose subsequent activities have made him the foremost Alaskan explorer and mountaineer of the present day.

Mount Steele (16,400 feet)—in the eastern part of the St. Elias Range. Climbed in 1935 by an expedition headed by Walter A. Wood, of New York. In the same year a National Geographic Society expedition, under Washburn's leadership, made a detailed winter survey of the range, but attempted no high ascents.

Mount Lucania (17,150 feet)—one of the giants of the St. Elias Range; the second highest mountain in Canada and fourth highest in the Alaska-Yukon region. Climbed in 1937 by Washburn and Robert Bates. In descending from Lucania toward the east, they also accomplished the second ascent of Mount Steele.

Mount St. Agnes (13,250 feet)—in the little-known Chugach Range. Climbed in 1938 by Washburn, Norman Dyhrenfurth, Norman Bright and Peter Gabriel.

Mount Sanford (16,210 feet)—highest summit of the Wrangell Range. Climbed in 1938 by Washburn and Moore. At the time Sanford was the highest unconquered peak in North America. Its ascent was of an unusual nature in that it was accomplished largely on skis.

Mount Bertha (10,182 feet)—in the Fairweather Range. Climbed in 1940 by another Washburn expedition, which included the leader's wife.

Not the least result of these numerous Alaskan expeditions has been the development of a group of ardent and expert American mountaineers. Climbers like Washburn and Moore, Houston, Bates and Wood—to name only a few—are no mere haphazard adventurers, out to "do" a peak and then forget it. They have explored, studied and mapped as they went, and virtually every expedition has added its share to our growing knowledge of America's last great frontier. One of the most important innovations has been the frequent use of airplanes, not only for transporting men and supplies over the tremendous stretches of wilderness, but for reconnoitring and picture-making as well. Some of the finest work yet done in the field of aerial photography has been accomplished over these peaks and glaciers of the remote north-west.

The story of Alaskan mountaineering, however, is still very

much in the writing. Each year brings tales of new mountains climbed, but none except McKinley and Steele has been ascended more than once, and uncounted hundreds remain which have never been attempted at all. Outstanding among the still virgin summits is Mount Wood, in the eastern section of the St. Elias Range, which, at 15,880 feet, is today the highest unclimbed peak in North America. It was attempted in 1939 by Walter Wood and several companions, in an expedition that fell only 1,800 feet short of the summit; and plans are currently being made for a renewed assault, either this year or next. Other great unclimbed peaks are Mount Vancouver (15,700 feet) and Mount Hubbard (14,980 feet), also in the St. Elias Range, and the slightly lower Mount Hunter, in the Alaska Range near McKinley.

The airplane, the aerial camera and the untiring work of many mountaineer-explorers have, in one short decade, accomplished wonders in opening up the great mountain fastnesses of Alaska and the Yukon. But the frontier is not yet gone, and we may rest confident that the day is far off when summer hotels will line the glaciers and peaks like Logan and St. Elias become "an easy day for a lady." Meanwhile the wilderness waits—for anyone who hears its challenge.

Far different from the Alaska-Yukon ranges are the Rocky Mountains of Canada. Extending for some 450 miles along the Alberta-British Columbia boundary, this magnificent chain of peaks has long been familiar to mountaineers, and virtually all its principal summits have been ascended, not only once but many times. Today it represents as close an approach as exists in the Western Hemisphere to the great mountain playground of the Alps.

Large sections of the Canadian Rockies are easily accessible, because the range is cut through, at two widely separated points, by the main transcontinental lines of the Canadian Pacific and Canadian National Railroads. Along these lines are many famous and flourishing summer resorts, notably Banff and Lake Louise on the C.P.R. and Jasper, 150 miles farther north, on the C.N.R. Largely owing to the enterprise of the railroads, trails have been made and camps and shelters established throughout the more frequently visited sections, and in the larger centres all manner of equipment and service —and even trained Swiss guides—are available to climbers. In the summer of 1939 a paved motor-highway was completed between Lake Louise and Jasper, giving easy access to a vast unspoiled region which before could be reached only by long pack trips.

Most of the important first ascents in the Rockies were made between 1890 and 1910, when the gradual opening up of the region attracted the attention of many noted climbers. Not the least of these was Edward Whymper, who at the age of sixty-five, forty years after his conquest of the Matterhorn, had still not lost his love of mountains nor—more remarkable— the strength to climb them. Between 1901 and 1905 he travelled extensively in western Canada, and, although by this time he was less a mountaineer than a legend, he pioneered several lesser peaks and did much to bring this new alpine region to the attention of the public. His ascents there were his last before his death in Chamonix in 1911.

By 1925 virtually every major peak in the range had been ascended, most of them on many occasions and by various routes. There are no giants to compare with McKinley, Logan and their satellites, far to the north-west, but four summits are more than 12,000 feet in height, forty-seven are more than 11,000 and almost seven hundred exceed 10,000. Some idea of the great mountaineering activity in this region may be gleaned from the fact that today not one peak over 11,000 feet remains unclimbed and only a very few of 10,000 or more— these chiefly in the out-lying districts. Most of the well-known summits in the vicinity of the big resorts are ascended many times every summer.

The chain of the Canadian Rockies is divided into almost equal thirds by the two railroad lines. North of Jasper, on the Canadian National, the country is still in a primitive state, and would-be climbers must be prepared for long pack trips and camping under canvas. This region is crowned by Mount Robson (12,972 feet), the monarch of the whole range and one of the most impressive and difficult peaks on the continent. After many unsuccessful attempts by earlier climbers the summit of Robson was first attained in 1913 by A. H. MacCarthy and W. W. Foster, later conquerors of Mount Logan, in company with the famous Austrian guide, Conrad Kain. Since then much reconnoitring has been done on the mountain, but there have been very few complete ascents.

Between Jasper and the Banff-Lake Louise district the range continues in a succession of magnificent massifs. This stretch comprises the heart of the Canadian Rockies, and in it are found the three peaks, besides Robson, which exceed 12,000 feet in height—Mount Columbia, North Twin and Mount Clemenceau—as well as twenty-nine peaks over 11,000 feet. One of the dominating features of the region is the Columbia Icefield, unique among the great watersheds of the continent. Catching the out-flow from scores of glaciers, the vast reservoir drains, in turn, to three different oceans: through the Columbia River to the Pacific, through the Athabasca to the Arctic, and through the Saskatchewan to Hudson Bay and the Atlantic. Until very recently this wilderness of rock and ice had been seen by only a few surveying and mountaineering parties, but today it may be traversed by automobile along the new Jasper-Lake Louise highway.

The region bordering the Canadian Pacific line, in the southern third of the range, is by far the best-known and most frequented district. Hotels and camps abound, and there are facilities for climbing unmatched by those of any other mountain resorts of the continent. Lake Louise is ringed by a magnificent series of peaks which offer climbs of every kind and every degree of difficulty. Among the best-known are Victoria, Lefroy, Temple, Hungabee, Deltaform and Mitre, all but the last more than 11,000 feet high. Mount Louis, a formidable rock spire not far from Banff, is considered one of the most difficult rock climbs in America. Further south, in wilder but easily accessible country, Mount Assiniboine rises in a spectacular, isolated pyramid reminiscent of the Matterhorn. All of these mountains have been climbed many times but, like the famous peaks in the Alps, familiarity has enhanced rather than spoiled their magic.

West of the Rockies and roughly paralleling them are four great mountain chains which are known collectively as the Interior Ranges of British Columbia. Individually they are designated as the Purcell and Selkirk Ranges and the Monishee and Caribou Mountains. Because of their proximity to the Pacific Ocean they receive more rainfall and are more densely forested than the Rockies, and, as a result, are considerably less easy of access. Exploration of the region began only in the 1870's, and it was not until 1916 that it was first visited by mountaineers. In the past few years several of the higher peaks have been ascended, particularly in the Purcells and Selkirks, but plenty of virgin summits remain for the climber who would be a pioneer as well.

Even wilder than the Interior Ranges is the Coast Range of British Columbia, which borders the Pacific for nine hundred miles from the Alaskan Panhandle to Vancouver. The greater part of this chain is an unmapped wilderness of peaks, glaciers and forests, as yet little known to mountaineers. Recently, however, several American and Canadian parties have penetrated its southern portion for exploration and climbing, and in 1936 Mount Waddington (13,280 feet), the highest point of the range, was climbed by Fritz Wiessner and William House, of the American Alpine Club, who were later to win fame on K2. An awe-inspiring steeple of ice-sheathed rock, Waddington was for many years considered a classic example of an unclimbable peak, and its conquest ranks among the outstanding mountaineering feats of the past decade.

So much for the mountains to the north of us. To the south —in Mexico and Central America—there are many peaks and ranges as well, but utterly different in every respect. Forest and glacier, precipice and ice-ridge are gone; in their place are high, arid plateaus, long slopes of sunbaked shale and lava, and the high, symmetrical snow-cones of great volcanoes.

The mountains of Mexico sweep southward from the United

States border in two roughly parallel chains—the Sierra Madre Oriental and the Sierra Madre Occidental. For some 750 miles they attain no great elevation or importance, but in the latitude of Mexico City the chains converge, and here there rises a group of tremendous volcanic peaks. The three principal ones are:

Orizaba (18,225 feet)—the third highest elevation of North America, topped only by McKinley and Logan. Rising from the steaming tropical lowlands near Vera Cruz, its great height and almost perfect symmetry make it one of the most beautiful mountains in the world. Its last eruptive period was between 1545 and 1566, and it is now considered to be extinct. The Aztecs called it Citlaltepetl—"mountain of the star."

Popocatepetl (17,850 feet)—the famous "smoking mountain" of the Valley of Mexico, dominating the horizon of the capital. It is a quiescent, but not extinct, volcano and the fifth highest peak of the continent, only Mount St. Elias coming between it and Orizaba. "Popo," as it is known to all Mexicans, was one of the first of the world's great mountains to be climbed. Cortez partially ascended it in his journey of conquest in 1519, and two years later a group of his soldiers pushed on to the summit to secure sulphur from its crater for the manufacture of gunpowder. This feat established a world's altitude record which endured for almost 300 years—or until the early days of Himalayan exploration.

Ixtaccihuatl (17,300 feet)—the immediate neighbour of "Popo," rising out of the same great volcanic uplift. Its tongue-twisting name—usually mercifully shortened to "Ixta"—is Aztec for "sleeping woman" and derives from the peculiar profile of its long summit ridge. "Ixta" is a thoroughly extinct volcano, not even a crater remaining.

Southern Mexico is largely mountainous country, but with few important peaks. In western Guatemala, however, the Cordillera rises again in a great tangle of volcanic cones. None of them as high as the giants of Mexico—Tajumulco, the loftiest, is about 13,500 feet—but they are far more numerous, and together form one of the most impressive groups of volcanoes in the world. Many of them are active. Beyond

Guatemala various ranges extend south-eastward through the rest of Central America, but the Cordillera does not again attain great heights until Panama is crossed and South America and the Andes begin.

All the major volcanoes of Mexico and Guatemala have long since been climbed. Few of them present any serious mountaineering difficulties other than that of altitude, and, owing to their gentle slopes, the ascent as far as the snow-line can usually be made on horseback. The most interesting feature of their ascents is the startling transition from tropical to arctic weather conditions in a few hours and a few thousand feet.

Between the ice-peaks of Canada and the fire-peaks of Mexico the mountains of the western United States rise in rank after rank from our northern to our southern boundaries and from Central Colorado to the Pacific. Spread over twelve states and a million square miles, they present a continental uplift that, for grandeur, variety and sheer extent, is matched only by the great ranges of inner Asia. The Rocky Mountains, the Sierra Nevadas, the Cascades, vast as they are, are only three among the many great chains that comprise the whole, and they themselves in turn are composed of almost numberless lesser chains and ranges. The Rockies alone, for example, contain more than one hundred separately defined and named groups.

Historically, these mountains have played a tremendous role in the making of our country. There would be no American West, as we know it, without their peaks, canyons and passes, and the great intervening plateaus. Yet we may read the records of a hundred and more years and find next to nothing of mountaineering as such. The explorer and soldier, the trapper, prospector, rancher and railroad-builder: all these have had a dominating part in the winning of the West. Of the climber —of the conquest of the high summits—there is scarcely a word.

The reason is not far to find. Vast though these mountains are, they are for the most part simple in contour and of subdued relief. They are composed of great range-masses rather than of great individual peaks, of rugged, slowly rising highlands rather than steep ridges and sudden, soaring cliffs. To be sure, there are lofty summits aplenty. Colorado alone boasts forty-six surpassing 14,000 feet in height and three hundred of more than 13,000 feet. California has eleven and one-hundred-and-fifty respectively. But there is not a Matterhorn or Robson among them, let alone a Logan or K2. The majority of them were first climbed years ago, by men who had never even heard of the technique of mountaineering, and today all but a few are accessible to anyone willing to make the effort of a stiff uphill walk.

As a result, most of the recent activity in our western mountains has been of the nature of hiking and camping trips rather than of actual climbing. Difficult rock routes, to be sure, may be found on many peaks by one who is searching for them; but there is almost always an easy side, and, except in a few isolated instances, glaciers, precipices and other truly alpine features are wholly lacking. The accomplished mountaineer can find more problems and hazards to test his skill on the 500-foot highlands along the Hudson River than on all of California's Mount Whitney, the highest elevation in the country.[1]

While he would well wish it otherwise, the climber who is after truly big game must go beyond the boundaries of our own country. Those with more modest ambitions, however, need not despair. Our western mountains may offer him no "famous firsts" and few "routes of the sixth degree of difficulty," but they are sound mountains nonetheless—broad and high and beautiful mountains. Tramping them, he will learn that the American out-of-doors is compounded of other things than filling stations, Bar-B-Q stands and clover-leaf intersections. And knowing them, he will perhaps become a truer

[1] Two of the most difficult ascents made in the United States during the past few years were of summits that could by no stretch of imagination be called mountains at all. One was the climbing of Devil's Tower, an almost vertical fluted shaft rising from the prairie of northeastern Wyoming, which was accomplished by Fritz Wiessner, William House, and Laurence Coveny in 1937. The other was the ascent, in 1939, of Shiprock, a sheer volcanic outcropping in the New Mexican desert, by a party from the Sierra Club, of San Francisco. Devil's Tower rises a mere 867 feet above its base, Shiprock only 2,000, but both present far greater climbing problems than most mountains many times their height.

mountaineer than if he had spent a night lashed to the north face of the Matterhorn with sixteen pitons and a prayer.

Climbing is engaged in throughout the United States wherever mountains exist—which means in some thirty-six states from Maine to California. In the following paragraphs only a few peaks and ranges will be dealt with, and those very briefly. The selection has been based not merely on their height or extent, but on their attractiveness to would-be climbers. Almost all of them lie within, or include, areas that have been designated as National Parks or National Forests, and detailed information about them—as well as about many others not included here—may be had from the National Park Service of the Department of the Interior, in Washington.

In the far north-western corner of the country is the Cascade Range, extending for some five hundred miles through the states of Washington and Oregon. It connects the Coast Range of British Columbia, to the north, with the Sierra Nevadas of California, to the south. Its higher summits are volcanic in origin, but all are either extinct or dormant. Receiving the full sweep of the moist Pacific winds, the Cascades are densely forested on their lower slopes and, higher up, possess the largest glaciers and snowfields to be found in the country. King of the range is Mount Rainier, near Seattle, a magnificent snow-dome whose 14,408 feet make it the third highest mountain in the United States. Rainier is famous not only as a peak for climbing, but as an all-year ski playground, its summit ice-cap and encircling glaciers covering some fifty square miles. Farther south, along the Washington-Oregon boundary, the Cascades are cut through in the deep gorges by the Columbia River. Beyond it the dominating peak is Mount Hood (11,253 feet), the highest elevation in Oregon.

Beginning at the California state-line, the northern Sierra Nevadas are, like the Cascades, largely volcanic. Here rise the graceful, snowy cone of Mount Shasta, beloved of postcard manufacturers, and, near by, Mount Lassen, whose eruptions in 1914 and 1915 make it the most recently active volcano in the United States. Further south the Sierras lose their volcanic character, but gain in sweep and elevation culminating in Mount Whitney's 14,502-foot summit. An interesting aspect of this, our nation's loftiest peak, is that it stands only a few miles to the north-west of Death Valley, which, at 276 feet below sea-level, is the lowest point of the western hemisphere. In spite of their great uplift, however, Whitney and its neighbours rise in gentle gradients, particularly to the west, where the tree-line mounts to 12,000 feet and there is little bare rock below the summit ridges. Offering far more challenge to climbers is the region of Yosemite Falls, in the centre of the state, where a maze of spectacular granite spires and domes provide rock-climbing of the first order, though at no great altitude.

The Sierras were first thoroughly explored and made known to Americans by the distinguished naturalist and solitary wanderer, John Muir. Their lower slopes are covered with magnificent stands of timber, notably the giant sequoias, and their upland valleys abound with lakes, cascades and waterfalls. They are our loveliest, as well as our highest, mountains, and for camping and tramping can be excelled nowhere in the world.

Some five hundred miles east of the Cascades and Sierra Nevadas, and separated from them by the Great Basin region of Nevada, Utah and Idaho, lie the Rocky Mountains. The Rockies are the heart of the West, and the broadest, most rugged section of the mountain backbone of North America. Unlike their Canadian continuation in the north, they are in no sense a single, unbroken chain of peaks, but rather a huge complex of many chains and ranges, often widely separated by great rolling tablelands. Considered as a whole, they form the principal natural division of the United States. The so-called Continental Divide roughly follows their highest crests, northwest to south-east, from the Canadian to the Mexican border, all the rivers of its eastern side draining to the Gulf of Mexico and all on the western to the Pacific Ocean.

In the northern Rockies, which comprise the ranges of Montana and northern Idaho, the most spectacular peaks and finest mountain scenery are to be found in the Lewis

Range, which lies largely in Glacier National Park. Bold, rocky summits, together with many small glaciers and countless lakes, make this section one of the most attractive and frequented playgrounds of the West. Central Montana is a region of rounded and unimpressive uplands, but in the southern part of the state, north-east of Yellowstone Park, the Beartooth Mountains present a jagged uplift of great wildness and scenic splendour. Granite Peak (12,850 feet) their highest elevation, was not climbed until 1923 and is considered one of the most difficult ascents in the Rockies.

Yellowstone Park, in the north-west corner of Wyoming, is bisected by the Continental Divide, but is a great geyser basin rather than predominantly mountainous. Immediately south of it, however, the Central Rockies thrust upward in a series of magnificent, bold peaks known as the Teton Range. The Tetons are not large in extent, covering only some 400 square miles between Jackson Hole, Wyoming, and the Idaho stateline, but their three principal summits, Grand Teton (13,747 feet), Mount Owen and Mount Moran, are considered by experienced mountaineers to provide the best rock climbing of any mountain-group in the country. Farther south, the Wind River Range of western Wyoming has also proved attractive to climbers. Gannet Peak (13,785 feet), highest summit in the state as well as in the group, was first ascended only in 1922, and the near-by rock-spires of the Titcomb Needles still offer several difficult first ascents. Other important mountain chains of the Central Rockies include the Bighorn and Absaroka Mountains of Wyoming and the Wasatch and Uinta Mountains of eastern Utah. They do not, however, offer climbing comparable to that in the Teton and Wind River groups.

South of the Wind River Range the main backbone of the Rocky Mountains is cut by the broad plateau of the Wyoming Basin. This gateway between the ranges was formerly the route of the historic Oregon Trail and is now traversed by the Union Pacific Railroad. Beyond it, the so-called Southern Rockies sweep southward across the breadth of Colorado and New Mexico.

The mountains of Colorado are the highest and most extensive of the whole system, range following range in bewildering number and complexity. Here are concentrated four-fifths of all the peaks in the country exceeding 14,000 feet in height, as well as a host of others so numerous that even today many have not yet been named. Loftiest of the ranges are the Sawatch Mountains, in the west-central part of the state, which culminate in Mount Elbert (14,420 feet), the second highest elevation of the United States. Other noteworthy summits of the Colorado Rockies include Long's Peak, in Rocky Mountain National Park, north of Denver; the famous Pike's Peak, near Colorado Springs, which has an auto road to the top; and Lizard Head, a spectacular pinnacle in the San Miguel Mountains, which defied all attempts at ascent until 1920.

Most of the Colorado peaks, however, present few climbing difficulties. Pike's Peak was first surmounted in the early years of the last century, and Long's Peak, in the past seventy-five years, had probably been ascended by as many people as any other mountain of equal height in the world. There are today no unclimbed summits over 14,000 feet and very few of more than 13,000.

The southernmost Rockies, in New Mexico, boast several lofty ranges, but few peaks of individual prominence. Except for occasional "special" ascents, like that of Shiprock in 1939, they are seldom climbed.

Extending from eastern Colorado to western Pennsylvania, the plains of the Mississippi Basin form one of the greatest flat areas of the globe. They are broken in widely separated localities by small uplifts, such as the Black Hills of South Dakota and the Ozark Mountains of Missouri, but it is not until 1,500 miles have intervened that the earth's surface again buckles upward into the second extensive mountain region of the United States. This region, known generally as the Appalachian Highlands, stretches in a series of ranges from Maine to Georgia, roughly paralleling the Atlantic coastline and one to three hundred miles inland. It is one of the oldest mountain systems in the world—weathered, rounded and heavily forested—and nowhere attains either the elevation or ruggedness of the western ranges. Only a handful of its loftiest summits rise above timberline, and none of them approaches the zone of perpetual snow.

The best-known of the Appalachian ranges are those of the New England states. Maine's Mount Katahdin (5,267 feet), which lifts its isolated peak some eighty miles north of Bangor, is in the heart of the largest wilderness area remaining in the East. South-west of it, in northern New Hampshire, are the historic White Mountains, subdivided into the Presidential and Franconia Ranges. The White Mountains have been a famous summer playground for more than a century and in recent years have also become a popular centre for winter and spring ski-ing, Mount Washington (6,288 feet), the highest elevation, boasts a hotel on its very summit, with both a motor road and a cog railway connecting it with the state highways below. For those who prefer their mountains unmechanized there is also a labyrinth of beautiful footpaths, both above and below treeline, and convenient shelters scattered among the slopes and ravines.

Except for infrequent and scattered cliffs neither the White Mountains nor any of the other eastern ranges provide climbing in the alpine sense. Up to timberline, at about 5,000 feet, the going is principally through great slanting forests and along the rocky margins of brooks and rivulets; on the bare ridges above, it is over tumbled masses of broken boulders. The only hazard is the weather, which even at the comparatively low elevations of the Appalachians is subject to sudden and violent changes. Indeed, the meteorological station on the summit of Mount Washington has records of wind velocities up to the almost incredible figure of 231 miles per hour, this last—made on April 12, 1934—the highest that has been officially recorded anywhere in the world. Too many hikers and campers have met with accidents, and even death, through taking these unspectacular and usually gentle mountains too casually. Snow and lightning and winds of twice hurricane force are matters to be reckoned with, whether they are encountered on the fearsome crags of Nanga Parbat or on the familiar trails above Gorham and Pinkham Notch.

South and west from New Hampshire virtually every state of the Altantic Seaboard presents at least one attractive mountain area. Vermont has its Green Mountains, Massachusetts its Berkshires, New York its Adirondacks and Catskills, Pennsylvania its Poconos and rambling Alleghenies. Below the Potomac River the Blue Ridge Mountains, famous for their new Skyline Drive, sweep across all of western Virginia, merging with the Great Smokies along the Tennessee-North Carolina boundary. Here are found the loftiest mountains of of the Appalachian chain, Carolina's Mount Mitchell, at 7,242 feet, being the highest elevation in the United States east of the Mississippi. Lying in a lower latitude than the New England ranges, the Smokies, despite their greater height, seldom rise above timberline; the surrounding country, however, is still in a primitive state and offers exceptional opportunities for the best sort of outdoor life.

Large sections of all the Appalachian ranges lie within the boundaries of National Forests or State Parks, and their maintenance in a state of wild and profuse nature, in the very heart of the world's greatest industrial region, is one of the most splendid examples of intelligent conservation to be found in any country. Perhaps the most remarkable feature of the whole area is the so-called Appalachian Trail. This is a footpath extending from the summit of Mount Katahdin, in Maine, to the summit of Mount Oglethorpe, in Georgia, and traversing en route almost all the principal mountain regions of the East. Maintained jointly by the various state governments and many local climbing and hiking clubs, it avoids cities and highways and provides a wilderness thoroughfare more than two thousand miles in length.

Mountaineering, we have seen, is a sport that was long in developing. In the United States it has been longer than elsewhere. The most obvious reason for this is our lack of a first-class, easily accessible mountain playground such as the Alps provide for Western Europe; another, equally important, is that throughout most of our history we have been too occupied with combating and taming the wild places of our country to think of them in terms of pleasure and recreation. To the pioneer, as to the peasant or tribesman, a mountain is an obstacle to be crossed, circumvented or ignored. Only to men of a highly developed civilization, possessed of leisure, imagination and a love of sport, does it become something to be surmounted as an end in itself.

Climbing in America has still not attained the popularity it enjoys in most European countries, but recent years have seen a tremendous spreading of its appeal, and today mountaineering clubs are active in many sections of the country. The better-known among them include the American Alpine Club, with headquarters in New York City; the Appalachian Mountain Club, of Boston; the Sierra Club, of San Francisco; The Mazamas, of Portland, Oregon; and The Mountaineers, of Seattle. Of these, the American Alpine Club most closely resembles the original Alpine Club of London, maintaining high standards of membership and sponsoring important expeditions. The others, with much larger memberships, are chiefly concerned with climbing and general out-door recreation in or near their own localities. All publish regular journals, which, taken together, present a complete and up-to-date picture of current mountaineering activity in this country.[1]

The future of American climbing would seem to lie in two rather widely separated realms. The major ventures of the past decade—on Nanda Devi and K2 and in the great ranges of Alaska—show clearly that our more expert alpinists possess both the will and the skill to challenge the world's highest unclimbed peaks. As these words are written the state of the world is unfortunately not such that men can cross oceans and continents for the climbing of mountains. But the time will come again when they can, and, when it does, it is certain that American expeditions will again be laying siege to the unconquered giants of Central Asia. It may even be that a changed world may at last give us our first fling at Everest.

[1] See Reading List.

Such ambitious undertakings, however, will still be only for the few. Like their counterparts in the past, of which we have read in this book, they will comprise the highlighted spectacular chapters in the story of men and mountains. But, in the most fundamental sense, they will be far less important than a second type of climbing in which Americans are indulging more and more.

This climbing is done without benefit of erudite papers and geographic society awards. It is done within the limits of our own United States, from Mount Katahdin to Mount Whitney, from the rhododendron forests of the Great Smokies to the snow-cap of Rainier. It involves no records, no "firsts," no conquering the unconquerable, but merely a small group of congenial companions with stout boots on their feet, grub in their knapsacks and a week or a week-end or a day at their disposal. Each year more Americans are visiting their National Parks and National Forests. Each year more of them are venturing deep into the woods and high upon the hills. Most of them would not know a piton from a bergshrund or a Mummery Crack from a hanging glacier. But they know more important things than these.

They know what it is like to stand on a bald bleak knob in the sky, while the sun goes down and the pinprick lights twinkle on in the shadowed valley below. They know the struggle of heart and lung and limb on the long upward pull and the sharp sudden thrill of a summit gained at last. They know that the fabled ambrosia and nectar of the gods were really nothing more than a cheese sandwich and a canteen of spring water. They know what sleep can be, on pine needles by a campfire, in the purple night. And knowing these things they know the love of mountains, *for their own sake*, which is at bottom all that mountaineering has ever meant, or ever will.

XII

AXE, ROPE AND TROUSER-SEAT

THE CRAFT OF MOUNTAINEERING

IN THE PRECEDING pages we have seen mountaineering in many and various guises—as a sport, as exercise and competition, as exploration and scientific research, as physical and spiritual adventure. In addition to all these it is a body of knowledge and experience and a technique based upon them. In short, a craft.

In the broad sense of the term mountain craft embraces an enormous field. It applies primarily, of course, to climbing, as such, but extends far beyond it to include every aspect of how men live and act on the high places of the earth. It is concerned equally with ends and means, practice and theory, half-hour scrambles on a riverside bluff and Himalayan expeditions complete with oxygen tanks, aneroid barometers and 300 porters. It encompasses such weirdly unrelated subjects as geology and acrobatics, astronomy and first aid, map making and bed making, paleontology and cooking.

Large volumes can be, and have been, written on any one of a hundred aspects of mountaineering knowledge and technique, and this chapter makes no claim to presenting even a fairly complete outline of the subject. Neither is it in any sense a manual on "how to climb." Indeed, though it is largely concerned with facts, those facts may almost be said to be secondary. Its purpose will be well served if it simply makes clear how much more there is to mountaineering than a mere going uphill and down again and indicates in some measure the breadth and richness and infinite variety of the climber's world.

The Nature of Mountains

In the organic sense—insofar as plant, animal and human life are concerned—mountains are perhaps the "deadest" regions on earth. Geologically, however, they are the most alive. More than any other features of the earth's surface they present visible evidence of the immense physical forces which have moulded, and are still moulding, the face of our planet. These forces are of two kinds. The first consists of heat and pressure within the core of the earth, which result, over enormous periods of time, in the folding and buckling of the earth's surface and the thrusting up of great rock-masses into highlands and ranges. This may be called the creative force in mountain-making. The second, or destructive, force, is found in the atmosphere, and manifests itself in the relentless levelling process of denudation and erosion. The geologic history and present form of the earth's high places are determined by these two agencies—the one building them up, the other tearing them down. Between them they create for mountains a life-cycle of vast duration and unvarying pattern.

The age of the earth's present ranges varies greatly. Some, like the Appalachians of the eastern United States, date back to remote geological times and show their antiquity in low, rounded outlines, moulded by the winds and snows of uncounted millions of years. Others, like the Alps and Himalayas, are of comparatively recent origin—a mere two or three million years—and exhibit their youth in their height and striking boldness of contour. There are many evidences, indeed, that the Himalayas are still in active process of being built up and that Everest and its neighbours will, in spite of constant denudation, be even higher a thousand centuries hence than they are today. In terms of mountaineering, young, uneroded mountains are always of greater importance and interest than their older counterparts.

The actual physical structure of mountains also shows wide diversity. The rocks of the earth's crust are usually divided by geologists into three groups: (1) *igneous rocks* (granite, diorite, basalt, lavas, etc.), which have been formed directly by solidification of molten matter; (2) *sedimentary rocks* (limestone, sandstone, dolomite, clay, shale, etc.), which are formed from the sediment or fragments of other rocks; (3) *metamorphic rocks* (gueiss, schists, slates, etc.), a mixed type generally believed to be sedimentary rocks that have been subjected to great heat or pressure. All three types are found in mountains sometimes in fairly simple form, more often in bewildering complexity. If any generalization can be made it is that the cores and upper reaches of most peaks are usually of granite or some similar igneous mass, their outer and lower slopes of stratified sedimentary or metamorphic rocks. A notable exception, however, is to be found in no less a mountain than Everest, which apparently is built up throughout of fossil-bearing limestone.

Because of their height and consequently exposed position, as well as the agency of gravity, mountains present a vast complex of natural phenomena which are not found elsewhere on the earth. They are not only subject to frequent and severe storms, but can also be the actual cause of storms, owing to their effect on the temperature and moisture of the atmosphere. Their climate is colder than that of the lowlands, their winds stronger, their air more rarefied. Also, every peak, whether or not it is still being pushed up from below, is falling to pieces at the top from the effects of weathering, with the result that rocks, ice and snow are forever pouring down its sides, sometimes in mere trickles, sometimes in vast avalanches. Truly high summits are almost invariably ringed with glaciers—great, creeping drainage systems whose behaviour bears little resemblance to that of snow and ice at lower altitudes. Finally, the architecture of the peaks themselves is on a uniquely vast and complex scale. They are built of rock and snow and ice, to be sure. But they are built also of slopes, precipices, buttresses and ridges; gullies, chimneys, ledges and cornices; crevasses, gendarmes, névés and bergschrunds; humps, domes, spires and pinnacles. Seen from afar a great mountain may appear to be merely a sudden upward prolongation of the earth's surface; once approached, however, it becomes in a very real sense a world in and to itself.

Climbing in General

"In mountaineering," writes the distinguished climber-scholar, Geoffrey Winthrop Young, "there is only one principle: that we should secure on any given day the highest form of mountain adventure consistent with our sense of proportion. All else is more a matter of practice than of principle."

In other words, there are no immutable rules that apply to all mountains and all mountaineers, no rigid formulas of "how" and "how not." Indeed, it is a large part of the charm of the sport that it is infinitely adaptable to the tastes and abilities of its followers. There are many fine peaks which can be climbed in a matter of a few hours, others which have been besieged for months on end, year after year, and still have not been won. There are ascents requiring the utmost in daring and acrobatic skill, others that are little more than a stiff, uphill walk. In fact, in frequented mountain districts such as the Alps a single summit will usually present several ways of approach, ranging from the very easy to the all but impossible. Mountaineering, therefore, is not an activity limited to "experts," or to young men, or to the physically powerful. A remarkable number of the great ascents in climbing history have been made by men well on into middle age, and self-knowledge and self-discipline have time and again proved themselves of more value than mere strength, agility or endurance. In the long run, judgment rather than muscle makes the mountaineer.

All climbing is concerned with two primary objectives. The first is getting to the top. The second is getting there—and back—*safely*. To say that mountaineering is a "dangerous" activity is meaningless; so are ski-ing and swimming and sailing and crossing Fifth Avenue in a traffic jam. What is true is that, more than in most sports, the element of danger is always present, and the climber whose judgment or performance is faulty may well lose not only the game but his life. It is from the recognition of this fact that mountain craft has developed as a science and an art. It cannot eliminate danger altogether—indeed, no true mountaineer would wish it to if it could. What it can and does do is to keep danger under control.

The dangers a climber faces are of three main kinds: that of falling himself, that of being struck by other falling objects, and that of the elements. All can take a great variety of forms. One can fall from rock or ice or snow, over a precipice or into a crevasse, two yards or two miles; the cause may be vertigo or a broken rope or improper balance or rotten rock or the sudden, unexpected action of a companion. Falling objects, too, can be either rock, snow or ice, ranging from a volley of pebbles scuffed down by a careless climber above to a gigantic avalanche peeling off the whole side of a mountain. The threat of the elements can manifest itself in even more ways: in cold and storms and blizzards, in the effects of altitude, in swift changes in the conditions of rock and snow, in the coming of night while a party is still far from food and shelter. Individual peaks, to be sure, often have their own special peculiarities and hazards. The dangers listed above, however, are common to every high mountain, and no climber will get far on any range in the world if he is not prepared to meet and, in a measure, deal with them.

One of the first things which every mountaineer must learn is the distinction between *danger* and mere *difficulty*; for the two are by no means synonymous. On the one hand, let us take the example of an expert climber descending a steep cliff-face *en rappel*. All that the uninitiated will see is a man dangling in space supported by two slender lengths of rope, and he will automatically jump to the conclusion that the man's situation is hazardous in the extreme. Actually, however, it is not hazardous at all. The climber is performing a standard manœuvre well-known to mountaineers for many years; his rope is well belayed above, its coils are properly adjusted about his body; his landing place has been selected and he is descending with smoothness and co-ordination. What he is doing is difficult, in that its performance requires practice, but it is not dangerous. In striking contrast to this let us take the instance of a novice climber during an ascent. Two alternative routes have presented themselves—one a steep and jagged ridge with disconcerting drops on either side, the other a sheltered gully of moderate gradient with excellent hand- and footholds. He selects the latter, and to all appearances his choice is the wise one, for he encounters no climbing problems whatever. Actually, however, the innocent-looking gully is a funnel frequently raked by rock avalanches, and he will be lucky if he escapes from it with his life. In eschewing the ridge and its difficulties the climber has unwittingly exposed himself to an immeasurably greater degree of danger.

Mountaineering has often been likened to navigation; in many respects it can also resemble a military campaign. In common with both it requires not only adept performance and the ability to meet unforeseen situations, but also careful planning in advance. Perhaps the most important of all preliminary considerations is the composition of the climbing party, for mountaineering, as we have seen repeatedly in the foregoing pages, is far less a matter of individual skill and effort, however impressive, than of intelligent teamwork. No novice or near-novice should climb alone, and even for the expert it is a practice better avoided. A party of two is acceptable for the usual type of ascent. Three is better yet, in that it provides double security on the rope, leaving two actively functioning members if one should get into difficulties. A larger group is liable to suffer from confusion and lack of coordination, and in most cases it is better to split such a party into sub-divisions of two or three men, each operating as a separate unit.

On most high or difficult ascents the average tourist-climber will be well advised to employ the services of a professional guide. There is no better way in which he can learn the fundamentals of mountain craft—provided he keeps his eyes open and his mind alert and does not merely follow blindly in his leader's footsteps. Still, it is not until he climbs guideless, in company with his fellow-amateurs, that he will become a true mountaineer. For then he will be required not only to follow where another has led, but to lead himself; to reconnoitre and choose routes; to tie knots and cut steps and manipulate the rope; above all, to share the responsibility of decisions on which the welfare, and possibly the lives, of a whole party depend. Many a first-rate climber has been developed in the course of modest outings on insignificant hills, during which, however, he was compelled to exercise his own initiative and judgment. None has ever been developed by being hauled up a great peak like a sack of potatoes.

To summarize: the essence of intelligent mountaineering consists of knowledge of conditions, knowledge of self, and the control of situations as they arise. A man who knows how to get to the top of a mountain may be an expert climber. A man who also knows when to turn back is a mountaineer.

Rock Climbing

Rock climbing is the most common form of mountaineering and involves a great variety of methods and techniques. In the strict sense of the term it may be said to begin where uphill walking ends—in other words, where the hands, arms, knees and body, as well as the feet, of the climber come into active play.

As in all other branches of the sport, the first requisite in a cragsman is sound judgment. Before beginning an ascent he must make his general choice of route (i.e., which side of the mountain he will attempt; which main ridges, faces, chimneys, etc., he will aim for and which he will avoid).[1] Once underway, moreover, he will find himself constantly confronted with the same problems and choices on a smaller scale. In difficult rock climbing virtually every movement requires a decision as to how it can best be made, and the advance selection of hand and footholds can be fully as important as the physical manœuvres that follow. In this connection it is essential for the novice climber to remember that a hold or stance cannot be judged by its outward appearance alone. Many rocks which look sound are actually rotten and will crumble away when pressure is applied; many which seem firmly fixed to the mountainside are in reality detached and precariously balanced, awaiting only the touch of hand or foot to break loose and topple downward. In rock climbing every hold should be carefully

[1] Steepness alone is by no means the measure of the difficulty of a climb. The slope of the rock strata is an important consideration, and a very steep pitch on which the strata slope upward will often provide a better route than a much gentler slope on which they slope down. This fact is well illustrated by Whymper's experiences on the Matterhorn.

tested before the full weight of the body is entrusted to it. Probably more serious mountaineering accidents have resulted from carelessness in this respect than from any other single cause.

The ordinary type of rock climbing is largely a matter of hand- and footholds, requiring judiciousness of choice and good balance and co-ordination when in motion. Not infrequently, however, a climber may be confronted by a stretch of rock which cannot be negotiated by the usual methods and for which special manœuvres must be employed. Sometimes, as on a narrow ledge or steep slabs, the pressure of the body against the rocks can give support which the hands and feet alone cannot supply. Other types of ledges, which offer no standing room at all, may be crossed by what is known as a hand-traverse—a Tarzan-like procedure in which the cragsman grasps the edge with his hands and moves himself along by them, his body and legs hanging free below. A knife-edged ridge, too narrow for standing erect or even for crawling, will frequently yield easily to a climber who straddles it and pushes himself along with his hands. Chimneys and cracks, in particular, lend themselves to ingenious forms of cragsmanship, as Mummery first demonstrated on the fearsome walls of the Chamonix *aiguilles*. Thus a narrow vertical fissure, though presenting no holds whatever, can often be scaled if the climber jams an elbow and knee into it and pulls himself up by them. Or, if the fissure is wider, but still has no holds, he may get his whole body inside and "chimney up" by the alternating pressure of back and feet against its two sides.

Two other climbing manœuvres often employed on difficult rock are those known as the "lay-back" and the *courte-échelle*. The "lay-back" is used on a steep stretch which offers no ordinary hand- or footholds, but where there is an underhold or vertical rock-edge within reach on which the climber can get a secure grasp. Pulling horizontally against the underhold or edge with his hands, he places his feet against the pitch to be climbed and, in effect, "walks" up it, his body meanwhile leaning out almost at right angles to the rock. In the *courte-échelle*, the first man of a party makes use of the bodies of his companion, or companions, to gain a stance or hold which would otherwise be out of his reach. The operation may consist merely of a boost from someone's hands, or it may involve the leader's climbing on the backs, shoulders or even heads of the other climbers. On occasion the axe is also brought into play to give additional artificial hand- or footholds.

One of the most remarkable developments in cragsmanship has been the perfection of a technique known as balance, or rhythm, climbing. It is based on the fact that equilibrium is much more easily maintained by a body in motion than a body at rest—a principle involved in many activities other than mountaineering. A dancer, skater or bicyclist, for example, is frequently in off-balance positions which he can maintain only because he is in constant motion from one to the other; if he were to attempt to hold one of them without moving he would immediately fall. So too with rock-scaling. A tiny finger-hold or quarter-inch ledge, which would afford no support at all to a stationary climber, can yet be made to serve his ends if he uses them but momentarily, for friction, on his way to another hold or ledge. Also, the climber himself can maintain equilibrium in otherwise impossible positions, if, while he is in them, he is already on his way to a counter-balancing position. The result is that by constant rhythmic movement and the ingenious use of friction an accomplished cragsman can often master short stretches of vertical or near-vertical rock which would be insurmountable by the ordinary methods of "stop-and-go."

In football and various other sports it is an oft-heard axiom that the best defence is a good offence. In mountaineering, however, the exact reverse is true. By far the most important aspects of the craft are those concerned with precaution and safety, and the climber who neglects them will inevitably come to grief, however great his strength, agility and daring.

Protective measures are nowhere more essential than in rock climbing, for this branch of the sport is most often carried on in high and exposed places where a minor mishap may quickly turn into a disaster. In general, these measures are more a matter of common sense than of arbitrary rules and vary greatly according to the situation at hand. There are, however, a few which are almost always applicable. One is to avoid routes on which there is obvious danger of stonefalls and avalanches, even though the alternative route may present much harder climbing. Another is never, during difficult climbing, to entrust the entire weight of the body to one hand- or foothold. At every point in his manœuvring the climber should have at least two secure points of contact with the rock surface, so that if one should break away or slip from his grasp he will still have the support of the other. It is also important that when strong pressure is applied to the rock with either hands or feet it is in a downward rather than an outward direction and takes the form of a steady push or pull rather than a sudden jerk. Ledges and proturberances which can support a 200-pound man moving easily and rhythmically will often break away under the abrupt lunge of a climber of half that weight.

In almost every climbing operation there is a correct and an incorrect position for the body. Most novices, during their first experience on steep rock, are apt to "hug" the mountain too closely, fearing that if they lean back from it they may lose their balance and fall. More often than not, however, this merely results in a cramped and tense position in which neither arms nor legs have free play, as well as in dangerous outward pressure on the rocks underfoot. There are, to be sure, certain times when it is necessary to press the thighs and chest closely against the rock. In general, however, the body should be kept in as near a vertical position as possible, and sufficiently far out from the rock to permit easy movement and clear vision both above and below.

The Rope

The rope plays so important a part in mountaineering that it has grown to be the very symbol of the sport. In rock climbing, and in particular, it comes into almost constant use, an understanding of its functions and manipulations is perhaps the most essential single requirement in any would-be cragsman.

The rope, properly employed, is *not* a substitute for good judgment or physical ability. Neither is it a leash for the stronger to lead the weaker, nor a sort of magic talisman insuring blanket immunity to the incompetent. It is, rather—again to quote Geoffrey Young—"the means by which the physical and moral efficiency of a party is pooled, and by which its margin of safety is extended so as to include all members of a party equally." The important words in this definition are "moral efficiency." For the rope's significance extends far beyond its mere physical function of tying the bodies of several climbers together; it ties them as well into a mental and spiritual unit and makes mountaineering, in the deepest sense, a collective rather than an individual enterprise. No climber, thus joined to his companions, can make snap decisions and take chances as he might if he were alone, for he is now, in everything he does, concerned not only with his own welfare but with that of others. The rope, on the one hand, may greatly increase his "margin of safety." But it increases his responsibility even more.

The rope most commonly used in mountaineering is of Manila hemp, a half-inch or so in diameter and between 80 and 125 feet long. There are a number of accepted knots for tying it around the body—both for end and middle men—and the distance between climbers may vary according to the nature of the ascent. It is essential, however, that the rope be allowed neither to drag slackly nor pull jerkily between them. As many as a dozen men have been known to climb on one rope, and as few as two. In the early days of the sport large roped parties were in vogue (witness the seven all tied together on the tragic first ascent of the Matterhorn), but modern practice favours smaller groups, with three usually considered to be the ideal number.

The order of climbers on a rope is of great importance and should be determined carefully according to the dictates of common sense. The man highest on the mountain at any given time is obviously the one who can give the most assistance to his companions. Similarly he is the one who can receive the least. On an ascent, therefore, the strongest member of a party should always go first; on a descent, last. The weakest member should be last on the ascent, but in the middle on the descent, when it would be inadvisable for him to lead. On difficult horizontal stretches the correct place for the weakest is also in the middle, where both the leader and last man can assure effective support. Too great emphasis cannot be placed on the responsibilities of the top man on a rope. The anchor for all below him, he is himself without anchor (unless pitons and karabiners are employed), and a slip or mis-step on his part can easily result in serious consequences.

In climbing of a more or less routine nature, when the rope is employed merely as a general precaution, all the members of a party will ordinarily be in motion simultaneously. On particularly difficult rock, however, the rope becomes an active protective device, and its proper use limits the movements of the group to one man at a time.

In such cases climbers frequently make use of the protective manœuvre known as the belay. The first step in belaying is for the anchor man on a team to take his position in the most protected and secure stance available. He then passes the rope either around his own body or a projecting mass of rock, or both, in such a way that a slip or fall by the man actually climbing will put the least possible strain both on the rope and on himself. In a "body belay" only the body is used, the shoulders and trunk of the belayer sharing the work of hands and arms. In a "direct belay" only a salience in the mountainside is employed, the rope passing around it in what is termed a "hitch." The most effective protection is usually attained by a combination of these two methods, in which the belayer makes full use both of the solidity of the rock and the strength and resilience of his own body. It is essential in performing a belay that there be no slack in the rope between belayer and climber; otherwise a falling climber will gain too much momentum before braking power can be exerted.

The belay, properly executed, can afford excellent protection to all but the topmost man on a rope. In difficult rock climbing some form of belay is interposed, whenever possible, between the leader and the others, usually through the use of pitons and karabiners, which the leader himself affixes as he climbs. Their purpose, however, is as much the protection of those below as that of the climber himself. Even the greatest strength and skill can rarely save a man if he has fallen any considerable distance before the rope goes taut.

One of the most ingenious and useful rope-manœuvres in rock climbing is that known as the rappel. Unlike the belay, it is an offensive rather than a defensive measure, and is employed only on descents, enabling a climber to negotiate cliff faces and overhands which would otherwise be impossible. For the rappel —"roping down" would be the nearest English equivalent—a supplementary rope is used, thinner than the ordinary rope and usually considerably longer. This is passed around a rock point or threaded through a firmly fastened rope-ring directly above the stretch to be descended, so that two equal lengths hang down the mountain. The climber then wraps a fold of the doubled rope around himself—under one thigh, diagonally across the body and over the opposite shoulder—and, facing in toward the mountain, proceeds to lower himself by letting the rope slip slowly first through one hand and then the other. The whole operation is based on the fact that the friction of the rope passing around the body takes almost all strain from the hands and arms. The weight of the rope itself acts as a brake, extremely powerful at the beginning of a descent when there are still two long strands dangling below the climber, becoming gradually less so as the strands shorten. In the case of steep or even vertical rocks the climber, in effect, walks backwards down the mountainside, his feet gaining what purchase they can from such points of support as may exist, his body leaning outwards against the braking power of the rope. On the descent of a bulge or overhang his body has no contact with the mountain at all, but hangs freely, supported in a sitting position by the rope under the thigh. In either case, however, the essence of the manœuvre lies in the opposite pull of the body and the rope wrapped around it. The hands are the controlling but not the force-producing agency, functioning in much the same way as if they were manipulating the brake on an automobile.

To the uninitiated the rappel can appear a hair-raisingly dangerous performance. It takes a deal of "doing," too, for a novice to stand at the top of a precipice or overhang and lean backward into space. Properly performed, however, it is no more hazardous than dozens of other less spectacular mountaineering operations, and ranks, indeed, as one of the oldest and most conventional manœuvres in the sport. In addition to dexterous handling of the rope, there are two important considerations involved in any rappel. First, it must be remembered that the rope is used doubled and that the length of a descent can therefore be no greater than half its length. Secondly, a climber roping down should always make sure that there is a landing place within reach and not trust to luck that one will appear when he is dangling in the air, literally at rope's end.

Snow and Ice

Snow and ice, as found on high mountains, assume such a bewildering variety of forms that it is almost impossible to formulate a set of rules for dealing with them. If any generalization can be made, it is that climbing on them requires somewhat less agility than rock clambering, but even greater experience and judgment.

The chief reason for this is that while rocks are more or less a constant, subject only to the slow influences of erosion and frost, snow and ice are in a constant state of flux, often changing both form and substance from day to day and hour to hour. Thus a cornice or snow-bridge high on a mountainside may provide a strong, safe highway during certain weather conditions, only to become during others a crumbling death trap. Similarly, a steep slope, perfectly safe for climbing in the cool of early morning, may well peel away in huge avalanches under the rays of the afternoon sun. No mountaineer should allow himself to forget that snow and ice—however massive and solid-appearing their outward forms—are not actually part of a mountain, as are the rocks, but merely a cloak or covering lying upon it. Freezing or friction may often hold them in position for long periods of time, but the downward pull of gravity is always there, and sooner or later every flake and crystal of them will complete its predestined journey to the valleys below. Glaciers, snow-slopes and ice-fields are not dead, changeless things. They are the drainage of the mountain, the source of streams and rivers, and a vital intermediate link in the endless living cycle of the watering of the earth. The mountaineer who has learned to think of them in terms of their functions—their "aliveness"—has taken the first great step in the mastery of snow and ice craft.

Most high peaks are flanked by glaciers, and these usually afford the most direct, sometimes the only, approach to the heights beyond. Basically a mountain glacier is a simple phenomenon—a large river of ice formed in high, cold altitudes and moving slowly down toward the lower, warmer altitudes along the path of least resistance. In the process, however, it is usually subject to so many variations of terrain and climate, and to so many forms of pressure and strain, that it becomes an organism of great complexity and many component parts. Most important of these components are:

The glacier proper—the lower, and larger, section of the ice-sheet, generally located in a valley and having a comparatively gentle slope.

Moraines—broken rock and debris carried down by the glacier and deposited in long heaps along its margins. Those at the sides of a glacier are known as lateral moraines; one at its snout as a terminal moraine; one between two confluent glaciers as a medial moraine.

The névé—a snowfield lying above the snow-line which acts as the source or feeder of the glacier.

The ice-fall—the steepest section of the glacier, usually at the point where it flows down from the mountain proper on to the slopes and valleys below. Because of the enormous pressure to which the glacier is subjected at such points, the surface of an ice-fall is invariably a chaos of humps and fissures, high ridges and deep chasms.

Seracs—towers or pinnacles of ice, sometimes of great size, squeezed up out of the glacier by pressure below. They are formed not infrequently in ice-falls and at points where crevasses intersect.

[Photo by E. Meerkämper. Courtesy Swiss Federal Railroads.

THE VOID BELOW
A great crevasse in one of the glaciers in the Pennine Alps, near Zermatt.

[Photo by K. Meuser. Courtesy Swiss Federal Railroads.

"HAVE WE VANQUISHED AN ENEMY?"

Crevasses—fissures and chasms formed by splitting of the glacier's surface. They can be either longitudinal or transverse, but most often lie roughly at right angles to the glacier's course.

The bergschrund—the great crevasse which separates the glacier proper from the upper glacier or ice-fall.

Ice-fields—large, almost stagnant bodies of ice on high valley floors, which receive the outflow of several glaciers.

Hanging glaciers—small ice streams formed high on the mountainside, which terminate before reaching the lower slopes or valleys—frequently at the brink of a precipice.

All these glacial phenomena, with the possible exception of moraines, present important and complicated problems to the mountaineer. In certain instances, notably that of a steep and badly crumpled ice-fall, the actual climbing may be extremely hard, and in the case of very large glaciers the ascent may well prove to be the acid test of a climber's stamina and endurance. For the most part, however—to return to our former distinction—danger rather than difficulty is involved; and the safety of a party depends primarily on a knowledge of conditions and constant alertness. Seracs often topple, particularly in the heat of the day, strewing the surrounding area with tons of falling ice. Hanging glaciers present a similar menace, not infrequently breaking away from the upper mountain in huge avalanches and pouring on to the main glacier below. Most dangerous of all are the omnipresent crevasses, threading the ice surface like the lines of a jigsaw puzzle and waiting like traps to catch the ignorant or unwary.

On the lower reaches of a glacier, where there is apt to be little or no snow, crevasses are usually plainly visible, and the only problem is how either to jump or circumvent them. Higher up, however, and especially on the névé, they are often completely hidden. Thus a careless climber, imagining himself to be on perfectly solid footing, may actually be treading on a thin and unsupported bridge of snow and find himself suddenly plummeting through it into an abyss below. In such terrain elaborate precautions are a prime necessity. The climbing party should be roped together, preferably three to a rope, and widely enough spaced so that there is never too much weight on any one point of the glacial surface. The leader, on whom, as always, the chief responsibility falls, must advance slowly and cautiously, studying the texture and conformation of the snow for any hint of crevasses beneath and stopping at every suspicious point to sound with his ice-axe. If the haft of the axe plunges downward through the snow without encountering any resistance he will be wise in assuming that it is merely the unsupported covering of a crevasse and therefore to be given a wide berth. The shortest distance between two points on a glacier is seldom a straight line. Indeed a straight line is more often than not the shortest distance to disaster.

Even when every precaution is taken glaciers remain unpredictable and treacherous things, and falls into crevasses are one of the commonest of mountaineering accidents. In such a mishap the victim should immediately swing his axe into a horizontal position, in the hope that it will jam against the crevasse walls and arrest his fall. His companions should throw themselves down at once, to avoid being pulled in after him, and simultaneously thrust their axes into the snow and hitch the rope around them for anchorage. The difficulty involved in extricating a man from a crevasse depends on the nature of the crevasse itself, the degree to which the victim can help himself and the number of persons in the party. An extra rope is usually of considerable help, especially if the rescuing is being done by a lone individual. Great care must obviously be taken by the rescuers that in working around the edge of the crevasse they do not fall through themselves.

On the upper reaches of a mountain, above the zone of glaciers, snow and ice may be found in a great variety of forms. Crevasses are for the most part absent, but a host of new problems present themselves in the form of steep slopes and walls, ice-coated ridges and couloirs, overhanging cornices, avalanches and the like. Also, the snow and ice themselves may assume many different forms and combinations. One slope, for example, may consist altogether of solid ice; another of snow on ice; others of snow on rock, ice on rock, new snow on old snow, snow with a crust of ice, melting or freezing snow, melting or freezing ice. To make things still more difficult, conditions are never constant, but alter continually with changes in weather and temperature and the rising and setting of the sun.

In climbing steep ice or snow-slopes the mountaineer's upward and downward progress is largely a matter of step-cutting with his axe. This can range from a fairly simple operation, in the case of sound snow, to an extremely laborious one, when the surface is of ice and scores of strokes must be made to effect one satisfactory step. On severe grades the staircase of steps is usually cut in zigzags rather than straight up or down, with an especially large step at each corner for security in turning. The tread of each step should slope very slightly inward and be deep enough to afford the climber support, not only in quick passage but also while engaged in cutting the next step. It is extremely important that the climber himself, in both step-cutting and step-taking, stand as nearly erect as possible. Leaning in toward the slope may give the illusion of security, but the resulting outward pressure of the feet can easily cause the snow or ice to break away beneath them. In the whole operation balance and rhythm of movement count for far more than strength.

Belaying is employed as a defensive measure in snow and ice climbing no less than on rock. Here, however, the rope is passed around the haft of the ice-axe, which is then embedded in the slope as firmly as possible and made to serve as the hitching point. The axe employed alone can also be a most important protective device, for its prong, thrust firmly into the slope, will generally check a slip before it develops into an outright fall. Other useful, though seldom indispensable, articles of equipment are crampons, or climbing irons. These consist of iron or steel frames, with projecting spikes, that are fastened to the sole of the shoe and permit the wearer to gain a purchase on ice or hard snow which would be impossible in ordinary nailed boots. On long uphill trudges of not too steep gradient crampons can take the place of step-cutting, but on extremely steep slopes they serve merely as an additional safeguard against slipping. Their chief disadvantage is that they are heavy and cumbersome to carry when not in use.

If, in step-cutting, snow-slopes call for laborious climbing, they also provide, in glissading, one of the most exhilarating experiences in mountaineering. The glissade, as the name implies, is simply a slide, and, as performed on long, smooth slopes, may perhaps be best described as ski-ing without skis. The climber, facing outward and throwing his weight back on his heels, descends as rapidly as he can while still keeping himself under control, his ice-axe, with spike thrust into the snow on one side of him, acting as combination rudder and brake. Stretches which would take two or three hours to descend by ordinary step-cutting methods can in this fashion often be negotiated in a few minutes. It is essential, however, that the snow be of the right consistency—firm but not ice-coated. If the surface is too slippery the climber will be unable to control or stop himself; if it is too soft he will be unable to gain momentum, and there will also be the serious danger of his starting an avalanche. Unlike ski-ing, a fall in glissading will not check one's speed, but increase it. It is therefore a manœuvre that should not be attempted by novices on steep slopes until they have first had experience with it on gentler grades.

In gullies and chimneys the chief ice and snow hazards which a climber faces are twofold—avalanches (which he may either start himself or which may descend on him from above), and slips on ice or *verglas*-covered rocks. On ridges the principal problem are cornices. Cornices, perhaps the most treacherous of all mountain phenomena, are masses of snow projecting from the main body of a ridge, usually on the side sheltered from the prevailing wind. Found for the most part in high and exposed places, they present two serious threats to the climber. The first is that of breaking away of their own weight and avalanching down upon him from above; the second is that of breaking away under his feet while he is moving along on top of them. Of the two dangers, the latter is more often encountered, and great care should be exercised in the climbing of any snow-ridge to make sure that one is actually treading the ridge itself and not merely a projecting shelf of unsupported snow.

This is rendered doubly difficult by the fact that a cornice is never recognizable to a man who is actually on one; it must be located in advance and given a wide berth, even at the cost of the most difficult and arduous climbing. Indeed, there is no more important "must" than this in all the lore of mountaineering, for a corniced ridge, innocent though it may appear from above, is seldom anything but a broad white highway to destruction.

The variety of situations and conditions to be found in snow and ice climbing is almost limitless, particularly when winter and arctic mountaineering are taken into consideration; and it is impossible in a few paragraphs to do more than hint at a few of those most commonly encountered. In general, however, it may be said that climate and weather play a larger part than in rock climbing and that the best time for an ascent is two or three days after a snowfall, in settled, but not melted, snow. Again and again the experiences of expeditions to the world's great ranges have shown that catching a mountain in the right condition is every bit as essential to success as the climbing abilities of the party itself. And times without number, on glacier and snowfield, ice-slope and cornice, the experienced and careful mountaineer has triumphed and survived while his perhaps stronger, but more reckless, brother came to grief—if not to his death.

Equipment and Clothing

A large part of the appeal that mountaineering holds for men is that it provides a form of escape from an over-mechanized world. Nowhere is this more evident than in the simplicity of mountaineering equipment and in the strong antipathy which most climbers feel toward mechanical gadgets and artificial climbing aids. The rope and ice-axe remain today, as they have been since the birth of the sport, the principal items of equipment, and both, in their ordinary functions, are far less "attacking" devices than safeguards against accident and injury. So too are the more rarely used crampons, or climbing irons, which, with them, comprise the average mountaineer's entire kit of tools.

The development of so-called "mechanized" climbing and the use of pitons, karabiners and the like have been discussed briefly in Chapter IV. For years now the pages of Alpine journals have been filled with violent arguments over the employment of such devices, and the air has been thick with such choice epithets as "old fogey," "reactionary," "trapeze artist" and "hardware-dealer," the selection depending on the point of view of the writer. It is doubtful if either side will ever win the argument. There will always be those to whom a mountain wall presents a challenge to be met by any form of human ingenuity—mechanical or otherwise—and there will always be others to whom a steel spike driven into mountain rock is nothing less than desecration. As in all aspects of mountaineering, the question resolves itself largely into a matter of the taste and sense of proportion of the individual concerned. Perhaps the most reasonable point of view is that which holds mechanical aids to be justifiable when used defensively (as a belaying point, to secure climber or rope during particularly difficult manœuvres, etc.), but condemns them as offensive weapons, designed to provide a steeplejack's field-day on otherwise unclimbable rock.

A mountaineer's clothing, naturally, varies greatly according to the season, weather and type of climbing. In general, however, it must be warm and sturdy, and still so designed as to allow full freedom of movement. The boots—perhaps the most important individual item—should be stoutly made, but neither too heavy nor too stiff, and the soles should be well nailed, so as to give ample purchase on both rock and snow. For certain types of ice work, as we have seen, crampons are often used in addition to the boots. On very steep rock, on the other hand, the boots are best discarded and rope-soled shoes (*Kletterschuhe, scarpetti*) or sneakers used in their place. This type of footgear is, indeed, absolutely essential on such difficult ascents as those of the Chamonix *aiguilles* and most of the Dolomites, as well as for cliff-climbing of the sort practised in England and the United States. On snow or ice, however, or for long climbs over varied terrain, it is not only useless, but dangerous.

As for the rest of a climber's clothing, experience has shown that several light garments are usually preferable to one heavy, bulky one. The breeches or trousers, to be sure, should be of strong material—even the best of mountaineers will find himself doing some of his climbing on his knees and the seat of his pants—but, for the most part, light, wind-resistant clothing is far preferable to that which features sheer weight. In high climbing it is essential that the socks and gloves be warm and not too tight, for it is the hands and feet which are most susceptible to frostbite. For strenuous rock climbing, where the hands come into constant play, the only practical glove is a woollen one with all the finger tips cut off. Dark glasses should be worn during all snow climbing, when the sun is bright, and are often advisable as well on bare, glaring rock. On high ascents it also is wise to apply some type of grease or cream to the face as a precaution against wind and sunburn.

The general equipment used in mountaineering depends, of course, upon the nature of the ascent and may include anything from a penknife and handkerchief to motion picture cameras and oxygen tanks. By and large, however, it does not differ greatly from that used on ordinary hiking or camping trips. The rucksack—that galling but inescapable companion of all mountain adventure—should preferably be on the large side, so that the climber's burden will be well distributed; but it should not bulge out too far from the body, lest it throw him off balance or catch against projecting rocks. It is usually advisable to carry along a small amount of food and extra clothing, even on climbs of only a day's duration, for there is always the possibility of the party's being delayed by storms or other unforeseen occurrences. On longer ascents a tent, sleeping bag and cooking utensils are essential—particularly in little-frequented districts where no huts or shelters exist—while on truly large-scale expeditions the needs of the climbers become almost as numerous and complex as those of an army on the march. In all cases the gear should be as light and compact as possible, for the finest supplies and equipment in the world will profit a party nothing if they are too heavy or cumbersome. The dictionary defines a foot-pound as "a unit of energy, or work, equalling the work done in raising one pound against the force of gravity the height of one foot." One may quickly, and to one's sorrow, learn as much about the nature of foot-pounds on a mountainside as in the physics laboratory.

Climber and Mountaineer

The preceding pages have merely skimmed the surface of the great body of knowledge and technique which comprise the craft of mountaineering. For its theory, in detail, the reader is referred to the many expert books on the subject, some of which are mentioned in the reading list at the end of this volume. For its practice, there is no other schoolroom than the mountains themselves. This chapter will have amply served its purpose if it has done no more than indicate the boundless variety of the mountain world and, in some degree, made clear the fundamental distinction between a climber and a mountaineer.

Proficiency merely in climbing is for the most part based on the same factors as proficiency in other active sports. It demands good health and a degree of natural aptitude; strength, agility and endurance; co-ordination of the body and discipline of the nerves; and a certain amount of technical knowledge derived from experience. It is concerned almost exclusively with physical activity, and its purpose is to take a man up a mountain and then back again, as quickly and safely as possible. In short, to climb is to go up or to go down.

Mountaineering, however, is something much more than this—something both simpler and far more complex. In its broadest aspects it is concerned with every field of human knowledge and experience that bears any relation to life and activity on the high places of the earth. Time and again throughout the history of the sport—and, indeed, throughout almost any individual ascent—we see the mountaineer changing his role to fit the changing circumstances and situations in which he finds himself. One moment he is a cragsman, clinging to a dizzy precipice; the next he is a meteorologist studying the barometer; again a homesteader searching for a secure spot to pitch his tent and sleep. He is geologist, cartographer, trail-scout, botanist, cook, rope-splicer, photographer, explorer, guide, follower, philosopher, friend. He is not merely a climber, but a man at home on a mountain.

Yet the principle underlying all this activity is simplicity itself. It is—once again to quote Geoffrey Young—"the pursuit of the happiest kind of adventure which is consistent with the degree of one's experience, with one's sense of proportion, and with one's respect for noble scenery and a noble sport." In other words, the making of a mountaineer depends not so much on what a man does, as on what he is; not on what vertical cliffs and dizzy summits he has conquered, but on what he carries with him in his mind and heart.

XIII

BEHIND THE RANGES

Something hidden—go and find it;
Go and look behind the Ranges.
Something lost behind the Ranges;
Lost and waiting for you. Go!

RUDYARD KIPLING

So MEN HAVE gone—alone, in pairs and small groups, in great expeditions—searching out the high, hidden places of the earth. They have climbed the cliffs of England, the rugged ranges of North America, the gleaming rock and ice-spires of the Alps. They have journeyed thousands of miles to the Caucasus, the Andes, the lost peaks of Africa and the vast uplifts of Central Asia. They have sought out the summits of the Arctic and Antarctic and of the islands of the sea. Wherever in the world great mountains stand there have been men who lifted their eyes to them and spoke the words of challenge and consecration: "We must get to the top."

Some have got to the top, some have not. Some have found victory and fulfilment behind the ranges, others disappointment and defeat—and sometimes death. All have found danger and privation, long drudgery and backbreaking work. But all, too, have found in their struggles something profoundly worth the doing—for its own sake; and in the long run it has always been the motivating spirit of the climbers, rather than their actual achievements, which is the important and meaningful thing. Some of the most magnificent exploits in mountaineering history have fallen far short of their goal. Men have achieved greatness no more in their victories than in their defeats. That is the mountain way.

The story of the conquest of the earth's high places is not merely a story of mountains, but of mountains *and* men. The Matterhorn without Whymper, McKinley without Hudson Stuck, Everest without Mallory, Kanchenjunga, Nanga Parbat and K2 without the brave men who have climbed and fought and failed upon them would be simply inorganic masses of rock and snow. It is their human associations that are the significant thing to us, not the composition of their stone or the angle of their ridges or the number of feet which their summits tower above the level of the sea. It is that men have struggled there, aspired there.

In something over three-quarters of a century the climbing of great mountains has grown into one of the most stirring adventures of modern times. Happily, it is an adventure of which the end is not in sight. Everest still looks down on earth's conquerors—unconquered. So do the whole royal family of "Eight-thousanders" and uncounted hundreds of other great Himalayan peaks. The Andes, the Antarctic and the sprawling ranges of Alaska and Central Asia still hold hosts of lofty virgin summits which will remain as a challenge to climbers for years to come. Furthermore, exciting, if unauthenticated, rumours keep recurring to the effect that in certain dark corners of inner China and Tibet are mountains even greater than the greatest Himalayas, on which no white man has ever gazed. It is just possible that such reports may be true. More likely they are legends. But whatever the future reveals, the work, the sport, the adventure of mountain climbing are far from over. Great as have been the exploits of the past, still greater ones are yet to come.

But it is not only in Everest and the "Eight-thousanders," big expeditions and "famous firsts," that the future of mountaineering lies. For every climber who blazes a new trail to the unknown heights of Asia and Alaska there will be thousands who follow the familiar routes up familiar peaks—to the summits of the Alps, the Rockies, the hills of Scotland and New England, wherever mountains rise high and challenging above the valleys. They will set no records. Their names will not be printed in newspapers or alpine journals. But they too will know discovery and adventure; and they will be no less mountaineers because the peaks they climb have been climbed and conquered before.

For a mountain is never "conquered." The Matterhorn today can hurl down murderous cannonades of stones as fiercely as in the days of Whymper. The Jungfrau and Mount Rainier can still annihilate a man by the crumbling of a ledge or the tremor of a snowpatch. Even such supposedly domesticated little ranges as the White Mountains or Adirondacks can on occasion become formidable with wind and cold, snow, storm and darkness. There is no royal road to the mountain-tops, but only the road of skill and knowledge, care and enterprise, patience and hard work; and of no field of human activity can it be said more truly that a man receives according to what he gives. He who comes to his mountain with sound body, clear eyes and open heart will seldom be disappointed. He will find adventure on its slopes, mystery and wonder on its summit whether he be the thousandth to stand there or the first.

In general, mountaineering makes its appeal to the best and least selfish elements in men's natures, and the great majority of the world's famous climbers have also been admirable human beings. Yet even earth's loftiest places are not, alas, the exclusive domain of heroes and philosophers. Indeed, we have only to recall Whymper on the summit of the Matterhorn, rolling stones down on his rivals, or the young Nazis on the Eigerwand, breaking their necks for the greater glory of *Führer* and *Vaterland*, to realize that mountains can bring out the worst, as well as the best in men.

But bring it out they inevitably do—whatever is there, whatever a man is. Climb with a companion for a week or a day, or even for a few hours; hear him swearing in a gully and panting on a ridge; feel the quiver of his muscles as he pays out the rope to you along a ticklish ledge; see the expression in his eyes as he sits beside you on a hard-won summit, with a squashed tomato sandwich in his hand and the world at his feet—and you may well discover that you have learned more about him than in twenty years in office, shop or factory. And perhaps about yourself as well.

Men go to the mountains because they need the mountains—because they find behind the ranges things that are hidden from them in the life of the plains. "Our present world," the distinguished climber, Frederic Harrison, once said, "is a world of remarkable civilization, but it is not very natural and not very happy. We need some snatches of the life of youth—to be for a season simply happy and simply healthy. We need to draw sometimes great draughts of simplicity and beauty. We need sometimes that poetry should not be droned into our ears, but flashed into our senses. And, man, with all his knowledge and his pride, needs sometimes to know nothing and to feel nothing, but that he is a marvellous atom in a marvellous world."

These eloquent words of a man who knew and loved mountains were written a good many years ago. But surely they ring no less true today, in a world darkened with strife and hatred, disillusionment and despair.

Indeed there has been no time in human history when mountains and mountaineering have had so much to offer to men. We need to re-discover the vast, harmonious pattern of the natural world of which we are a part—the infinite complexity and variety of its myriad components, the miraculous simplicity of the whole. We need to learn again those essential qualities in our own selves which make us what we are: the energy of our bodies, the alertness of our minds; curiosity and the desire to satisfy it, fear and the will to conquer it. The mountain way may well be a way of escape—from cities and men, from turmoil and doubt, from the perplexities and uncertainties and sorrows that thread our lives. But in the truest and most profound sense it is an escape not *from* but *to* reality.

That men have climbed the Matterhorn and McKinley, Aconcagua and Nanda Devi—and that they will eventually climb Everest itself—means little. That they should want to climb them and try to climb them means everything. For it is the ultimate wisdom of the mountains that a man is never more a man than when he is striving for what is beyond his grasp, and that there is no conquest worth the winning save that over his own weakness and ignorance and fear.

"Have we vanquished an enemy?" asked Mallory.

And there was only one answer:

"None but ourselves."

It is not the summit that matters, but the fight for the summit; not the victory, but the game itself.

APPENDICES

APPENDIX I

A NOTE ON VOLCANOES

STRICTLY SPEAKING, a volcano is any opening in the earth's crust through which heated internal matter is brought to the surface. Virtually all volcanoes, however, assume the form of hills or mountains, sometimes of great height, and it is to these rather than to the actual volcanic mechanism that the term is commonly applied.

Volcanic mountains are of three general types—active, dormant and extinct. They share a common origin in that all were originally built up by their own eruptions, but in their present state they present wide differences in shape, structure and behaviour. Of the extinct type, some—such as Chile's Aconcagua and Mexico's Ixtaccihuatl—no longer even possess craters or lava cones and may more accurately be called peaks of volcanic origin than actual volcanoes. Others—Kilimanjaro and Chimborazo, for instance—although long since cold at their cores, still retain all the typical external features of volcanoes and are universally referred to as such. Peaks of the dormant type, of which many of our own Sierra Nevadas and Cascades are examples, are similarly cones which have been long inactive, but in their case the internal mechanism still exists which makes them *capable* of further eruption. In many cases it is almost impossible to determine whether a peak is extinct or merely dormant.

Active volcanoes differ greatly from one another, both in the frequency and nature of their eruptions. The great Hawaiian craters, for example, are almost continuously active, but rarely violently so. On the other hand, there are mountains such as Vesuvius and Pelé which remain quiescent for centuries, only to break out suddenly in paroxysms of earth-shaking violence. There is a great variety too in the amount and character of discharge. Some volcanoes confine themselves to the pouring down of great streams of lava; other eject steam, ashes, cinders or mud, still others huge chunks of earth and rock. Almost all eruptions, however, are accompanied by the release of great quantities of suffocating vapours, and it is these, more perhaps than any of the others, that have been responsible for the high death roll in most of the famous volcanic disasters of history. At the present time there are some 400 volcanoes on the earth specifically recognized as active, but the actual total figure, including such little-known regions as Antarctica, Alaska and Patagonia, is probably a great deal higher.

The geographic distribution of volcanoes is extremely wide. For the most part, however, they are found fairly close to the sea and in regions where the folding and faulting of the earth's crust is still in active progress. Thus a volcanic zone is very likely to be also an earthquake zone, although there is no direct cause-and-effect relationship between the two phenomena. Many great volcanoes are known to exist beneath the sea, and on a few occasions whole islands have been formed as the result of violent submarine explosions.

All the great land masses have had their share of volcanic activity. Europe, in historic times, has probably had the least, and Vesuvius is today the only live fire-mountain on the continent. The Mediterranean islands, however, have several active peaks—notably the famous Etna and Stromboli—and Iceland, some 500 miles off the northern tip of Scotland, is one of the most persistently eruptive regions in the world. The two loftiest peaks of Africa, as we have seen, are basically volcanic, though extinct. (These, incidentally, provide an exception to the rule that almost all volcanoes are near the sea.) The guardian twins of remote Antarctica, Erebus and Terror, are lava-peaks beneath their permanent sheath of ice and snow—the former still violently eruptive, the latter cold.

Western and Central Asia are almost devoid of volcanoes, as are eastern North and South America, with the exception of parts of the West Indies. The Pacific shores of these continents, however, form part of the greatest volcanic chain in the world. Beginning at the southernmost tip of South America this chain appears and reappears throughout the whole length of the American cordillera —in the Andes of Chile, Bolivia, Peru and Ecuador, in Guatemala and south-central Mexico, in northern California, Oregon and Washington, and along the Alaskan coast. Following the long curve of the Aleutian Islands the volcanic belt then bridges the Bering Sea and sweeps southward again through Japan, Formosa, the Philippines and East Indies, all the way to northern New Zealand. There are, to be sure, many gaps in the vast arc, sometimes of considerable extent; but its general pattern is unmistakable, and when one includes the great firepeaks of the outlying Hawaiian Islands it is no exaggeration to say that fully three-quarters of the earth's major volcanoes rise within sight of the Pacific Ocean.

A NOTE ON VOLCANOES

By and large, volcanoes are not mountaineers' mountains. Most of the accessible ones have been climbed, to be sure, and the giants—Aconcagua and Cotopaxi, Kilimanjaro, Kenya and others—have been the scene of great and celebrated exploits. Almost all are so formed, however, with their symmetrical cones and broad, gentle slopes, that they offer little of climbing interest and few problems other than those of distance and altitude. World-famous summits such as Fujiyama, Popocatepetl, Etna and Mauna Loa, in spite of their height, can be easily gained by anyone with adequate legs and lungs. Still others, scarcely less renowned, are little more than hills.[1]

Volcanoes in their purely volcanic sense, rather than as mountains, do not, of course, come within the scope of this book. Nevertheless it is impossible to leave the subject without at least brief mention of the greatest eruptions. Of these, three stand out above the others as major events in world history.

First, of course, there was the eruption of Vesuvius, in the year 79, which completely buried the Roman cities of Pompeii, Herculaneum and Stabiae and wiped out a large part of their population. To this day it remains one of the famous holocausts of history, and probably no subsequent volcanic upheaval has matched it in destruction of life and property. What is less well known is that Vesuvius has also been violently active on various other occasions, notably in 1631 when its fiery overflow again caught men unprepared and took almost 20,000 lives.

Another major upheaval was that which took place as recently as 1902 on the French West Indian island of Martinique. The 4,400-foot volcano, Pelé, climaxed a week of minor activity with a series of shattering explosions that sent millions of tons of lava and ash cascading down on the surrounding countryside. The nearby town of St. Pierre, largest in the colony, was completely destroyed, and every ship in its busy harbour, with a single exception, was either sunk or consumed by flames. Between thirty and forty thousand people lost their lives, and the carnage was so terrible that for some time after there was much talk of completely evacuating the island.

For sheer physical fury, however, no cataclysm in historic times has approached that of Krakatoa. A small mountainous island of the East Indies, not far from the coast of Java, Krakatoa, during midsummer of 1883, began experiencing profound and increasingly violent volcanic disturbances, and finally, on August twenty-six

[1] The height of a live volcano is apt to vary considerably from year to year, according to whether its activity builds up or tears down the crater rim.

and twenty-seven was convulsed by a series of eruptions that were literally felt around the world. More than half the island was blown into the sea. Geysers of solid rock and earth shot up seventeen miles and more into the air, and ashes, cinders and dust still higher, into the farthest limits of the stratosphere. The principal volcanic cone, which originally had risen to a height of some 2,500 feet, was reduced almost to sea level. Small cones and island masses round about vanished entirely, while new ones appeared where none had been before.

The noise of the explosions was heard at points as much as three thousand miles away—by far the greatest distance at which sound-waves have ever been detected. At Batavia, Java, a hundred miles distant, the sky was black as night at midday, and for months after the whole world experienced unusually brilliant sunrises and sunsets, due to the quantity of dust and ash which had been dispersed through the atmosphere. No less remarkable, and far more serious, were a series of tidal waves which were generated in the ocean near the scene of the eruption and reached halfway around the earth before they spent themselves. Coastal towns, villages and settlements through the East Indies were inundated or washed bodily away, with an estimated loss of more than 36,000 lives. Fortunately Krakatoa itself and its immediately surrounding islands were uninhabited; otherwise the death toll would inevitably have been far higher.

APPENDIX II

ONE HUNDRED FAMOUS MOUNTAINS[1]

WITH LOCATIONS, ALTITUDES AND DATES OF FIRST ASCENT

NORTH AMERICA

Peak	Location	Altitude	First Ascent
McKinley	Alaska	20,300	1913
Logan	Yukon (Canada)	19,850	1925
Orizaba	Mexico	18,225	1848
St. Elias	Alaska	18,024	1897
Popocatepetl	Mexico	17,850	1521
Lucania	Yukon	17,150	1937
Foraker	Alaska	17,000	1934
Wood	Yukon	15,880	unclimbed
Fairweather	Alaska	15,300	1931
Whitney	California	14,502	1873
Rainier	Washington	14,408	1870
Pike's Peak	Colorado	14,108	1819
Grand Teton	Wyoming	13,747	1898
Waddington	Canada	13,280	1936
Robson	Canada	12,972	1913
Washington	New Hampshire	6,290	1642

SOUTH AMERICA

Peak	Location	Altitude	First Ascent
Aconcagua	Chile-Argentine	22,900	1897
Sahama	Bolivia	22,350	1939
Mercedario	Chile	22,300	unclimbed

[1] This is not a list of the hundred highest mountains. It includes merely one hundred selected peaks which are either important in their own right or have played a significant part in the history of mountaineering. The altitudes of many summits—particularly those in remote and little-known regions—have not yet been exactly determined. In these cases, the figures given are the most commonly accepted estimates.

SOUTH AMERICA—contd.

Peak	Location	Altitude	First Ascent
Huascaran	Peru	22,200	1908
Coropuna	Peru	21,700	1911
Illampu (Sorata)	Bolivia	21,500	1919
Tupungato	Chile	21,500	1897
Illimani	Bolivia	21,200	1898
Chimborazo	Ecuador	20,500	1880
El Misti	Peru	20,000	1878
Cotopaxi	Ecuador	19,600	1872
Sarmiento	Tierra del Fuego	7,000	unclimbed

EUROPE

Peak	Location	Altitude	First Ascent
Elbruz	Caucasus (U.S.S.R.)	18,465	1868
Dykhtau	Caucasus (U.S.S.R.)	17,050	1888
Shkara	Caucasus (U.S.S.R.)	17,040	1888
Koshtantau	Caucasus (U.S.S.R.)	16,875	1889
Kasbek	Caucasus (U.S.S.R.)	16,545	1868
Mont Blanc	Alps	15,782	1786
Ushba	Caucasus (U.S.S.R.)	15,410	1903
Monte Rosa	Alps	15,217	1855
Dom (Mischabel)	Alps	14,942	1858
Lyskamm	Alps	14,889	1861
Weisshorn	Alps	14,804	1861
Matterhorn	Alps	14,782	1865
Täschhorn (Mischabel)	Alps	14,700	1862
Dent Blanche	Alps	14,318	1862
Grand Combin	Alps	14,164	1859
Finsteraarhorn	Alps	14,026	1812
Grandes Jorasses	Alps	13,806	1864
Jungfrau	Alps	13,670	1811
Aiguille Verte	Alps	13,520	1865
Mönch	Alps	13,465	1857
Schreckhorn	Alps	13,386	1861
Obergabelhorn	Alps	13,365	1865
Eiger	Alps	13,040	1858
Ortler	Alps	12,802	1804
Monte Viso	Alps	12,609	1861
Wetterhorn	Alps	12,149	1854

EUROPE—contd.

Peak	Location	Altitude	First Ascent
Disgrazia	Alps	12,067	1862
Etna	Sicily	10,758	unknown
Olympus	Greece	10,000	unknown
Mont Aiguille	Alps	7,000	1492
Pilatus	Alps	6,995	1307(?)
Ben Nevis	Scotland	4,406	unknown
Vesuvius	Italy	4,000	unknown

ASIA

Peak	Location	Altitude	First Ascent
Everest	Himalayas	29,141	unclimbed
K2 (Godwin Austen)	Karakoram (Himalayas)	28,250	unclimbed
Kanchenjunga	Himalayas	28,146	unclimbed
Makalu	Himalayas	27,790	unclimbed
Cho-uyo	Himalayas	26,860	unclimbed
Dhaulagiri	Himalayas	26,795	unclimbed
Nanga Parbat	Himalayas	26,620	unclimbed
Gasherbrum (Hidden Peak)	Karakoram	26,470	unclimbed
Broad Peak	Karakoram	26,400	unclimbed
Gosainthan	Himalayas	26,305	unclimbed
Nanda Devi	Himalayas	25,660	1936
Masherbrum	Karakoram	25,660	unclimbed
Kamet	Himalayas	25,447	1931
Tirach Mir	Hindu Kush	25,420	unclimbed
Bride Peak	Karakoram	25,110	unclimbed
Minya Konka	Tibet	24,500	1932
Mustagh Ata	Pamirs	24,388	unclimbed
Jonsong Peak	Himalayas	24,340	1930
Kabru	Himalayas	24,000	1883(?)
Chomolhari	Himalayas	23,930	1937
Mustagh Tower	Karakoram	23,860	unclimbed
Pic Lenin (Mt. Kaufmann)	Pamirs	23,300	1928
Trisul	Himalayas	23,260	1907
Shilla	Himalayas	23,050	1851
Demavend	Persia	18,600	1837
Ararat	Armenia	17,043	1829
Fujiyama	Japan	12,395	unknown

AFRICA

Peak	Location	Altitude	First Ascent
Kilimanjaro	British East Africa	19,717	1889
Kenya	British East Africa	17,040	1899
Ruwenzori	British East Africa	16,793	1905

ELSEWHERE

Peak	Location	Altitude	First Ascent
Karstens Peak	New Guinea	16,730	unclimbed
Mauna Kea	Hawaii	13,825	unknown
Kinabalu	Borneo	13,698	(?)
Mauna Loa	Hawaii	13,675	unknown
Erebus	Antarctica	13,300	1906
Cook	New Zealand	12,350	1894
Gunnbjornsfeld	Greenland	12,139	1935
Forel	Greenland	11,100	1938
Kosciusko	Australia	7,328	unknown

APPENDIX III

GLOSSARY OF MOUNTAINEERING TERMS

(THE FOLLOWING LIST includes only the most common of the many special words and terms employed in mountaineering. The variety of languages from which they are drawn is an interesting indication of the international nature of the sport. The meanings of the initials below are as follows: F.—French; G.—German; I.—Italian.)

aiguille, F.—a rock spire or needle
alp—a mountain pasture
arête, F.—a ridge
belay—securing of a rope by hitching it over a projection or passing it around the body
bergschrund, G.—a large crevasse separating the main portion of a glacier from its upper slopes
bivouac—a temporary camp
boss—a knob of rock; a protuberance
cairn—a pile of stones set up to mark a summit or route
chimney—a steep, narrow cleft in a rock wall
chockstone—a large block of rock wedged in a chimney
col, F.—a pass, or the low point of a ridge
cornice—a projecting mass of snow, as on a ridge
couloir, F.—a gully
courte-échelle, F.—clambering on the body or head of another climber
crampons, F.—climbing irons. Iron or steel frames, with projecting spikes, that are attached to the soles of the boots for use on steep snow or ice
crevasse, F.—a deep crevice or fissure in a glacier, caused by its downward movement
espadrilles, F.—rope-soled climbing shoes
gendarme, F.—a rock tower, usually on a ridge
glissade, F.—sliding down a snow-slope
ice-fall—the steepest section of a glacier, usually taking the form of a wildly jumbled mass of ice
joch, G.—a pass, or the low point of a ridge

karabiner, G.—a metal snap-ring, usually used in conjunction with a piton, through which the rope may be passed for greater security during difficult climbing

kletterschuhe, G.—rope-soled shoes

moraine—rock and debris carried down by a glacier

névé, F.—a snowfield lying above the snow-line, usually the source of a glacier

pitch—a short, steep section of rock

piton, F.—a metal spike which may be driven into rock or ice to afford support for hand, foot or rope

rappel, F.—roping down. The manœuvre of letting oneself down a steep place by means of a supplementary rope

scarpetti, I.—rope-soled shoes

scree—small stones and rock debris, usually found in the form of slopes at the foot of steep rock faces

serac, F.—a tower of ice, usually found on glaciers

snow-bridge—an arch of snow joining two sides of a crevasse

traverse—the horizontal or diagonal crossing of a mountainside. Also the crossing of a peak or pass from one side to the other

verglas, F.—thin veneer of ice on rock

APPENDIX IV

READING LIST

THOUSANDS OF BOOKS and articles have been written about mountains and mountaineering. They cover every imaginable phase of the subject and, together, comprise a vast treasury of factual information, technical theory and high—and true—adventure. The following list is in no sense a complete bibliography, but represents merely the author's selection of certain books which he feels would be of most interest to the general reader. Highly technical and specialized works are omitted, as are all books written in foreign languages which have not been translated into English. With the exception of a few foreign publications, all volumes which have been used in the preparation of this book are included.

The list is divided into three principal sections, as follows: (1) books on mountaineering in general; (2) books dealing with specific mountains and expeditions; (3) journals and guides.

GENERAL

Mountain Craft, edited by Geoffrey Winthrop Young. The definitive English work on the subject and a "must" for any mountaineering library.

Mountaineering, edited by Sydney Spencer. An encyclopedia of the sport, with contributions by many authorities, mostly English.

Mountaineering, by Claude Wilson. A general consideration of climbing regions and climbing technique by a veteran of the English Alpine Club.

The Complete Mountaineer and *Modern Mountaineering*, by George D. Abraham. Mostly on technique.

Mountaineering Art, by Harold Raeburn. A pioneer Himalayan climber considers his craft.

Mountain Memories: A Pilgrimage of Romance, by Sir William Martin Conway. A record of thirty years of exploration and climbing in all parts of the world.

The Romance of Mountaineering, by R. L. G. Irving. A veteran English climber on the history and significance of mountaineering.

The Mountain Way, edited by R. L. G. Irving. An anthology of prose and verse about mountains and mountain climbing.

Ten Great Mountains, by R. L. G. Irving. A selection of the great adventure stories of mountaineering.

The Making of a Mountaineer, by George Finch. Experiences and observations of one of the foremost modern English climbers.

Mountains and Men, by Leonard H. Robbins. Tales of the great ascents (through 1930) by a popular American writer.

The Mountain Scene, Peaks and Valleys, A Camera in the Hills, My Alpine Album, by F. S. Smythe. Four volumes of photographs taken by the author during his long climbing career in Europe and the Himalayas.

NORTH AMERICA

ALASKA

The Conquest of Mount McKinley, by Belmore Browne. The most complete and authoritative book on North America's highest mountain.

The Ascent of Denali, by Hudson Stuck. The story of the first ascent of McKinley by the man who accomplished it.

To the Top of the Continent, by Frederick Cook. Dr. Cook's concocted story of his "ascent" of McKinley.

The Ascent of Mount St. Elias, by Filippo de Filippi. The winning of the great Alaskan peak by the expedition of the Duke of the Abruzzi.

Travels in Alaska, by John Muir. Includes many descriptions of mountains and glaciers.

CANADA

The Glittering Mountains of Canada, by J. Monroe Thorington. History and description of the Canadian Rockies.

A Climber's Guide to the Rocky Mountains of Canada, by Howard Palmer and J. Monroe Thorington. (Third edition published in 1939.)

In the Heart of the Canadian Rockies, by Sir James Outram. Exploration and first ascents by one of the foremost pioneers in the field.

Climbs and Explorations in the Canadian Rockies, by Hugh Stutfield and J. N. Collie. The adventures of two other noted pioneers.

Mountaineering and Exploration in the Selkirks, by Howard Palmer. The authoritative work on this great Canadian range.

READING LIST

A Climber's Guide to the Interior Ranges of British Columbia, by J. Monroe Thorington.
Round Mystery Mountain, by Sir Norman Watson and E. J. King. Ski exploration in British Columbia, especially around Mount Waddington.
Where the Clouds Can Go, by Conrad Kain. Autobiography of a famous Austrian guide who made many of his greatest climbs in the mountains of Canada.

WESTERN UNITED STATES

Our Greatest Mountain, by F. W. Schmoe. Mount Rainier.
Mount Rainier: a Record of Exploration, by Edward S. Meany.
Wy' East "The Mountain," by F. N. McNeil. A chronicle of Mount Hood.
The Mountains of California, My First Summer in the Sierra, Steep Trails, by John Muir. Three of the many books written by the noted naturalist on the mountains of our West.
Mountaineering in the Sierra Nevada, by Clarence King. One of the earliest and most famous American mountain books, first published in 1872.
A Journal of Ramblings Through the High Sierras, by Joseph LeConte. Another early account of the mountains of California.
Guide to the John Muir Trail and the High Sierra Region, by Walter A. Starr, Jr.
The Teton Peaks and Their Ascents, by Fritiof Fryxell. Key to the best rock-climbing in the American Rockies.
Fourteen Thousand Feet, by J. L. J. Hart and Elinor Kingery. The Colorado Rockies.
The Rocky Mountain National Park, by E. A. Mills.
The Call of the Mountains, by LeRoy Jeffers. Rambles among the mountains of the western United States and Canada.

EASTERN UNITED STATES

Appalachian Mountain Club White Mountain Guidebook. The definitive guide to the most important of our eastern ranges.
The Book of the White Mountains, by J. Anderson and S. Morse. One of the best of the recent books on the region.
Mount Washington Reoccupied, by Robert S. Monahan. A record of scientific investigation on New England's highest summit.
Bradford on Mount Washington, by Bradford Washburn. A boy's book.

SOUTH AMERICA

Travels Among the Great Andes of the Equator, by Edward Whymper. The great climber's adventures and ascents in the mountains of Ecuador.

The Highest Andes, by Edward FitzGerald. The conquest of Aconcagua and Tupungato.

From the Alps to the Andes, by Mattias Zurbriggen. Autobiography of the famous guide who was the first up Aconcagua.

The Bolivian Andes, by Sir William Martin Conway. A record of exploration and climbing in the late 1890's by one of the foremost mountaineers of his day.

Aconcagua and Tierra del Fuego, by Sir William Martin Conway. Conway's expedition to the southernmost Andes.

A Search for the Apex of America, by Annie S. Peck. Exploits of a famous lady-mountaineer in Peru and Bolivia, including the conquest of Huascaran.

Inca Land, by Hiram Bingham. Includes an account of the first ascent of Coropuna.

EUROPE

EARLY DAYS IN THE ALPS

The Life of Horace Benedict de Saussure, by Douglas Freshfield (in collaboration with Henry F. Montaignier). The story of the father of mountaineering as told by an illustrious climber of later days. (De Saussure's own writings are not available in translation.)

Travels Through the Alps, by J. D. Forbes. Adventures of one of the foremost pioneer climbers of a century ago.

The Story of Mont Blanc, by Albert Smith. History of the mountain and an account of his own ascent (in 1851) by the first and greatest press-agent of mountaineering.

Mont Blanc Sideshow : the Life and Times of Albert Smith, by J. Monroe Thorington.

The Annals of Mont Blanc, by C. E. Mathews. A history of the mountain through the nineteenth century.

Where There's a Will There's a Way, by the Rev. Charles Hudson and E. S. Kennedy. A notable ascent of Mont Blanc in 1855.

Wanderings Among the High Alps, by Alfred Wills. Experiences of another noted pioneer.

Hours of Exercise in the Alps, by John Tyndall. Climbing adventures of the famous scientist, including the first ascent of the

READING LIST

Weisshorn. (Other Alpine books by Tyndall are *The Glaciers of the Alps* and *Mountaineering in 1861*.)
The Alps in 1861, by A. W. Moore. Stories of many great ascents by one of the outstanding climbers of the nineteenth century.
Peaks, Passes and Glaciers, by the members of the Alpine Club of London. (Three series.) Famous Alpine ascents of mountaineering's Golden Age, described by the men who made them.
The Early Mountaineers, by Francis Gribble. Stories of the great first ascents in the Alps.
Pioneers of the Alps, by C. D. Cunningham and A. Abney. Biographies of the foremost Alpine guides of the early days.
Scrambles Amongst the Alps in the Years 1860–69, by Edward Whymper. The Alpine career of the greatest climber of his time, including the complete story of the Matterhorn. A mountain classic.
The Ascent of the Matterhorn, by Edward Whymper. The same as the above, but with Whymper's other climbs omitted.
Edward Whymper, by F. S. Smythe. A biography.
The Playground of Europe, by Sir Leslie Stephen. Another classic, the name of which has become synonymous with Switzerland.

THE ALPS IN MORE RECENT TIMES

Conway-Coolidge Climbers' Guides, edited by Sir William Martin Conway, W. A. B. Coolidge and others. Standard guides to the Alps for more than half a century. (Published in pocket editions.)
Alpine Guides, by John Ball. Another famous series of guide-books. (In three large volumes.)
The Alps in Nature and History and *Alpine Studies*, by W. A. B. Coolidge. Two of the author's many books on various aspects of the Alps.
My Climbs in the Alps and Caucasus, by A. F. Mummery. The career of the man who revolutionized the technique of climbing. A veritable mountaineer's bible.
The High Alps Without Guides, by A. G. Girdlestone. A record of various exploits in the early days of guideless climbing.
The Italian Alps, by Douglas Freshfield. One of the earliest books by the great climber whose active career spanned half a century.
Above the Snow Line, by Clinton Dent. Mountaineering sketches by a well-known pioneer-climber of the Alps and Caucasus.
The Alps from End to End, by Sir William Martin Conway. Conway's "grand tour" of the Alps in the 1890's.
Peaks and Precipices, by Guido Rey. Records of many great ascents, mostly in the Dolomites, by a noted Italian mountaineer.

The Matterhorn, by Guido Rey. Whymper's mountain forty years after.

Alpine Pilgrimage, by Julius Kugy. The career of a distinguished German mountaineer.

Climbs on Alpine Peaks, by Abate Achille Ratti. The climbing adventures of the young priest who later became Pope Pius XI.

Adventures of an Alpine Guide, by Christian Klucker. Life story of one of the most famous professionals.

On High Hills, by Geoffrey Winthrop Young. Reminiscences of a lifetime of climbing. An aristocrat of mountain books.

The Mountains of Youth, by Arnold Lunn. Contains much on winter mountaineering and skiing.

Climbs and Ski Runs, by F. S. Smythe. Mountaineering adventures in the Alps, Great Britain and Corsica by one of the foremost English climbers of the present day. (This is only one of several books on European mountaineering by Mr. Smythe.)

Climbs on Mont Blanc, by J. and T. de Lépiney. (Translated by Sydney Spencer.) New and precarious trail-blazing by two young French experts.

They Climbed the Alps, by Edwin Muller. Accounts of various famous ascents by a contemporary American writer.

Climbing Days, by Dorothy Pilley. A lively personal account of recent climbing excursions in the Alps.

Among the Alps with Bradford, by Bradford Washburn. A boy's book.

ELSEWHERE IN EUROPE

British Mountain Climbs, by George D. Abraham. Deals with climbing districts and routes.

Rock Climbing in the English Lake District, by O. G. Jones. One of the best of many books on the region.

Norway: the Northern Playground, by W. C. Slingsby. The standard work on mountaineering in Scandinavia.

The Exploration of the Caucasus, by Douglas Freshfield. The definitive work on the subject and one of the great books of mountaineering history.

ASIA

EARLY HIMALAYAN EXPLORATION

Climbing and Exploration in the Karakoram Himalayas, by Sir William Martin Conway. Pioneering on the grand scale.

Climbing in the Himalayas and Other Mountain Ranges, by J. Norman

READING LIST

Collie. Accounts of various Himalayan journeys including the Nanga Parbat expedition on which Mummery lost his life.

Round Kanchenjunga, by Douglas Freshfield. Narrative of a famous trip of exploration and a classic of its kind.

Five Months in the Himalaya, by A. L. Mumm. Adventure and exploration in the early days.

Karakoram and Western Himalaya, by Filippo de Filippi. An account of the K2 expedition of the Duke of the Abruzzi.

In the Ice World of the Himalayas, by Fanny and Hunter Workman. One of many books written by the remarkable American couple who were among the pioneers of the Himalayas.

Approach to the Hills, by C. F. Meade. Recollections of a veteran mountaineer who blazed many new Himalayan trails.

Wonders of the Himalaya, by Sir Francis Younghusband. Reminiscences covering many years and expeditions.

Himalayan Wanderer, Kulu and Lahoul, 20 Years in the Himalayas, by Gen. C. G. Bruce. Three books of mountain memories by one of the foremost explorers of the great range.

MOUNT EVEREST

Mount Everest: the Reconnaissance, by Lt. Col. C. K. Howard-Bury and others. Official account of the preliminary expedition of 1921.

The Assault on Mount Everest, 1922, by Gen. C. G. Bruce and others. Official account.

The Fight for Everest, 1924, by Lt.-Col. E. F. Norton and others. Official account.

The Epic of Mount Everest, by Sir Francis Younghusband. A résumé of the expeditions of 1921, 1922 and 1924.

The Story of Everest, by Capt. John Noel. Account of the same three expeditions by the photographer of the 1922 and 1924 exploits.

After Everest, by T. H. Somervell. Reminiscences of a famous "Everester."

George Leigh-Mallory, by David Pye. A memoir.

Attack on Everest, by Hugh Ruttledge. Story of the 1933 expedition recounted by its leader.

Camp VI, by F. S. Smythe. The 1933 adventure.

Everest: the Unfinished Adventure, by Hugh Ruttledge. Official account of the 1936 attempt.

Everest, the Challenge, by Sir Francis Younghusband. A discussion of the various expeditions, including an account of the 1936 attempt.

First Over Everest : the Houston-Mount Everest Expedition, 1933, by Air-commodore P. F. M. Fellowes and others. Over the top of the world by plane.

OTHER RECENT HIMALAYAN EXPLOITS

Himalayan Campaign, by Paul Bauer. Account of the great Bavarian attacks on Kanchenjunga in 1929 and 1931. Translated and condensed from the original German by Sumner Austin.

The Kanchenjunga Adventure, by F. S. Smythe. Story of the Dyhrenfurth expedition of 1930. Includes an account of the conquest of Jonsong Peak.

Kamet Conquered, by F. S. Smythe. The "highest yet" of 1931.

The Naked Mountain, by Elizabeth Knowlton. Account of the German-American Nanga Parbat expedition of 1932.

Nanga Parbat Adventure, by Fritz Bechtold. The disastrous exploit of 1934.

Himalayan Quest, by Paul Bauer. Includes accounts of several successful climbs of 1936 and of the Nanga Parbat tragedy of 1937.

Nanda Devi, by Eric Shipton. The discovery of the route to the mountain, in 1934, by the author and H. W. Tilman.

The Ascent of Nanda Devi, by H. W. Tilman. The conquest, two years later, of what remains today the highest mountain ever climbed to the top.

Blank on the Map, by Eric Shipton. Exploration in the farthest Karakoram.

Himalayan Assault, by Henri de Segogne and others. The French attempt on Gasherbrum in 1936.

Helvellyn to Himalaya, by F. S. Chapman. Climbing adventures in many lands, culminating in the first ascent of Chomolhari.

The Everlasting Hills, by J. Waller. Account of the 1938 attempt on Masherbrum, in the Karakoram.

The Throne of the Gods, by Arnold Heim and August Gansser. Story of a recent journey of exploration and scientific investigation.

Peaks and Lamas, by Marco Pallis. A subjective account of two recent Himalayan expeditions by a man who is both a mountaineer and a student of Tibetan Buddhism.

Five Miles High, by Members of the First American Karakoram Expedition. Edited by Robert Bates. The story of the splendid 1938 attempt on K2.

Images de L'Himalaya. A portfolio of magnificent Himalayan photographs, mostly by Vittorio Sella. (Published in France, but available in this country.)

ELSEWHERE IN ASIA

Men Against the Clouds, by R. L. Burdsall and A. B. Emmons. The conquest of Minya Konka, in Tibet, by a party of Americans.

The Ascent of Mount Stalin, by Michael Romm. A Soviet expedition to one of the great peaks of the Pamirs.

Mountaineering and Exploration in the Japanese Alps, by the Rev. Walter Weston. The definitive book on mountaineering in Japan.

AFRICA AND ELSEWHERE

Across East African Glaciers, by Hans Meyer. The first ascent of Kilimanjaro.

From Ruwenzori to the Congo, by A. F. R. Wollaston. Early exploration.

Ruwenzori, by Filippo de Filippi. Account of the great expedition of the Duke of the Abruzzi to The Mountains of the Moon.

Snow on the Equator, by H. W. Tilman. Experiences of fourteen years as a planter and mountaineer in East Africa. Includes ascents of Kilimanjaro, Kenya and Ruwenzori.

In Coldest Africa, by Carveth Wells. Travels among the high ranges by a well-known American explorer.

The High Alps of New Zealand, by the Rev. W. S. Green. Adventures of a noted clergyman-mountaineer.

Climbs in the New Zealand Alps, by Edward FitzGerald. The conqueror of Aconcagua on the other side of the world.

The Conquest of Mount Cook, by Freda Du Faur. The climbing of New Zealand's highest peak.

Unclimbed New Zealand, by John Pascoe. A record of recent mountaineering adventures.

Exploration of Mount Kina Balu, by John Whitehead. An expedition to the great mountain of North Borneo.

The First Crossing of Spitzbergen, by Sir William Martin Conway. Mountaineering in the Arctic.

The Heart of the Antarctic, by Sir Ernest Shackleton. Contains an account of the ascent of Mount Erebus.

JOURNALS AND GUIDES

Journals of mountaineering are published by scores of clubs and organizations all over the world. Among the most important, in English, are:

Alpine Journal, published semi-annually by the Alpine Club, London. In existence since 1857.
Himalayan Journal, published annually by the Himalayan Club, of Calcutta.
Canadian Alpine Journal, published annually by the Alpine Club of Canada.
American Alpine Journal, published annually by the American Alpine Club, New York. First issued in 1929.
Appalachia, published semi-annually by the Appalachian Mountain Club, Boston. First issued in 1879.
Trail and Timberline, published monthly by the Colorado Mountain Club, of Denver.
Sierra Club Bulletin, published annually by the Sierra Club of San Francisco.
Mazamas, published annually by The Mazamas (climbing club), of Portland, Oregon.
The Mountaineer, published annually by The Mountaineers (climbing club), of Seattle.

In addition to their journals, most mountaineering clubs issue guide-books and maps of the regions in which they are particularly interested. In the United States considerable material is also published by the National Park Service of the Department of the Interior, the WPA Federal Writers' Project, and the various state governments.

INDEX

INDEX

Abruzzi, Duke of the, 19, 86, 140 ff, 152, 155, 241, 242
Absaroka Mts., 256
acclimatization, 215, 233
Aconcagua, 112, 114, 122 ff, 293, 295
Adirondack Mts., 259
Agassiz, Louis, 40
Aiguille (Mont), 31
aiguilles of Chamonix, 28, 71, 282
airplane expeditions, 108, 109, 230, 246
Alaska Range, 240
Albert, King of the Belgians, 19
Aletschhorn, 29, 41
Aleutian Range, 239, 240
Allegheny Mts., 259
Almer, Christian, 58, 60, 69
Alpine Clubs
  Alpine Club of London, 43, 68, 75, 260
  American Alpine Club, 193, 197, 260
  Appalachian Mountain Club, 260
  Deutsch-Osterreichischer Alpenverein, 76, 130
  Mazamas, The, 260
  Mountaineers, The, 260
  Sierra Club, 260
Alps, the, 18, 22 ff, 263
  Albula, 29
  Austrian, 30
  Bergamasque, 29
  Bernina, 30
  Cottian, 26
  Dauphiné, 26, 31
  Graian, 27
  Japanese, 88
  Julian, 29
  Lepontine, 29
  Maritime, 26
  New Zealand, 89
  Pennine, 28 ff
  Rhaetian, 30
  Silvretta, 30
  Tarentaise, 27
Altai Mts., 87, 148
Altyn Tag Mts., 87
Ampato, 119
Ancohuma, 120
Anderegg, Jakob, 69, 73
Anderegg, Melchior, 69, 73

Anderson, Pete, 98 ff
Andes, 86, 111 ff, 237, 287, 294
Antarctica, mountains of, 86
Apennine Mts., 82
Appalachian Highlands, 257 ff
Appalachian Trail, 259
Ararat (Mount), 17
Aschenbrenner, 186
Assiniboine (Mount), 249
Aten, Arthur, 101
Atlas Mts., 17, 134
Austen, Colonel Godwin, 191
Australia, mountains of, 89

balance climbing, 270
Balkan Mts., 83
Balmat, Jacques, 35 ff
Baltoro Spires, 191
Barrill, Edward, 96
Bates, Robert, 193 ff, 246
Bauer, Paul, 19, 90, 170, 175 ff, 188, 190
Beartooth Mts., 256
Beaufoy, Colonel, 39
Beauman, E. B., 159
Beetham, Mr., 219
belaying, 273, 274, 279
Ben Nevis, 81, 82
Bennen, 43, 56
Berkshire Mts., 259
Bernese Oberland, 29, 39, 77
Bernina (Piz), 30
Bertha (Mount), 246
Biener, Franz, 58, 60
Bietschhorn, 29, 41
Bighorn Mts., 256
Bingham, Hiram, 19, 119
Birnie, Captain E., 159, 160, 227
Blackburn (Mount), 242
Black Hills, 257
Blanc (Mont), 27 ff, 33 ff, 69, 70 ff
Blue Ridge Mts., 259
Blümlisalp, 29
Bona (Mount), 245
Bourrit, Marc Théodore, 36 ff
Breithorn, 28
Bride Peak, 153, 191, 192
Bright, Norman, 246
British Columbia, Ranges of, 250

INDEX

British mountaineering, 81, 82
Broad Peak, 172, 173, 191, 200
Brocklebank, T. A., 229
Brown, Professor T. G., 165
Browne Belmore 95 ff
Bruce, General C. G., 153, 162, 213 ff
Bruce, Geoffrey, 14, 223 ff
Buchan John (Lord Tweedsmuir) 19
Buet, 28
Bullock C. H., 206, 209, 210
Burdsall, Richard, 160, 193, 194
Burgener, Alexander, 69, 73

Caribou Mts., 250
Carnicero, 118
Carpathian Mts. 83
Carpé Allan 108, 109, 243, 245
Carrel, Jean-Antoine, 51 ff, 69, 116, 123
Carrel, Louis, 69
Carter, H. A., 165
Cascade Range, 254, 293
Castor, 28
Cathedral Peaks, 240
Catskill Mts., 259
Caucasus Mts., 17, 83 ff
Cervin (Mont), see Matterhorn
Cervino (Monte), see Matterhorn
Chapman, F. Spencer, 170
Charlet, Armand, 70
Charmoz, the, 28, 71
Chettan, 180
Chimborazo, 115, 116, 293
Chomolhari, 170
Chomolönzo, 210
Chomolungma, see Everest
Cho-uyo, 172, 173
Chugach Range, 240, 246
Clemenceau (Mount), 249
clothing, 282, 283
Clydesdale, Marquis of, 230
Collie, J. Norman, 153
Columbia (Mount), 249
Columbian Icefield, 249
Conway, Sir William Martin, 72, 86, 120, 123 132, 152, 155, 191
Cook, Dr. Frederick, 95 ff
Cook (Mount), 89
Coolidge W. A. B., 19, 72
Cordillera Blanca, 118
  Central, 115
  de Huayhuash, 118
  Occidental, 121
  Oriental, 119
  Real, 120
cornices, 280, 281
Coropuna, 119
Cotopaxi, 115, 116, 295
Coveny, Laurence, 253
crampons, 279, 281, 282

Cranmer, Chappell, 197 ff
Crawford, C. G., 213, 218
crevasses, 277 ff
Crillon (Mount), 245
Cromwell, Eaton, 197 ff
Croz, Michel-Auguste, 58 ff

dangers of mountaineering, 266 ff
d'Angeville, Henriette, 39
da Vinci, Leonardo, 31
de Filippi, Filippo, 141
Deltaform (Mount), 249
Denali, see McKinley
Dent Blanche, 28, 41
Dent, Clinton, 85
Dent d'Herens, 28, 49
Dents du Midi, 28
de Saussure, Henri Bénedict, 19, 34 ff
de Ville, Antoine, 31
Devil's Tower, 253
Dhaulagiri, 149, 153, 172, 173
Disgrazia (Monte della), 29, 41, 43
Djebel Toukhal, 134
Dolent (Mont), 28
Dolomites, 20, 87, 282
Dom, 28, 41
Donkin, W., 84, 85
Douglas, Lord Francis, 61 ff
Drakensberg Mts., 135
Dru, the, 28
Dunn, Robert, 242
Durrance, Jack, 197 ff
Dyhrenfurth, Gunther, 158, 170, 173, 179 ff, 192
Dyhrenfurth, Mrs. Hettie, 179, 192
Dyhrenfurth, Norman, 246
Dykhtau, 84

Ecrins, les, 27
Eiger, 29, 77
Eigerwand, 77 ff
Elbert (Mount), 257
Elbruz, 84
Emmons, Arthur, 160, 165
Empedocles, 17
equipment for climbing, 281 ff
Erebus, 87, 294
Escobar, A. M., 116
Etna, 17, 82, 294, 295
Everest, Sir George, 204
Everest (Mount), 13 ff, 147, 149 ff, 172, 173, 192, 204 ff, 263, 264, 287

Fairweather (Mount), 241, 245
Fairweather Range, 241, 246,
Farmer, E. F., 175
Fellowes, Air-commodore, 230
Finch, Capt. George, 213 ff
Finsteraarhorn, 29, 41

INDEX

FitzGerald, Edward, 89, 123 ff
Foraker (Mount), 94, 96, 240, 245
Forbes, J. D., 39, 42
Forel (Mount), 86
Foster, Colonel W. W., 243 ff, 249
Fox, H., 84, 85
Franconia Range, 258
Freshfield, Douglas, 72, 84 ff, 140, 142, 152 ff, 174 ff, 205
Fujiyama, 87, 295

Gabriel, Peter, 246
Gannet Peak, 256
Gansser, August, 171
Gasherbrum (Hidden Peak), 170, 172, 173, 191, 192, 200
Gaspard Père, 69
Géant, 28
geology of mountains, 263 ff
Gesner, Conrad, 31
Ghiglione, Piero, 121
glaciers, 276 ff
glissading, 280
Godwin Austen (Mount), see K2
Golden Throne, 191, 192
Gosainthan, 172, 173
Graham, W. W., 151, 158, 161, 174
Grand Combin, 28, 41
Grand Paradis, 27
Grand Teton, 256
Grande Casse, 27
Grandes Jorasses, 28, 41, 77, 80
Granite Peak, 256
Great Gable, 81
Great Smoky Mts., 259
Green Mts., 259
Green, Rev. W. A., 89
Greene, C. R., 159, 160
Greenland, mountains of, 86
Grépon, 28, 71, 72
Grivola, 27
Gross Glockner, 30
Gross Venediger, 31, 41
Guatemala, mountains of, 251
guideless climbing, 73, 267
guides and guiding, 34, 43, 69, 70, 123, 155, 266, 267
Gunnbjornsfjeld, 86
Güssfeldt, Paul, 72, 123, 125, 127

Hadow, Mr., 61 ff
Hadrian, Emperor, 17
Hall, Henry S., Jr., 243
Harper, Walter, 104 ff
Harris, Wyn, 227, 229
Harrison, Frederic, quoted, 289
Hartmann, Hans, 182 ff
Harz Mts., 82
Hayes (Mount), 240

Hazard, Mr., 219 ff
Hedin, Sven, 87
Heim, Arnold, 171
Helicon (Mount), 17, 83
Heron, Dr. A. M., 206
Herron, Rand, 184 ff
High Tatra Mts., 83
Himalaya Mts., 86, 147 ff, 263, 287
Hindu Kush Mts., 87, 148, 150
Hingston, Major R. W. G., 219
Hohe Dachstein, 30
Holdsworth, H. L., 159
Hood (Mount), 254
Hooker, Sir Joseph, 174
House, William 193 ff, 250, 253
Houston, Dr. Charles, 165 ff, 193 ff, 245, 246
Howard-Bury, Colonel C. K., 206
Hualcan, 118
Huascaran, 118
Hubbard, Father, 240
Hubbard (Mount), 247
Hudson, Charles, 19, 42, 43, 61 ff
Humboldt, Alexander von, 116
Hungabee (Mount), 249
Hunter (Mount), 240, 247
Huxley, Julian, 19

Ice-axe, 279, 281
Illampu, 120
Illimani, 120, 126
Irvine, Andrew, 204, 219 ff
Ixtaccihuatl, 251, 293

Japan, mountains of, 87
Jesus, 17
Jonsong Peak, 158, 180
Jungfrau, 29, 40, 288
Jura Mts., 82

K2 (Mount Godwin Austen), 147, 150, 152, 153, 157, 172, 173, 191 ff, 287
Kabru, 151, 158, 174
Kain, Conrad, 249
Kamet, 149, 159 ff, 192
Kanchenjunga, 147, 149, 152, 157, 172 ff, 287
karabiner, 74, 274, 282
Karakoram Range, 150, 152, 170, 172, 173, 190 ff, 287
Karstens, Harry, 104 ff
Kasbek, 84
Katahdin (Mount), 258 ff
Katmai, 103, 239
Kaufmann (Mount) (Pic Lenin), 157
Keen, Dora, 242
Kellas, A. M., 19, 153, 159, 175, 205 ff, 211

Kennedy, E. S., 42, 43
Kenya, 133, 135, 137, 295
Kilauea, 88
Kilimanjaro, 133, 135, 136, 293, 295
Kinabalu, 88
Klucker, Christian, 70
Knowlton, Elizabeth, 184
Knubel, Josef, 69, 73
Kosciusko (Mount), 89
Koshtantau, 84
Koven, Theodore, 109
Krakatoa, 295, 296
Kunlun Mts., 87, 148

Laing, A. M., 243
Lambart, H. F., 242
Lanti, Nicola, 125 ff
Lassen (Mount), 254
La Voy, Merle, 101
Lefroy (Mount), 249
Leone (Monte), 29
Leo Pargyal, 151
Lewis Range, 255
Lewa, 159
Lhakpa Chede, 223
Lhotse, 172, 210
Lick, Harry, 107
Linard (Piz), 30
Lindly, Alfred, 107, 108
Lizard Head, 257
Lloyd, Peter, 165, 231
Lochmatter, Franz, 69, 73
Logan (Mount), 241 ff
Longland, J. L., 229
Long's Peak, 257
Longstaff, Dr. Thomas, 153, 158, 159, 162, 205, 213
Loomis, W. F., 165
Louis (Mount), 249
Lucania (Mount), 246
Luft, Ulrich, 188
Lyskamm, 28, 41, 43

MacCarthy, Captain A. H., 242 ff, 249
Macdonald, Reginald, 50 ff
McGonogol, Charley, 98 ff
Mackinder, Sir Halford, 137
McKinley (Mount), 93 ff, 238 ff, 245 ff 287, 289
McPhee, Billy, 97, 99
Makalu, 149, 153, 172, 173, 210
Malaspina Glacier, 239, 241
Mallory, George Leigh-, 18, 90, 204 ff, 287, 290
Masherbrum, 170, 191
Matterhorn, 28, 44 ff, 68, 69, 72, 77, 80, 268, 272, 287-9
Mauna Kea, 88

Mauna Loa, 88, 295
Meade, C. F., 153, 159
Mechanization, 74, 75, 282
Meije, la, 27, 69
Mercedario, 122
Mer de Glace, 28
Merkl, Willy, 184 ff
Mexico, mountains of, 250, 251
Meyer, family, 39, 40
Meyer, Hans, 136
Meynet, Luk, 50 ff
Minya Konka, 160
Mischabel, 28, 64
Misti (El), 119
Mitchell (Mount), 259
Mitre, the, 249
Mitre Peak, 191
Mönch, 29, 41
Monischee Mts., 250
monsoon, 154, 165, 213 ff, 229 ff
Mont-aux-Sources, 135
Moore, A. W., 42, 72, 73, 84
Moore, Terris, 160, 245, 246
Moran (Mount), 256
Morgan, Robert, 243
Morris, Capt. C. G., 213
Morshead, Major, 206, 213 ff
Moses, 17
Mountains of the Moon, *see Ruwenzori*
Muir, John, 255
Muldrow Glacier, 98 ff
Mumm, A. L., 140, 142, 153
Mummery, A. F., 18, 71 ff, 152, 184, 269
Mustagh, Tower, 191

Nanda Devi, 149, 160 ff
Nanga Parbat, 150, 152, 157, 172, 173, 184 ff, 287
Nan Shan Mts., 87, 148
Napoo Yishay, 223
Natazhat (Mount), 242
nationalism, 75 ff
New Zealand, mountains of, 89
Noah, 17
Noel, Captain John, 213 ff
North Twin, 249
Norton, Lieutenant-Colonel E. F., 213ff
Nutzotin Range, 240

Obergabelhorn, 28
Odell, N. E., 19, 165 ff, 219 ff
Oglethorpe (Mount), 259
Olympus (Mount), 17, 83
Orizaba, 251
Ortler, 30, 41
Owen (Mount), 256
Oxygen, 216, 225, 233
Ozark Mts., 257

INDEX

Paccard, Michel Gabriel, 35 ff
Pacific Islands, mountains of the, 88, 294 ff
Pallis, Marco, 171
Palu (Piz), 30
Pamir Mts., 87, 148, 150, 158
Parker, Herschel, 95, 100 ff
Parnassus (Mount), 17, 83
Pasang Kikuli, 167, 199 ff
Pasang Lama, 199 ff
Pearson, Grant, 108
Peck, Annie S., 117
Pelé, 293, 295
Pelvoux (Mont), 27, 41
Petzoldt, Paul, 193 ff
Philip V of Macedon, 17
Pike's Peak, 257
Pilatus, 32
Pillar Rock, 81
Pioneer Peak, 152
Pisgah, 17, 163, 166
piton, 74, 273, 282
Pius XI, Pope (Abate Achille Ratti), 19
Pizzo Rotondo, 29
Pocono Mts., 259
Pollux, 28
Popocatapetl, 251, 295
Prem, Joseph, 121
Presidential Range, 258
Purcell Range, 250
Pyramid Peak, 152
Pyrenees Mts., 82

Queen Mary Peak, 191, 192

Raeburn, Harold, 206, 207
Rainier (Mount), 254, 288
rappel, 274, 275
Reid, Wilhelm, 116
Requin, 28
Rey, Guido, 72
Rheinwaldhorn, 29
Rickmer-Rickmers, W., 158
Robson (Mount), 248
rock climbing, 268 ff
Rocky Mts , 252, 255 ff
Rocky Mts., of Canada, 247 ff
Rongbuk Glacier, 209 ff
rope, use of, 271 ff
Roraima (Mount), 111
Rosa (Monte), 28, 41, 64
Roseg (Piz), 30
Rousseau, Jean Jacques, 32, 40
Ruskin, John, 40
Russell, Dr. Israel, 241
Ruttledge, Hugh, 162, 227, 231
Ruwenzori, 133, 137 ff

Sahama, 114, 121 ff
St. Agnes (Mount), 246
St. Elias (Mount), 140, 239, 240 ff
St. Elias Range, 240 ff
Salanctay, 120
Sanford (Mount), 246
San Miguel Mts., 257
Sarmiento (Mount), 132
Sawatch Mts., 257
Scandinavia, mountains of, 82
Scawfell, 81, 82
Scersen (Piz), 30
Schaller, Hermann, 181
Schneider, Erwin, 186
Schreckhorn, 29, 41
Selkirk Range, 250
Sella, Vittorio, 141, 174
Semchumbi, 223
Serra Roncador (Snoring Mts.), 111
Shackleton, Sir Ernest, 86
Shasta (Mount), 254
Shebbeare, E. O., 219
Sheldon, George, 197 ff
Sherpas, 155, 225 ff
Shilla, 151, 152
Shiprock, 253, 257
Shipton, Eric, 159 ff, 227 ff
Shkara, 84
Sierra Madre Mts., 238, 251
Sierra Madre Occidental, 251,
Sierra Madre Oriental, 251
Sierra Nevada de Santa Marta Range, 114, 132
Sierra Nevadas, 252, 254, 255, 293
Simler, Josias, 32
Simvu, 170
Sinai (Mount), 17
Siniolchu, 170
ski-mountaineering, 30, 108 ff
Smith, Dr. Albert, 40, 41
Smythe, Frank S., 90, 159, 179, 227 ff
snow and ice climbing, 275 ff
Snowdon, 81
Somervell, Dr. T. Howard, 162, 213 ff
Sorata, 118, 120
Soule, William, 242
Spain, mountains of, 82
specialization, 73
Spitzbergen, mountains of, 86
Stairs, Lieutenant, 139
Stanley, Henry, 138, 139
Stanley (Mount), 146
Steele (Mount), 246, 247
Stein, Sir Aurel, 87
step-cutting, 279
Stephen, Leslie, 26 ,42, 34
Strahlhorn, 28
Streatfeild, Captain N. R., 193, 194
Strom, Erling, 107 ff

Stromboli, 294
Strutt, Colonel E. T., 213
Stuck, Hudson, 19, 96 ff, 104 ff, 242, 287

Table Mountain, 135
Tajumulco, 251
Täschhorn, 28, 41, 72
Tatum, Robert, 104 ff
Taugwalder, Peter, Jr., 61 ff
Taugwalder, Peter, Sr., 61 ff
Taylor, Andy, 243 ff
Taylor, Billy, 98 ff
Tejbir Bura, 216
Temple (Mount), 249
Terror (Mount), 294
Teton Mts., 256
Tien Shan Mts., 148
Tilman, H. W., 162 ff, 231
Titcomb Needles, 256
Tolima, 115
Trench, Lieutenant, 198
Trisul, 153, 158
Tronador (El), 131
Tryfaen, 81, 82
Tucker, C. C., 84
Tuckett, F. F., 42
Tupungato, 130
Tyndall, John, 21, 42, 43, 45, 56, 57, 60

Uinta Mts. 256
Ushba, 84

Vancouver (Mount), 247
Vesuvius, 293 ff
Victoria (Mount), 249
Vines, Stuart, 123 ff
Viso (Monte), 26, 31, 41
Vosges Mts., 82

Waddington (Mount), 250
Wager, L. R., 227
Wakefield, Dr., 213, 218
Wasatch Mts., 256
Washburn, Bradford, 246
Washington (Mount), 258
Weisshorn (Mount), 28, 41, 43, 45
Weisskugel, 30
Welzenbach, 187
Wetterhorn, 29, 41 ff
Wheeler, Captain, 206, 210
White Mts., 258
Whitney (Mount), 253, 255
Whymper, Edward, 18, 42, 44, 116 123, 206, 248, 268, 287, 288
Wickersham, Judge, 95
Wieland, 187
Wien, Karl, 170, 182, 188
Wiessner, Fritz, 184, 193, 197 ff, 250, 253
Wildspitze, 30
Wills, Alfred, 42, 43
Wilson, Maurice, 236
Wind River Range, 256
Wolfe, Dudley, 197 ff
Wollaston, A. F. R., 86, 140, 206, 207
Wood (Mount), 246
Wood, Walter A., 115, 246
Workman, Dr. and Mrs. William Hunter, 152, 179, 191
Wrangell (Mount), 242
Wrangell Range, 240, 242, 246

Young, Geoffrey Winthrop, 19, 72, 272
Young, Jack, 160

Zemu Glacier, 176 ff
Zillerthal Mts., 30
Zinal-Rothorn, 28
Zugspitze, 30
Zurbriggen, Mattias, 69, 123 ff

www.ingramcontent.com/pod-product-compliance
Lightning Source LLC
Chambersburg PA
CBHW021832220426
43663CB00005B/219